It's a Print!

It's a Print!:
Detective Fiction
from Page to Screen

Edited by

William Reynolds
Elizabeth A. Trembley

Bowling Green State University Popular Press
Bowling Green, OH 43403

IT'S A PRINT!:
Detective Fiction from Page to Screen

No particular art form "holds an exclusive claim to the secrets of the soul or the wisdom of the ages. Therefore, no true hierarchy of the arts exists."

—Hal Himmelstein

Acknowledgments

Publication of this book would have been impossible without the assistance of more people than can possibly be mentioned; but some contributions have been particularly important. Our friends in the Mystery and Detective Fiction Area of the Popular Culture Association encouraged us throughout the process of turning dinnertime conversation into reality. Professors Charles Huttar and Peter Schakel of the Hope College English Department exceeded the bounds of generosity in reading, commenting, discussing, and advising. Myra Kohsel typed, formatted, proofread, and—as usual—made editorial suggestions of great value. Dr. Edward and Pauline Trembley provided continual support across the years and miles. As always, Maura, Kathleen, and Mary Reynolds gracefully accepted a husband's/father's scholarly enthusiasm and through their love made the effort worthwhile.

Contents

Introduction

Elizabeth A. Trembley

The mechanistic age of the twentieth century has required a mechanized medium for expression: the production of film—dependent from the start on machines such as cameras, projectors, lights, and now more heavily reliant on computers, sensitive films, miniaturization, and sophisticated sound recording devices—has flowered in this century not only as a means of popular entertainment, but as a critically acclaimed art form. The new cinematic art functions in a more complex fashion than any earlier art form: it occupies both space, like a sculpture, and time, like a symphony; it appeals to the sight like a painting, to the ears like a sonata, and to the mind like poetry. Despite such similarities, film nevertheless differs in its emphasis on visual imagery, the manipulation of its audiences' points of view, and the infinite reproducibility of its experience through the projection of light and sound.

Even though "one of cinema's most immediate effects was to supplant the novel as the foremost art form of narrative realism" (Sinyard vii), much about film production relies on forms of the older, more traditional arts. Nowhere is this reliance more important than in the role of fiction, drama, and even poetry as the basis for many narrative films. Approximately 30 percent of all American movies are adapted from novels and the majority of all films produced in the world are based on material originally produced for other media (Beja 77-79). Such adaptation forms the central pillar for the varied essays collected in this anthology, though the subjects addressed all lie within the realm of detective and mystery narrative.

In approaching a study of film adaptation of fiction, the literary critic almost naturally begins by comparing the two products. Any adaptation from page to screen makes change inevitable. But of what nature should the change be and to what degree should it occur? Most film critics agree that the integrity of the original work should be preserved, though at the same time filmmakers must freely adapt and create, in a new medium, a work with its own

1

integrity. Though both media are essentially narrative constructions, they present narrative in entirely different representational systems. How, then, do the fundamental elements of fiction translate? Or can they?

Traditionally, critics of both film and literature have emphasized the differences between the media, perhaps to maintain what they felt to be the integrity of their disciplines. George Bluestone spoke for many when in 1957 he wrote, "the novel is a linguistic medium, the film essentially visual" (vi), implying that never the twain shall meet. He continued:

> what is peculiarly filmic and what is peculiarly novelistic cannot be converted without destroying an integral part of each. That is why Proust and Joyce would seem as absurd on film as Chaplin would in print. And that is why the great innovators of the twentieth century, in film and novel both, have had so little to do with each other, have gone their ways alone, always keeping a firm but respectful distance. (63)

Because of such fundamental differences, many critics, such as Luhr and Lehman, have remarked that the mediums' "artistic configurations differ massively, so massively as to make ontological comparison aesthetically impossible" (174). In general, critics have agreed to disdain film adaptation of fiction as a lower form of film because of this inter-media dependence. As Joy Gould Boyum recently put it, "In short, nobody loves an adaptation" (15).

We believe, however, that the situation is not so dire, that there is validity in discussing the issue of adaptation, of comparing works unquestionably related but produced in two such different media. This can be seen by exploring the similarities in the creation and presentation of connotative images, the manipulation of the elements of narrative, and the possibility for and importance of achieving fidelity to the text in film adaptations of literature.

Semiology, the study of systems of signs, helps a great deal when considering the adaptation of verbal productions into visual arts. Both "film and literature tend to be fundamentally representational arts which have a natural tendency to reflect this world-out-there" (Boyum 31). Attention to semiotic issues can diminish the massive differences so apparent between the two mediums, allowing us to compare presentations of narrative despite artists' use of differing sign systems. When a filmmaker adapts a piece of fiction for film, he or she functions as a translator of the semiotics of words into the semiotics of film. The richness of connotation and trope associated with the semiology of literature might seem at first glance to be missing from the sign systems of film. In literature, words—arbitrary arrangements of letters into recognizable patterns—stand as the signs for objects, emotions, and experience. These words change from language to language, though the things they represent do not. The semiology of film functions with a fundamental difference: in film the signifier and the signified are nearly identical. While the word "foot" bears little resemblance to the five-toed appendage, a picture projected onto the screen reproduces one almost exactly. This near relationship between the sign and the thing it symbolizes suggests that the filmmaker has less creative leeway in deciding how to present material to his audiences.

However, in film, the gap between signifier and signified which allows for creative play does exist. First, though film presents its "readers" with visual images, it still requires that they internalize those images to create meaning. The reader's perception of a novel is also visual—through scanning a printed page, but also through visualization of the events. In both cases, the meanings which readers contribute to the art, which they remember long after the experience ends, lie in their own recreation of the elements before them.

Second, the creative gap between signifier and signified occurs in film during the presentation of photographic images, one after the other, in time. Because visual images, like verbal ones, have culturally determined connotations, film has a wide-ranging connotative ability. First, the "connotation of a specific shot depends on its having been chosen from a range of other possible shots. . . . the connotative sense we comprehend stems from the shot being compared, not necessarily consciously, with its unrealized companions in the paradigm" (Monaco 131). Each frame may be considered—like a painting, or a photograph, or a sentence describing an action, or an imagistic poem—as something which presents a singular, static, and suggestive product. These are the blocks which build the edifice of narrative, whether in film or literature. Just as we ask ourselves why the author of a poem or novel chose a certain word over another, we ask ourselves why a filmmaker chose one particular visual image over another.

It is the combination of such individual images that opens the most expansive possibilities for filmic tropes. While on one level connotations of visual images operate in a paradigmatic setting—

what shot the filmmaker chose considered in comparison with all the possibilities left unchosen—on another level connotations function syntagmatically, or in connection with all the other images chosen for presentation.

> When the significance . . . [of a shot] depends not on the shot compared with other potential shots, but rather on that shot compared with actual shots that precede or follow it, then we can speak of its syntagmatic connotation; that is, the meaning adheres to it because it is compared with other shots that we do see. (Monaco 131)

It is in this comparative linking that traditionally literary figures begin to appear in visual presentation. For instance, synecdoche—a comparison of the part with the whole—applies to film when we see many marching feet cross the screen: we know an army now moves off to war. Metonymy—the association of details with ideas—also functions in film with great strength: the presentation of a man releasing a hypodermic syringe as he rolls down his sleeve suggests drug addiction.

So, though the differences in the two mediums, one verbal and one visual, are indeed substantial, the creation of images through manipulation of the semiological systems does suggest that the mediums might successfully be studied together. Even though Josef Von Sternberg, director of the film adaptation of Theodore Dreiser's *An American Tragedy*, believed that "literature cannot be transferred to the screen without a loss to its value [because] the visual elements completely revalue the written work" (qtd. in Luhr and Lehman 190), revaluing does not preclude comparison. A successful work of fiction can be turned into a successful film, and both can be distinct works of art, because "while the subject, or story, of both works is identical, their *content* is nevertheless different. It is this different *content* that is adequately expressed in the changed form resulting from the adaptation" (Balázs, qtd. in Beja 79). When one thinks of film and literature as primarily narrative arts, "intent on creating images and sound in the reader's mind, then film will appear much more obviously literary itself" (Richardson 12).

Many of the elements of narrative central to literary presentation seem to become problematic in a visual medium. Scholars of film adaptation often organize their studies by these elements, comparing how each medium dealt with them in its version of the same story. The most widely discussed of these are plot, character, point of view, and style and tone (Kaminsky, McDougal).

Almost everyone agrees that plot must not change—or must change only in negligible degrees—when a book is adapted to fiction. Beja describes the common attitude thus: "books and films with the same titles ought to be virtually identical, and . . . if they are not, then something unclean has to have happened along the way" (88). However, plots often suffer fundamental changes, dictated by the limited running time of a film. Small events, sub-plots, and occasionally major episodes never see the final version of film, because deemed inessential by producers: they were never dramatized, or fell onto the cutting room floor in an editor's or director's drive to shave time. Therefore, because the "criticism of films using novels as a source will frequently center on their 'fidelity' to the events of the novel, not on their artistic integrity" (Luhr and Lehman 192), many critics—professional and amateur—view adaptations with dismay. "References are constantly made to what is 'left out' or 'changed,' instead of what is there" (Luhr and Lehman 192).

While a novel's plot usually receives a trimming in adaptation to the screen, subtleties of characterization often are highlighted through cinematic presentation. McDougal argues that in film "characters tend to have a specificity their literary counterparts often lack" (113). Many critics, like Richardson, would agree. "One of film's greatest and most often noted assets is its sensitivity to appearance, its built-in capacity to characterize things and people directly, in pictures, rather than through description or analysis" (56). Those filmmakers who hope to present the characters as an author wrote them find themselves faced with countless opportunities to do so instantaneously, visually.

Perhaps the most problematic element of fictional presentation of narrative, and one closely tied to plot and characterization, is point of view. At first glance, film and literature once again seem far apart. Most narratives are subjective, presented to the reader through the perceptions of a first person narrator or through a third person narrator whose omniscience seems tied to the characters' subjective perceptions. Film, on the other hand, appears objective: it shows you what exists, only rarely presenting people's interpretations of events. But, in fact, most narrative films do adapt a visual subjectivity in point of view. Certainly objective per-spectives—including long shots, deep focus, and a static camera—do appear in film where they "make any mediation between audience and event invisible. . . . In such cases the integrity of the pro-filmic event is assumed—shots are chosen to give the viewer a better view of what is going on within it" (Luhr and Lehman 33). However, for the most part, narrative film adapts a subjective posture: the camera moves to follow its object, as does the human eye; and close-ups together with shallow focus mimic the concentrated focus of humans on one object at a time.

The subjectivity of film does retain at least limited omniscience, however, because presentation of a first person narration becomes highly problematic in film. In literature, first person narration develops the relationships between events, other characters, and the narrator as the readers essentially *hear* the narrator's thoughts on each scene. But that represented voice cannot be reproduced on film without extensive and distracting use of voice-over narration. Instead, film remains largely omniscient, adopting whichever point of view best presents the actions, thoughts, and reactions of important characters. A typical example lies in the over-the-shoulder shots used in filming conversations. As one person speaks, the camera often looks over the shoulder of the listener, presenting viewers with the listener's visual point of view. If the listener then becomes the speaker, either by verbalizing a response or simply by reacting with silent body language, the camera will shift to look over the shoulder of the first speaker, so viewers see the new speaker's reaction to what the first said. Occasionally soundtrack narration will appear in film to strengthen the sense of a particular character's perception of events, but this occurs only rarely and in special cases. Filmmakers control our perceptions through use of a subjective point of view, yet only rarely allow us to enter the thoughts of any of the characters we see on the screen.

The relative rarity with which film-makers can present characters' thoughts or internal monologues raises questions about any film's ability to represent the author's original words—his style and tone—faithfully. Harold Foote, a writer of novels, plays and screen adaptations of the works of Harper Lee, Truman Capote, William Faulkner, Erskine Caldwell, and Flannery O'Connor, believes that "adapting the work of other writers is . . . the most difficult and painful process imaginable. . . . When you try to get inside the world of another writer, you're under constant tension not to violate this person's vision" (7). Stanley Kubrick, director of the film version of Burgess's *A Clockwork Orange*, remarked extensively on the importance of fiction's stylistic content and film adaptation:

to take the prose style as any more than just a part of a great book is simply misunderstanding just what a great book is. . . . Style is what an artist uses to fascinate the beholder in order to convey to him his feelings, emotions, and thoughts. These are what have to be dramatised, not the style. The dramatising has to find a style of its own, as it will do if it really grasps the content. (qtd. in Beja 80)

Though Foote and Kubrick disagree on technique, both agree that cinematic fidelity to the original fiction is an admirable, if not essential, goal for adapters. Ultimately, in fact, all questions about how the elements of fiction "translate" into filmic language point us toward consideration of whether or not fidelity is fundamental to commendable adaptation.

Many people understand the fidelity issue as of central importance. Critics trained in a literary tradition, as are most of our contributors, continually struggle with this issue. Morris Beja describes the common attitude of "readers with a great deal of literary sophistication" thus: "whether or not a given film based on a cherished novel succeeds *as a film*—as a cinematic work of art—is a matter not of the slightest interest, compared to the question of whether or not it is 'faithful'" (88). Fans of fiction watching a screen adaptation look at everything "framed in a double vision" (Boyum 53) of memory and expectation. In adaptations viewers tend to look for similarities between film and their *memories and impressions* of the fiction. In response to such audience loyalty to text, some film critics argue that a film, whether adapted from fiction or not, must stand alone as a separate piece of art, that any consideration of an adaptation in connection with the original text sets up a false dichotomy. Neither an approach which emphasizes literary connections nor one which ignores such roots seems best suited to studying adaptation.

A true cinematic adaptation is a completely different product from a film based loosely on the gimmick or plot or character of a certain fiction. Films produced primarily to represent visually what an author has created verbally form what is, in essence, a genre of their own. The cinematic adaptation's ties to fiction constantly contribute to the shape of the film. As Neil Sinyard explains, "the great screen adaptations are the ones that go for the spirit rather than the letter of the text; or explore a unique affinity between the personalities of the original writer and the present filmmaker; or use the camera to interpret and not simply illustrate the tale" (x). Nevertheless, an understanding of the different semiologies of the two mediums and of the various ways each exploits narrative elements to control audience perception leads the careful critic to discuss such adaptations separately—neither the integrity of the film as an independent work of art nor the integrity of the film's representation of the original verbal work can be ignored.

Such exploration of dramatizing fiction faithfully, of the development of film adaptations as a genre of their own, drives the essays included in our collection. Because, in many ways, mystery is a uniquely plot-bound genre, the considerations of film adaptations of such fiction might tend to focus solely on transfigurations of plot. However, the critics collected here have moved beyond this to discuss many of the more sophisticated issues addressed in this introduction. These essays address a wide range of topics, including varied types of adaptations possible from fiction, thematic manipulations, reconstructions of character, verbal and visual figurative language, the translation of first-person point of view, feminist perspectives on cinema and popular culture, and the ways adaptations reflect the societies which produced them. In so doing, they create lively discussions of the films inspired by fiction and provide enriched understanding of the fiction itself.

Investigating film adaptations of fiction can bring a scholar into deep waters. Comparison can erode both film and novel because both mediums are so individual—the critic must be highly aware of how each uses its own language system to portray similar actions, setting, characters, point of view, and style. "The making of a film using a novel as a source does not involve 'reproducing' the novel—any Xerox machine can do that. It involves an attempt to use whatever 'events' that theoretically precede the novel itself as the basis for the visually created 'events' of the film" (Luhr and Lehman 187). But examination of the way a filmmaker uses elements of fiction often illuminates both products.

> Of course, what a film takes from a book matters, but so does what it brings to a book. When it brings dedication and talent . . . the resulting film is then not a betrayal and not a copy, not an illustration and not a departure. It is a work of art that relates to the book from which it derives yet is also independent, an artistic achievement that is in some mysterious way the "same" as the book but also something other: perhaps something less but perhaps something more as well. (Beja 88)

That phenomenon, the transformation of fiction into a product so similar and yet so foreign, presents the mystery which we have tried to solve with the essays gathered together here.

Holmes Is Where the Heart Is:
The Achievement of Granada Television's
Sherlock Holmes Films

Elizabeth A. Trembley

The 32 Sherlock Holmes films which Michael Cox produced for Granada Television maintain the integrity of Doyle's texts in ways which other adaptations, including the famous series of films featuring Basil Rathbone and Nigel Bruce, do not. Even when the films depart from Doyle, they consistently add to or change the stories in ways implicit in the original works.

After over a century of popularity, the Sherlock Holmes legend has achieved proportions far different from the tales invented by Conan Doyle. The popular image of Holmes shows him isolated and untouched by the horrors of crime, arrogantly explaining his methods to Dr. Watson, the bumbling fool who worships him. This Holmesian icon gained its shape first from William Gillette's stage productions and later from 147 film portrayals of the eccentric sleuth and his biographer-roommate. Of these, Basil Rathbone's and Nigel Bruce's classic work became the dominant cinematic representation of Doyle's creation, a representation which towers beyond the fiction. Because of the pervasiveness of the film icon, many people are surprised when they read the actual texts and discover what Doyle really created. Holmes, though supremely competent, appears realistically human: emotional, musical, addicted to cocaine, and bothered by failure. Watson stands an astute observer, a competent writer and physician, and a devoted friend to Holmes. These traits become explicit in Doyle's depiction of the complex, intricate relationship which the two share, based not on Watson's mindless worship, but on mutual respect and dependence.

Despite overwhelming textual evidence regarding the true nature of the characters, the cultural misconceptions about Holmes and Watson seemed unassailable for over 40 years because of the popularity of the Rathbone-Bruce portrayals. No serious contender to these appeared until England's Granada Television began to film Doyle's work. Led by producer Michael Cox, Granada released three series, totalling 32 films, unique in their fidelity to Doyle's original texts.[1] While many adaptors have used the difference between media as justification for abandoning texts and creating whole new plots and characters, Cox viewed maintaining the integrity of the original text across two media as his central challenge. Even when he departed from Doyle, he consistently added to or changed the stories in ways implicit in the original texts. His achievement lies in what one might vaguely call "capturing the spirit" of Doyle's work.

In discussing the adaptation of Doyle's fiction to film, I am not primarily interested in the transference of plot details from one medium to the other, though this is the issue upon which many evaluations of adaptation focus. Suffice it to say that Cox's work has received almost universal praise for maintaining Doyle's plot construction—something which few other films had ever even attempted. Cox himself reports, "We did depart from the text at times. We added things or changed things. There's often a difference between what works on the page and what works in a dramatic medium. I hope that we've never done anything which went against the spirit of what Conan Doyle wrote" (personal interview). Transference of narrative detail may provide the foundation for effective adaptation, but the filmmakers' attention must also focus on the less tangible aspects of a story.

The longevity of Doyle's fiction does not derive from the clever or careful construction of his plots but from such intangible aspects. Readers and critics alike have long admitted the errors, inconsistencies, and unlikelihoods which riddle the Holmes stories. Fans of Doyle's writing, however, willingly suspend their critical natures when engaged in a tale involving Holmes and Watson. Clearly, the power of the narrative lies in some other aspect of the author's work. While the character of Holmes stands out as the central attraction of Doyle's fictional world—a fantasy figure eminently powerful, pursuing his vocation with supreme competence—such "superheroes" abound in fiction, especially in detective fiction. The spirit of Doyle's work emanates more completely from Dr. Watson, the character who filters *everything* we see about Holmes and his adventures. Watson acknowledges the sleuth to be as mysterious as any criminal case, and, it appears, as unsolvable; readers therefore find the detective continually intriguing. Nevertheless, Watson exudes an unflinching devotion to

Holmes based on their mutually reliant friendship, encouraging readers to feel the same loyalty.

The intangible spirit of the original, the source of power which affects audiences—these become the most important aspects of a text which a successful film adaptation must convey. If we accept that the source of power in Doyle's Holmes stories lies not so much in plot as in the two main characters and their relationship, then we must ask whether Granada's films capture and convey those characters and that relationship in a different medium. The mastery of Cox's films lies in his ability to maintain the centrality of Watson as narrator and in his careful depiction of Watson's relationship to a very human Holmes. In shifting from fiction to film, Cox necessarily switches sign systems, and what was formerly conveyed in dialogue and description must now appear in visual imagery and spoken words. Exactly how he does that provides the subject for this investigation of the achievement of Granada Television's Sherlock Holmes films.

First among the various elements of Doyle's fiction which seem essential to the power of his works is the centrality of Watson as first-person narrator, the source of all the readers' perceptions throughout the fiction.[2] Therefore, maintaining this centrality is essential to successfully adapting Doyle's stories to film. Perhaps the most remarkable achievement in Granada's films is the preservation of the sense of first-person narrative in a visual and essentially objective medium. Most earlier screen versions abandon Watson's central role, providing only objective looks at the sleuth and his sidekick; however, without the inclusion of this subjective point of view, the essential flavor of Doyle's work has always been lost. While one of the "distinguishing characteristics of film is its total control over point of view, a control that allows the careful film maker to dictate exactly what shall be seen, and how, and when, and in what context" (Richardson 54), creating a film which adheres to a first-person perspective has proven almost impossible, and impractical when achieved. In fact, only one film has been made completely from the first person point of view: Robert Montgomery's *The Lady in the Lake* (1946). While it achieved literal representation of the narrator's perspective, that film's constant use of voice-over and mirror shots to allow audiences to see the main character/narrator proved confining and has not been repeated.

Instead of employing such unwieldy literal tactics to establish the continual presence of a narrative "I," Granada's films achieve a first-person tone through a combination of more subtle effects. In several stories a voice-over of the narrative "I"—Dr. John Watson—is heard at the beginning and the end of the film, and sometimes intermittently in the middle. This implies the literary technique of limited omniscience, which is further developed through the use of camera shots which capture the sense of limited omniscience by showing scenes which the narrative "I" saw, enacted, or imagined. To produce this effect, the camera and soundtrack often actually double as the "eye" and "ear" of the narrative "I," providing "subjective camera and sound" and producing the effect of the literal view of the first person narrator. Thus,

> the point of view in subjective camera is not that of an "it," but of an "I," a definite presence relating something to the viewer as an "I" would relate something to a "you." Subjective sound is similar: when a character hears something, the character is no longer a "he" or a "she" but an "I" telling "us" what he or she is thinking or hearing. (Dick 180)

Such film techniques which imply the presence of a specific personality conveying something to viewers permit the transference of first-person narrative from a fictional sign system to that of cinema.

Cox establishes Watson as central narrative presence from the initial scenes of the first Holmes film, *A Scandal in Bohemia*, using in quick succession the techniques discussed above. Though the producer has edited together many different shots taken from varied camera angles, they work together to create one perspective—Watson's. The opening scene, shot with what appears at first to be an objective, omniscient camera, shows burglars ransacking Irene Adler's house, then fleeing when confronted by the woman and her coachman. As the camera freezes in close-up on Irene's puzzled face, a voice-over begins as Watson reports, "to Sherlock Holmes she was always *the* woman. The beautiful Irene Adler of dubious and questionable memory." Though Watson was not present during this ransacking scene, he learns about it later—in both fiction and film—from the Prince who reports that "burglars in my pay ransacked her house" (Doyle, "Scandal" 161). The juxtaposition of the voice-over and this scene establishes the burglary scene as occurring within the limited omniscience of the narrator, an imagined flashback visualized by the person who now tells us this story from a vantage point somewhere in the future. Given this introduction, the whole film, in fact, becomes a flashback with

Watson as the controlling source of information. The first scene implies his knowledge of and narrative presence in scenes in which he is not actually physically present—a narrator telling a story after the fact. Cox clearly presents this film from the beginning not as a visual representation of the events, but an interpretation of the episodes as Watson envisioned or remembered them after they occurred, including Watson's imagining of events which he did not see or hear about in detail.

This establishment of Watson as the central narrative presence in the film continues in the next scene of A Scandal in Bohemia. Though many of the subsequent shots are objective, they are still clearly connected to Watson as the controlling perspective. As we watch Watson exiting a cab in Baker Street and entering 221B, his voice-over continues: "My practice had caused me to be absent in the country for several days. As usual, after leaving Holmes for any length of time, I returned filled with apprehension as to his mood." Watson dramatizes this as he silently climbs the steps and pauses before the door to the sitting room, debating whether to disturb his friend. By showing us Watson's movements and silent facial expressions, the objective camera succeeds in silently communicating the additional information about Watson's arrival which the first-person narrator included in the fiction.

When Watson finally does open the door to his rooms, the objective camera shots suddenly become entwined with the subjective camera—the "I" and the camera "eye" join. This makes even more forceful our sense of Watson's perspective as we now see exactly what Watson sees as he scans the sitting room for the first time after a long absence. Subjective camera shots of the details Watson notices are intertwined with objective shots of his silent facial reactions to those details—however, all shots remain essentially bound to the doctor. Watson looks at the back of Holmes's head as the sleuth sits entranced before a roaring fire. A close-up of his face shows smiling hopes for a reunion collapsed into hurt at his friend's silence. The camera then shows Watson's focus on the open window admitting cold air and driving rain; the objective shot of his face clearly indicates annoyance at such foolish circumstances. Next Watson notices the hypodermic syringe and empty vial on Holmes's desk. The concluding shot reveals Watson's face pinched with disappointment and anger as he explodes sarcastically, "What is it tonight? Morphine or cocaine?" Immediately the shot again assumes Watson's subjective point of view of the back of Holmes's head as the sleuth slowly turns through profile to full frontal close-up. Ironically (and intentionally), this impressive dramatic moment binds the audience even more tightly to Watson as the controlling presence in the film—Watson's first view of the legendary sleuth is also the camera's, and thus provides the audience with their first view as well.

Only at this point, with Watson's role as the source of narrative fully established, do we get the first shot which does *not* include Watson either in voice-over, as an actor, or as source of the visual point of view—we see Sherlock Holmes's face, once again turned toward the fire, as he responds to Watson's question. This camera separation from Watson lasts only a few seconds, however, for as their conversation continues, the film begins a series of "over-the-shoulder" shots, designed to include both characters in the scene's make-up, and to create the visual perspective of each on the other as the conversation continues. Since the opening shots have established the entire story as a memory being conveyed by a narrator who exists somewhere in the future of this narrative, such shots separated from Watson's perspective do not disrupt his role as narrator. While not every shot in the many Holmes films includes Watson's perspective, the majority of them do, and the doctor's centrality in Doyle's narrative process is preserved.

A scene from *The Resident Patient*, also part of the first series, similarly emphasizes this commitment to the impression of first-person narration in film. At the end of the story, the camera shows Holmes playing the violin and Watson trying to write. Their conversation reveals that Watson is actually starting to draft his account of the adventure we have just witnessed. When Holmes expresses dismay with Watson's chosen title, "The Brook Street Mystery," Watson banishes him from the room, and with brooding frustration attempts to begin his story. As the film ends, the camera assumes Watson's literal view as he struggles to come up with a title for the story we have just witnessed. We do not watch Watson as he drafts, crosses out, sighs, writes more, crosses out, and tries again; instead the "eye" joins the "I" one more time and we see only what Watson does, his own hand holding a pen to the page. The filmmakers here achieve an explicit link between the audience's point of view and Watson's which restrospectively colors the contents of the film.

The films even carefully establish Watson as the narrator of scenes in which Holmes sleuths alone. Some of these occur as flashbacks which we see as Holmes narrates the scenes to Watson, who visualizes the story Holmes tells him. This technique of

Holmes narrating to Watson and to the audience at the same time stems directly from Doyle's stories—the film's scenic structure mirrors that of the original text. For instance, in *A Scandal in Bohemia*, the camera follows Holmes on his solitary investigations at Briony Lodge, which temporarily seems to divorce the film from Watson's perspective. However, this scene ends by fading to Holmes narrating the story to Watson as the sleuth removes his costume and make-up—clearly we have been learning about the scene along with Watson, and his integrity as narrator is maintained. Similarly, *The Naval Treaty* cuts abruptly from one afternoon to the next morning, passing over the time Holmes spends sleuthing on his own. He returns to Baker Street wounded, and as he eats his breakfast, tells his night's adventures to Watson. Announced by a fade, the film then presents us with the events Holmes describes.

This commitment to the power of Doyle's narrative style does not diminish in the project's second and third series. Episodes from *The Return of Sherlock Holmes* and *The Casebook of Sherlock Holmes* continue to reinforce Watson's fundamental role in the tales. For instance, the first scenes of *The Abbey Grange* reconfirm Watson's fundamental presence as the "I" source of the "eye" providing the vision for audiences. The opening wide shot features an objective camera, focused on Watson sleeping in his bedroom. Suddenly the door opens and Holmes creeps in to wake him. At this point the film presents a subjective shot—clearly the reclining Watson looking up at the bending Holmes—as Holmes murmurs, "Come, Watson. The game is afoot." The camera then returns to the original wide shot as Holmes leaves and Watson, after a second's consideration, falls back into bed. Almost immediately Holmes pops back through the door—with the clairvoyance of a parent waking a sleeping child for school—and cries, "Into your clothes and come!" before banging the door in exit. Through all this the camera moves only once to provide Watson's "eye"; otherwise it remains stationary in his room as Holmes passes in and out of the shot, clearly establishing a connection to Watson's experience.

Though less clearly connected to the first-person narrator of the texts, the construction of other scenes of Holmes working without Watson continues to foster a link between the audience and Watson through the camera's eye. *The Problem of Thor Bridge*, from *The Casebook*, opens with Holmes silent and alone in his sitting room. After several seconds of this objective camera view of Holmes, Watson enters and, stopped by Holmes's concentration, silently gazes at his friend. The next shot of Holmes is clearly meant to be subjective—the camera's eye shows us what the narrative "I" sees— and it is the same view that the earlier objective camera provided its audience. So the link between viewer and Watson is once again established. Similar openings punctuate films throughout all three series—many do not introduce Watson immediately into the narrative, but nonetheless skillfully link the camera's perspective with the doctor's. Actor Edward Hardwicke expressed the intention of the filmmakers when he remarked, "Dr. Watson is really always the audience. I think that he presents what the viewers . . . want— that's their viewpoint."

Watson's central role as source of narrative in the fiction foregrounds his relationship with Holmes and introduces the human traits of the sleuth—the second important source of "spirit" in Doyle's texts. Throughout all three series, Cox's films convey this as well. For the first time on film we see Sherlock Holmes as Doyle wrote him—through Watson's often admiring, occasionally bewildered, and alternately amused, concerned, fearful, and compassionate eyes—and that Watsonian filter touches us, influencing what we perceive about the great detective. Many of Watson's observations in the fiction suggest Holmes's more human characteristics, and Cox's films also emphasize these, reestablishing this side of the sleuth who has been so often misrepresented as a purely rational thinking machine. For instance in the first film, *A Scandal in Bohemia*, Cox imports Doyle's original dialogue into a skillfully edited sequence of shots to emphasize visually the same implications that the text makes verbally. In the story, Watson, realizing an important client will soon arrive, tries to leave, causing Holmes to remark, "Not a bit, Doctor. Stay where you are, I am lost without my Boswell. And this promises to be interesting. It would be a pity to miss it" (Doyle, "Scandal" 164). In the film version the subjective and objective camera shots—all linked to Watson's experience—capture Holmes's emotions as they are implied in the original dialogue. As Watson tries to leave, Holmes cries, "Not a bit of it, Doctor. Stay where you are." Here the dialogue ends momentarily as the camera shows Watson turning from the door to look at Holmes questioningly. The camera then cuts to Watson's subjective "eye": a close-up of Holmes considering Watson's confusion. His next line, "I am lost without my Boswell," emerges in soft explanation of his earlier harsh order. The subjective camera lingers on the silent Holmes for an instant, his eyes in full contact with the camera (thus also with Watson and with the audience) allowing the implications of this allusion to reverberate. Suddenly Holmes shakes off the mood like a dog sprays water and resumes his energetic advice, finishing off Doyle's dialogue; and with that the camera leaves the intimacy of subjectivity and returns to an objective perspective.

In the second series, *The Second Stain* also provides an example of how Watson's perception grants audiences a clear vision of Holmes's more human traits. Upon accepting a case which involves an important letter stolen from a prominent government official, Holmes privately tells Watson with great glee that a successful solution will be the "crowning glory of my career." Yet, later, after discovering that criminals had blackmailed the official's wife into stealing the letter, Holmes gives up this glory by pretending the letter had never disappeared. While Doyle's story leaves Holmes's motivations and emotions ambiguous—neither Watson nor Holmes comments upon them any further—Cox eliminates that ambiguity in the final seconds of the film by creating a further connection between Watson and the audience. As they leave the site of the case, Watson approaches Holmes with a puzzled look, clearly wondering, as is the audience, about the motives for the detective's actions. Before Watson can ask his question, however, Holmes grants his answer in a gesture visible only to Watson (and therefore to the audience): with an uncharacteristic, wild whoop of joy, Holmes leaps into the air and down several steps. The camera freezes on this moment of airborne abandon, Holmes laughing and free, Watson amazed and pleased. As Granada's credits roll over this frame we know with Watson that it was Holmes's compassion that led him to save a marriage at the expense of his own "crowning glory." At issue here is not the fact that Cox eliminated the ambiguities of Holmes's actions. Such ambiguity may have occurred simply through Doyle's hasty writing—he could have forgotten the force behind Holmes's early comments just as he occasionally confused the first name and marital status of his narrator. What is significant is that Cox has built from the text a film which succeeds cinematically because of its more acceptable closure, but which nevertheless maintains the central essence of Doyle's work: the centrality of Watson as narrator, and the vision of Holmes's humanity as presented through that narrator's eyes.

This technique continues in *The Casebook of Sherlock Holmes*, as evidenced by the adaptation of "The Adventure of the Illustrious Client." Here Doyle stresses Holmes's vulnerability through

Watson's reaction to the injuries Holmes receives at the hands of murderous thugs. Watson's chill of fear poignantly portrays the intensity of feeling which characterizes his relationship to Holmes. "I think I could show you the very paving-stone upon which I stood when my eyes fell upon the placard, and a pang of horror passed through my very soul" (Doyle, "Illustrious" 993). When the medical man actually visits the injured sleuth, all professional suavity disappears in concern for his friend, a concern which Holmes acknowledges.

> I stole into the darkened room. The sufferer was wide awake, and I heard my name in a hoarse whisper. The blind was three-quarters down, but one ray of sunlight slanted through and struck the bandaged head of the injured man. A crimson patch had soaked through the white linen compress. . . .
>
> "All right, Watson. Don't look so scared," he muttered in a very weak voice. "It's not as bad as it seems." (993)

Here Doyle breaks into narrative to describe what happened to Holmes. Later in the story, Holmes "was seated in his familiar chair, looking very pale and exhausted. Apart from his injuries, even his iron nerves had been shocked" (998). Doyle's specifics create a shadowed, almost gothic, ambience of anxiety and depletion.

Cox's film of this story creates the same darkened atmosphere through visual and aural details. When Watson enters the room, his facial expression conveys his concern, adding poignance to Holmes's whispered admonition that he should not "look so scared." While the film presents all the details of Doyle's setting, it does so in a single shot of the room, perhaps leaving viewers less affected than readers. To translate the intensity of emotion depicted in the fiction, the film adds new dialogue:

> "It's all right, Watson, don't look so scared."
> "You mustn't talk."
> "Nonsense. Need to."
> "Holmes. I supposed it was that damned Austrian. Give me the word and I'll go and thrash the hide off him."
> "Good old Watson. No, no, no no."

Throughout all this Holmes whispers with his eyes closed, his body and usually animated face immobilized, the lips barely moving. His words and delivery emphasize the gravity of Holmes's wounds, the unnaturalness of his condition, and Watson's angry concern. Audiences see Holmes and Watson struggling together through a traumatic situation as Doyle envisioned it—a far cry from anything which the Rathbone-Bruce films offer.

Most of these examples of how Cox's films capture the power of Doyle's work rest on the producer's fundamental adherence to the author's texts. However, as he admits himself, Cox occasionally departs from Doyle's texts, adding to them to enhance the transfer of the narratives' spirit to their new filmic medium. When Cox needs such creative adaptation, however, he uses tremendous sensitivity to the body of Doyle's text as inspiration for shaping new sequences. The triumph of Cox's work lies in such creative adaptation and the attention it pays to the "spirit" of Doyle's work, if not to the letter of the text.

The effectiveness of such creative adaptation is best illustrated by concentrating on a single example of Cox's technique of enhancing Doyle's depiction of Holmes's humanity and the relationship which he and Watson share. For this reason I will devote the rest of this article to Cox's treatment of the effects on Sherlock Holmes of the deadly narcotic *radix pedis diaboli* (the devil's-foot root), in particular, the filming of the hallucination experienced by Holmes while on the drug, which Doyle mentions but never describes.

In Doyle's short story "The Adventure of the Devil's Foot," Holmes's health has become so precarious that he must rest or suffer a complete breakdown. He and Watson visit Cornwall to relax, but instead discover a series of devilish crimes: a young woman found dead, her face contorted with fear, and her two brothers driven senseless with fright. Soon another brother turns up dead, and Holmes must discover not only the culprit, but the method by which the criminal assaulted his victims. Having deduced a bizarre theory about a combustible poison, Holmes determines to prove his ideas by trying the poison out on himself and Watson. When inhaled, the devil's-foot root stimulates the fear centers of the brain, causes the victim to hallucinate, and leads to madness or death.

Both Watson and Holmes undergo this ordeal, but Doyle remains silent about the details of their experience. The author could not provide the contents of Holmes's hallucination because Watson narrates the story; interestingly, Doyle also relates very little about Watson's experience. The doctor tells us only of his sense of the "vaguely horrible . . . monstrous and inconceivably wicked . . .

whose very shadow would blast my soul" (965). This lack of detail increases the dramatic effects of the fiction by allowing readers to envision their own personal nightmares. But Doyle ultimately directs his readers' attention to Holmes's experience, for it is this which most alarms Watson and spurs him to action. Watson tells us, "[I] had a glimpse of Holmes's face, white, rigid, and drawn with horror—the very look which I had seen upon the features of the dead. It was that vision which gave me an instant of sanity and strength" (965), and the intrepid Doctor pulls his friend from the lethal fumes.

The importance which Doyle places on Holmes's experience supports Granada's decision to dramatize Holmes's hallucination.[3] The choice to produce this psychological, symbolic scene propels this film beyond simple translation, adding elements which enhance the themes Doyle introduced. Because the devil's-foot root stimulates the fear centers of the brain, any person's hallucination will be the product of his own personal, perhaps even subconscious, fears. The film hallucination suggests that Sherlock Holmes fears three things: first, physical death; second, the loss of the rational deductive abilities which constitute his identity; and third, the destructive potential of guilt. While Granada created the text of Holmes's hallucination, all these issues appear prominently in Doyle's original story.

Holmes's concern with physical danger becomes immediately apparent in the film through his running away from something, indicated by his backward glances. The ground appears to tilt in these early shots as the camera rolls to disrupt the parallel between the matched horizontal axis of the horizon and of the lens. As Monaco points out, this bond represents the metaphysical bond between the camera (or the observer) and the subject, and the disruption of this parallel destroys the stability of this bond (170). The image is altered metaphysically—we no longer believe in the "reality" of what we see and realize we have entered the world of the detective's hallucination. The camera angles suggest he is running toward a group of ancient stone structures, at once monuments to death and providers of a sort of immortality by its chronicling of those long gone. Editing causes Holmes to flash in and out of the picture, suggesting the ease with which he could disappear from the earth, the suddenness of death. The memories of his struggles with Moriarty (including Moriarty's warning, "You must stand clear, Mr. Holmes, or be trodden underfoot") and their mortal combat atop the Reichenbach Falls (and here Granada used film clips from its own *The Final Problem*) reinforce the idea that the passage between life and death is controlled by the most delicate balance. By envisioning what might have easily happened at the Falls—his own plunge into the abyss—Holmes faces the precariousness of his existence.

Holmes's concern with physical death clearly develops from the events in Doyle's story. In it Holmes explores two particularly gruesome deaths caused by the very drug the sleuth inflicts on himself, so it is not unlikely that he harbors some concern as to how his experiment will turn out. There might be a distinct disadvantage to proving his theory about this drug correct! Moriarty and his message also connect with plot details from "The Devil's Foot." In "The Final Problem," Holmes ran from the murderous Professor, hoping to avoid Moriarty until the police capture him. In "The Devil's Foot" Holmes also runs from someone who has warned him to stop detecting or suffer for it: the Harley Street specialist who diagnosed Holmes's oncoming breakdown and ordered him to take a complete rest. Holmes avoids the doctor's advice until he is threatened with permanent disqualification from work, and only then grudgingly agrees to the Cornish retreat. When the murder investigation appears in Cornwall, Holmes leaps into it with alacrity, despite Watson's severe warnings. In both cases, detecting crime has endangered him; it nearly cost him his life with Moriarty, and now it threatens him with grave illness in Cornwall.

The second fear which appears in Holmes's hallucination is the loss of rational, deductive abilities. The tilting ground indicates the loss of the equilibrium so necessary to objective, rational work. Holmes first appears in the hallucination running from something rather frantically, the state of his emotional distress indicated by his disheveled hair and clothes. The loss of objectivity also appears when he looks into a mirror and sees not only himself but himself as a child and the oncoming Moriarty. When faced with these memories, Holmes attempts to cover his eyes, to shield himself from their horror. These attempts bring blood from his eyes: the refusal to observe results in the loss of the ability to observe. The film's incorporation of Blake's Nebuchadnezzar also implies the loss of reason. Nebuchadnezzar is the fallen Babylonian king who, punished by God, was "driven from men . . . did eat grass as oxen, and his body was wet with the dew of heaven, till his hairs were grown like eagle's feathers, and his nails like bird's claws" (Daniel 4:33). Becoming unreasonable, like a beast, is a fate more fearful than death for Sherlock Holmes.

Doyle's original text also focuses on the loss of rationality and the horrors of mental breakdown. While the loss of his special mental abilities would be a horrible fate for Holmes, even less rational people like Watson fear insanity more than death. Watson abhors the madness of the stricken Tregannis brothers, but seems relatively unmoved by the death of the sister. The "most sinister impression" (959) is made upon Watson when the carriage carrying the demented brothers passes him and Holmes. Watson glimpses "a horribly contorted, grinning face glaring out at us. Those staring eyes and gnashing teeth flashed past us like a dreadful vision" (959). Yet when examining the dead body of Brenda Tregannis, who died in a paroxysm of fright, Watson thinks she "had been a very beautiful girl. . . . [and] was handsome, even in death" (959). Even given Watson's well-known appreciation of women, this seems odd. Others in the story associate the brothers' madness with the devil. Both Mortimer Tregannis and the Vicar call the situation "devilish!" Mortimer continues at length, not even mentioning the death of his sister: "It is not of this world. Something has come into that room which has dashed the light of reason from their minds" (958).

Holmes's situation in the story threatens just such a mental disintegration. The visit to Cornwall is occasioned by Holmes's ill health, which brings "the threat of [his] being permanently disqualified from work" (955). In Holmes's mind, choosing to quit practicing deduction equates to the inability to deduce. Determined not to lose the special skills which structure his identity, he risks his health to continue his work. Nevertheless, when he embarks on the case, he clearly is not his usual self. He must rest frequently, claiming that lack of evidence makes further work impossible. His excuses, however, reveal his true fear for his own state of mind: "To let the brain work without sufficient material is like racing an engine. It racks itself to pieces" (960). Although in other stories the sleuth has often lectured Watson on the importance of sufficient evidence, never has he portrayed his mental health as being in such a precarious state.

The third fear suggested by the hallucination is Holmes's apprehension of the damaging effects of his own guilt. Guilt of any degree must be particularly abhorrent to a person like Holmes who prides himself on logical action and on excising guilty persons from society. This reversal of positions—from pursuing criminals to fearing guilt in the self—first appears in the hallucination as Holmes, the hunter, apparently becomes the hunted. Holmes is the one running, looking behind him for some pursuing agent, shaking his head fearfully at an approaching dread, his hands and head coated in blood. While the role of the hunted does not necessarily imply guilt (many detectives and private investigators are stalked by criminals), other images within the hallucination connect guilt to that role.

Four other people figure in Holmes's hallucination—Professor Moriarty, Cain, Nebuchadnezzar, and, by allusion, Oedipus—and all four are guilty men who share both the power of the hunter and the terrors of the hunted. Moriarty pursues Holmes throughout London and across Europe, attempting to kill the detective even as the professor flees from the authorities of Scotland Yard. Cain, jealous of his younger brother's success with God, lures him into a secluded spot and kills him, only to be immediately pursued not only by an avenging God, but potentially by other men as well. Nebuchadnezzar seeks out for slaughter those men who will not worship the idols he erects, yet finds himself chased by disquieting visions of the vengeance of God. Oedipus is the most famous character to undergo this ironic change in status; he relentlessly trails the murderer of Laius only to discover that he, as agent of the gods, pursues himself.

These four images not only imply the guilt of the hunter who becomes the hunted, but they also all suggest specific sources of Holmes's potential guilt. When dealing with a hallucination, we must remember that the unconscious mind operates by symbol and image, not by logic or rationality. Thus, while Holmes may not consciously feel guilty, the sleuth's unconscious recognizes the similarities between Holmes's actions and those of the men whose guilt is more apparent. All are murderers, and Cain and Oedipus are particularly sinister as killers of kin. The hallucination links, by juxtaposition, Cain's murder of Abel to Holmes's deadly duel with Moriarty atop the Reichenbach Falls. Regardless of the rational justification for Holmes's actions, the fact remains that Holmes did hurl the professor to his death. Additionally, because critics have often identified Moriarty as Holmes's dark half, or evil "twin," the only man who ever came close to being Holmes's equal, the hallucination suggests Holmes feels fratricidal for his self-defensive actions. Granada's filmmakers clearly indicate Holmes's connection with Cain by having actor Jeremy Brett mirror Cain's physical stance in the interweaving shots: both clutch at their hair with their hands. The connection between Holmes and Oedipus also appears in the bleeding eyes. In addition to killing Moriarty, Holmes has also nearly killed Watson with this horrible drug experiment, and has endangered himself through his relentless and prideful pursuit of detection.

Even more important than the guilt implied in these hallucinated images is the punishment each man received for his actions. Prideful Nebuchadnezzar fell to the ground a reasonless beast and Cain found himself forced to wander for life, both punished by a vengeful God. Oedipus both blinds and banishes himself, acting even more severely than the gods required. Moriarty dies, pushed into the abyss by the agent of justice, Sherlock Holmes. Each of the criminals Holmes sees in his hallucination has received punishment for his crime, thus his case is closed. But for the murder of Moriarty and the careless treatment of Watson's life and his own, Holmes has received no punishment, made no reparation. Psychologists tell us of reparation's essential role in controlling guilt, even unconscious guilt—without the opportunity to pay for a "crime," or otherwise "make up for it" to the offended party, guilt continues to eat away at one's psychological equilibrium. Without this chance for reparation, Holmes's unconscious, irrational guilt will become an ever more dangerous, fearful power within him.

The textual basis for introducing the issue of unconscious guilt into Holmes's hallucination lies in his uncharacteristic, uncalled for displays of emotion following his vision. Immediately after recovering from the shock of the devil's-foot experiment, Holmes apologizes to Watson. "I owe you both my thanks and an apology. It was an unjustifiable experiment even for one's self, and doubly so for a friend. I am really very sorry." Watson is much moved by this—"I had never seen so much of Holmes's heart before" (965). Later, Holmes lets the murderer go, arguing, "I have never loved, Watson, but if I did and if the woman I loved had met such an end, I might act even as our lawless lion-hunter has done. Who knows?" (970). Such sentimentality and empathy are characteristic of persons attempting to make reparation for committed wrongs—consider the example of a child who, having angered a parent, behaves in a particularly kind or considerate way in order to earn new acceptance into his family's good standings. Likewise, an adult must eradicate the harmful effects of guilt and ensure smooth re-entry into society.

The hallucination crafted by Cox's team enhances the spirit of Doyle's text in several ways. Most importantly it provides sound psychological motivation for the odd behavior Doyle attributed to Holmes: his emotional outbursts to Watson are attempts at reparation which will stave off the negative effects of the guilt he so fears. Second, the film focuses on Watson's reaction to Holmes's experience, dramatizing through quickly shifting close-ups the intensity of emotion which passes between them. Finally, even though the hallucination's details clearly remain unknown to Watson, his centrality as narrator is essentially maintained. The last shot we see before the hallucination begins is subjective: Holmes looks directly into Watson's eyes, into the camera's eye, and into our own. The first shot after the hallucination is also subjective, from the unusual angle of Watson leaning over a supine and semi-conscious Holmes. Thus, though details are created and added to Doyle's work, the elements which grant the fiction its power continue to appear in the film.

About his project Cox remarks, "I think that Conan Doyle's writing describes one of the great friendships in literature. These men, totally different, manage to share a life together. We always looked for the moment at which Holmes and Watson could exchange a glance acknowledging that one had understood what the other was thinking" (personal interview). This sensitivity allowed Cox to succeed in identifying the spirit of Doyle's Holmes stories— the two main characters and the relationship they share—and in translating that from one medium to the other. No other film version of this fiction has ever achieved this degree of fidelity to the "text" because none has looked beyond the detective plot for the source of the stories' power and longevity. Doyle granted both detective and biographer tremendous humanity and an enviable devotion to each other, details which until recently had disappeared from the popular conception of Holmes. Now, however, Granada's films, produced by Michael Cox, recapture that power and transmit it to a visual medium, reminding viewers that Holmes and Watson are more than flat stereotypes: Doyle's characters really do have heart.

NOTES

[1]The three series are *The Adventures of Sherlock Holmes* (1984-85), *The Return of Sherlock Holmes* (1986-88), and *The Casebook of Sherlock Holmes* (1991). While the auteur theory of film criticism suggests that the director is the dominant creative power in the making of a film, in the production of Granada's series, the creative vision and consistency was provided not by the directors, who changed with every film, but by the man who conceived the project and oversaw the production of every

episode: Michael Cox. Therefore, throughout this article, I credit him with the central responsibility for the 32 Holmes episodes.

At least three additional Holmes films have been made by Granada since 1991. I do not include these in my study because not all have aired in the United States and because none involved Cox in the production.

[2]The one exception to this is the short story which Holmes narrates himself, "The Lion's Mane," which appeared in *The Case Book of Sherlock Holmes* (1927). It is important that fans and critics alike find this tale one of the most ineffective among Doyle's works.

[3]Following is a description of the hallucination sequence from Granada Television's film *The Devil's Foot*, directed by Ken Hannam and produced by Michael Cox.

Holmes places powder on the smoke guard, and as it flames up, the music—which has consisted of slow-moving chords punctuated with an exotic percussion—stops for a second. The hallucination begins in silence as this flame melts into the image of a glaring red sun. The music returns, slowly, electric, single notes, no chords, no percussion, but grows in volume and frenzy as the hallucination continues. An empty plain appears, tilting from right to left, the image alternating from normal color to treated images. Holmes appears, running across the expanse from left to right. He is disheveled, hair mussed, without coat or tie, sleeves rolled up. As he runs he glances behind him. The shot changes, showing a quoit, or stone structure of three uprights and a crossing stone. The shot changes again and now we are within the structure, looking out between two monoliths at Holmes running toward us. This exchange of shots occurs three times. As he runs, Holmes disappears from and reappears in the picture four times. The perspective cuts to waves crashing in turmoil. Again we see Holmes running toward us between the two uprights; then an oval mirror floats in front of that image to the center of the screen. A close-up of Holmes, with stormy sky in background, growing alarmed. Another glimpse of the waves appears, and fades out as the mirror fades in. The mirror itself then becomes a photograph of actor Jeremy Brett as a child, so presumably of Holmes as a child. The shot returns to the close-up on Holmes's face; he is distraught, shaking his head at something dreadful approaching. Cut to clip of Moriarty running at him for their confrontation at the top of the Reichenbach Falls. Switch back to the close-up of Holmes's face as he covers his eyes to block vision, and blood seeps through his hands. Two prints by William Blake appear, one of Nebuchadnezzar on all fours and one of Cain fleeing from the body of Abel. Another close-up of Holmes, his head dripping blood, but his eyes intact, looking in supplication at the sky. Cut again to print of Nebuchadnezzar. Repeat vision of Moriarty approaching, with a voiceover: Moriarty saying, "You must stand clear, Mr. Holmes, or be trodden underfoot." Cut to print of Nebuchadnezzar, then print of Cain. Another close-up of Holmes, only now no blood at all and the background indicates he is backed up against one of the upright stones of the quoit. His hands clutch his head like Cain in the print, then move to cover eyes again. Print of Cain returns. Cut to clip of Moriarty at last reaching him as their grappling above the Falls begins. Back to a close-up of Holmes warding unseen terror off with his hands, then Holmes and Moriarty going over the Reichenbach Falls. Again the close-up of Holmes frantically warding something off, followed by a return to the scene of the detective falling with his nemesis. The shot of the waves in turmoil is mixed with the falling image. Watson's voice then slowly intrudes, and the screen cuts to solid red. The music stops completely as Watson pulls Holmes out of the hallucination. We know we have left the hallucination and returned to Watson's perspective when the music ceases, and we see Holmes lying on the ground, struggling to wake up.

WORKS CITED

The Abbey Grange. Exec. Prod. Michael Cox. Dir. Peter Hammond. Dram. Trevor Bowen. Granada Television. 1986. *MYSTERY!* PBS. WGBH, Boston. 12 Feb. 1987.

Cox, Michael. Personal Interviews. 28 Nov. 1990 and 12 Feb. 1991.

The Devil's Foot. Exec. Prod. Michael Cox. Dir. Ken Hannam. Dram. Gary Hopkins. Granada Television. 1985. *MYSTERY!* PBS. WGBH, Boston. 3 Nov.1988.

Dick, Bernard F. *Anatomy of Film*. 2nd ed. New York: St. Martin's, 1990.

Doyle, Arthur Conan. "The Adventure of the Devil's Foot." *The Complete Sherlock Holmes* II. Garden City, NY: Doubleday, 1927. 954-70.

___. "The Adventure of the Illustrious Client." *The Complete Sherlock Holmes* II. Garden City, NY: Doubleday, 1927. 984-99.

___. *The Complete Sherlock Holmes*. 2 vols. Garden City, New York: Doubleday, 1927.

___. "A Scandal in Bohemia." *The Complete Sherlock Holmes* I. Garden City, NY: Doubleday, 1927. 161-75.

Hardwicke, Edward. "Edward Hardwicke on Conan Doyle's Popularity." Interview. PBS. WGBH, Boston. Attached to *The Problem of Thor Bridge*.

The Illustrious Client. Prod. Michael Cox. Dir. Tim Sullivan. Dram. Robin Chapman. Granada Television. 1991. *MYSTERY!* PBS. WGBH, Boston. 14 Nov. 1992.

Monaco, James. *How to Read a Film: The Art, Technology, Language, History and Theory of Film and Media*. New York: Oxford UP, 1977.

The Naval Treaty. Prod. Michael Cox. Dir. Alan Grint. Dram. Jeremy Paul. Granada Television. 1984. *MYSTERY!* PBS. WGBH, Boston. 28 Mar. 1985.

The Problem of Thor Bridge. Prod. Michael Cox. Dir. Michael Simpson. Dram. Jeremy Paul. Granada Television. 1991. *MYSTERY!* PBS. WGBH, Boston. 28 Nov. 1992.

The Resident Patient. Prod. Michael Cox. Dir. David Carson. Dram. Derek Marlowe. Granada Television. 1985. *MYSTERY!* PBS. WGBH, Boston. 13 Feb. 1986.

Richardson, Robert. *Literature and Film*. Bloomington: Indiana UP, 1972.

A Scandal in Bohemia. Prod. Michael Cox. Dir. Paul Annett. Dram. Alexander Baron. Granada Television. 1984. *MYSTERY!* PBS. WGBH, Boston. 14 Mar. 1985.

The Second Stain. Exec. Prod. Michael Cox. Dir. John Bruce. Dram. John Hawkesworth. Granada Television. 1986. *MYSTERY!* PBS. WGBH, Boston. 26 Feb. 1987.

The Patriarchy Restored:
BBC Television's Adaptation of
Dorothy L. Sayers's *Strong Poison*,
Have His Carcase, and *Gaudy Night*

William Reynolds

The 1987 television adaptations of Strong Poison, Have His Carcase, *and* Gaudy Night *reshape Dorothy L. Sayers's characters into stereotypical figures and conventionalize her account of the relationship between Peter Wimsey and Harriet Vane. Despite a generally effective treatment of Sayers's mystery plots, the series transforms her carefully developed account of a male-female relationship grounded in equality into a standard mass-market romance.*

More than 50 years after the publication of her last novel, Dorothy L. Sayers has maintained her reputation as a first-rate writer of detective fiction. Yet one debate refuses to be silenced: that involving Harriet D. Vane, the heroine of *Strong Poison* (1930), *Have His Carcase* (1932), *Gaudy Night* (1936), and *Busman's Honeymoon* (1937).[1] For 30 years Harriet received little attention save as a foil to Sayers's detective Lord Peter Wimsey; and despite Sayers's own comments, their courtship and marriage was regarded as little more than a standard convention of popular fiction.

Recent feminist critics, however, have centered attention on Harriet, and most have condemned Sayers for creating a strong, independent woman only to have her abandon her independence by capitulating to Peter and assuming the traditional female role of wife and mother. Nina Auerbach, for example, calls Peter's marriage to Harriet a "self-congratulatory, cloying idyll" (165). Other feminist critics defend Harriet; Susan J. Leonardi, for example, maintains that "Harriet Vane, that most sympathetic heroine, chooses marriage over female community or a single life . . . to find scope for her gifts as well as lifelong companionship" (97).

Such disagreement about Harriet's relationship with Peter is not possible with the 1987 television mini-series starring Edward

31

Petherbridge as Peter Wimsey and Harriet Walter as Harriet Vane; for the series does exactly what Sayers's detractors accuse her of doing. The adaptations deal effectively with the mysteries presented in the novels, but not with Sayers's carefully developed account of a male-female relationship grounded in equality—one relevant nearly 60 years after Sayers wrote it. Instead, these films reshape Harriet and Peter's love into a standard mass-market romance: emotional attraction, pursuit by Peter, temporary resistance by Harriet, and a resolution representing little more than dominance on Peter's part and submission on Harriet's.

The first indication of the series' lack of interest in what Sayers furnished is its omission of *Busman's Honeymoon*. This novel, which begins with a section entitled *Prothalamion* and ends with one called *Epithalamion* (alluding to two of the most famous marriage poems in English), concerns itself with far bigger issues than identifying a murderer. Even a cursory reading of this novel discloses that for Sayers the commitment and self-giving represented by Peter and Harriet's marriage constitute a natural, indeed a necessary, stage in their relationship—and, by implication, in other relationships as well. Moreover, this novel plays an essential role in completing Sayers's picture of Harriet and Peter as mature individuals and giving them what Catherine Kenney terms "psychological realism" (174).

This avoidance of Sayers's intent is equally obvious in the handling of the novels the BBC series chose to include: *Strong Poison*, *Have His Carcase*, and *Gaudy Night*. The options rejected by the series can be clarified by reviewing the genesis of the Wimsey-Vane novels. From 1922 to 1930 Dorothy L. Sayers worked at S.H. Benson, Ltd., at the time Britain's largest advertising agency, and did her writing—including the early Wimsey novels *Clouds of Witness* (1927), *Unnatural Death* (1927), and *The Unpleasantness at the Bellona Club* (1928) on the side. By 1930, she had gained enough financial security to quit her job and begin a full-time career as a freelance writer. Pleased with her one non-Wimsey novel, *The Documents in the Case* (1930), and eager to attempt still other types of serious fiction, she began *Strong Poison* with what she described seven years later as "the infanticidal intention of doing away with Peter; that is, of marrying him off and getting rid of him" ("Gaudy Night" 78).

Sayers points to the British and American public's growing appetite for Lord Peter as a key reason she turned from her intended path; and economic self-defense surely had something to do with it.

A worldwide depression was beginning to make itself felt, and her husband's income had almost disappeared. But Sayers furnishes another, far less mundane yet quite believable, version of what happened:

> I could not marry Peter off to the young woman he had (in the conventional Perseus manner) rescued from death and infamy, because I could find no form of words in which she could accept him without loss of self-respect. I had landed my two chief puppets in a situation where, according to all the conventional rules of detective fiction, they should have had nothing to do but fall into one another's arms; but they would not do it, and that for a good reason. When I looked at the situation I saw that it was in every respect false and degrading; and the puppets had somehow got just so much flesh and blood in them that I could not force them to accept it without shocking myself. ("Gaudy Night" 79)

Faced with this dilemma, Sayers decided "there were only two things to do: one was to leave the thing there, with the problem unresolved; the other, far more delicate and dangerous, was to take Peter away and perform a major operation on him. If the story was to go on, Peter had got to become a complete human being" ("Gaudy Night" 79-80). Sayers chose the second alternative—hardly a surprise for someone who within a few months of the publication of *Strong Poison* had called on mystery writers (obviously thinking primarily of herself) to accept "the necessity of creating living character" ("Present Status" 50) and produce books that "strike that interior note of essential mysteriousness which is part of the nature of things" (51-52). In short, being forced to keep Peter going a while longer did not force Sayers to abandon her Arnoldian desire to write fiction that would furnish what she would later term a "serious treatment of the sins and passions . . . which commonly form the motives for violent crime" (Introduction, *Tales* xii). Rather, she added to this goal the challenge of providing such a treatment from within the detective fiction genre.

Catherine Kenney observes that it is "difficult to know how closely Sayers's proffered explanation actually describes her conscious motivation" (86), and nowhere does Sayers indicate when in the process of writing *Strong Poison* she arrived at these conclusions. But, Kenney continues, "whether it was done consciously or not, the pattern that 'Gaudy Night' describes is in Sayers's fiction" (86). The pattern begins with Harriet and Peter's last scene together in *Strong Poison* when Harriet surprises Peter by rejecting his offer of marriage but does so without making it impossible for their relationship to develop further, continues in a muted way through *Have His Carcase*, and becomes fully realized in *Gaudy Night* and *Busman's Honeymoon*.

And it is this pattern which the BBC film series neglects. The film of *Strong Poison* simplifies but does no major violence to the mystery plot and, with the exception of one original scene, treats the Harriet-Peter plot in the same order as the novel. But the film's characterization is original; sharing Sayers's perception that Peter needs to be humanized, it begins the process in *Strong Poison* itself. In addition, the film does not accept Sayers's view that Harriet is "a human being from the start" ("Gaudy Night" 81) and sets about reshaping her as well.

Some of what the series intends as humanization is accomplished through minor additions to the film—chit-chat between Peter and Harriet about the personality of the warder watching over them, about Harriet's new novel, and about Peter's motivation for wanting to marry Harriet; Peter's touching Harriet's hand and saying "Damn" while she weeps; and Harriet's reciting in her own mind the last stanza of "To Althea, from Prison." But these segments, clearly intended to convince viewers that a romance can exist between Harriet and Peter, offer sloppy romanticism and surface emotion in place of rounded characterization.

Other alterations, beginning with the scene in which Peter meets Harriet for the first time and then unexpectedly announces that he intends to marry her, shape Harriet and Peter into what amount to new creations. In the novel, the trauma of her imprisonment and trial have deprived Harriet of her self-confidence and much of her ability to think straight. But her reaction to Peter's bolt from the blue is in line with a comment she has just made: "I thought Philip had made both himself and me ridiculous, and the minute I saw that—well, the whole thing simply shut down—flop!" (IV).[2] Viewing Peter's proposal as another attempt to make her "ridiculous," she groups Peter with those sad "imbeciles" who propose marriage to accused murderesses. So hasty and so wide of the mark is her analysis that one wonders how it can come from a writer of detective fiction who has followed the course of Peter's career and who is in the middle of a long conversation in which Peter again and again reveals both his powerful intellect and his serious commitment to her cause. Though it does not become clear till later, Harriet's lack of self-esteem accounts for what she says;

she is simply not prepared to believe that Peter means what he says about his feelings for her. But at the same time, two of Harriet's comments late in this scene hint at the kind of person she really is, the person Peter alone seems capable of seeing. She tells Peter, "I'm sorry—but one gets rather a bruised sort of feeling in my position. There have been so many beastlinesses." And when Peter answers, "I know. . . . It was stupid of me," she quickly replies, "No, I think it was stupid of me" (IV).

The Harriet of the film is very different. However amazed this Harriet may be by Peter's proposal, she is in complete command of herself—no sense that she is too worthless to be loved, no wild conclusions, and no intemperate words, only "Have I got this right? You are proposing marriage to me. . . . Do you do this all the time, Lord Peter?" Not until her third scene with Peter does she even ask Peter to explain himself more fully; and nowhere does she evince the concern for Peter's feelings apparent in the novel.

During the first two hours of the film, Peter is substantially the Peter of Sayers's novel. The major alteration comes in Peter's fifth scene with Harriet. This scene, unique to the film and the only scene between Harriet and Peter not to incorporate anything from the novel, opens with Peter telling Harriet that the mysterious white powder which seemed to show that Philip Boyes had committed suicide is only bicarbonate of soda. Toward the end of this scene Peter displays an honesty about his own feelings far beyond what he shows in the novel. He tells Harriet, "I was trying to think of something funny to say. I can't," and then drops his usual bravura to answer Harriet's "It would be awful to feel funny all the time" with "Yes, it would, wouldn't it." But in subsequent scenes, particularly the final conversation between Harriet and Peter, the film fails to develop the Peter it introduces here.

While the Harriet portrayed in the novel is afraid of the commitment involved in marriage, she also expresses her reservations in terms of Peter's situation and offers to live with him as his mistress. There is nothing unusual about such a suggestion in 1990's terms; but to see what it means, or came to mean, to Harriet, we need to leap ahead to the last chapter of *Gaudy Night* where she tells Peter, "It was myself I was sick of. How could I give you base coin for a marriage-portion?" (XXIII). This self-analysis goes a long way to clarifying why Harriet and Peter's first and last meetings in *Strong Poison* should be interpreted in terms of Harriet's lack of self-esteem. Though she is about to be exonerated of the murder charge, Harriet still thinks so little of herself that she is unable to think in terms of love. She offers to become Peter's mistress because, as she will tell him in *Gaudy Night*, the offer "meant nothing to me" (XXIII). So completely has Harriet lost her sense of self that she is, in fact, offering to repeat with Peter the very relationship she had with Philip Boyes, a relationship which she had given up her principles to enter into.

Once again, the film's Harriet is very different. Two things about this Harriet come through clearly. The first is that in this scene—as in the "proposal scene"—she shows herself far more insightful, more forceful, and (perhaps most important) more independent than the Harriet of the novel. Like the Harriet of the novel, the film's Harriet says that she wants to "be left alone," but new to the film is Harriet's announcement that she intends to travel. (In fact, this more dynamic Harriet does just as she says, for the walking trip to the southwest coast of England which opens the film version of *Have His Carcase* takes place a few weeks rather than the novel's seventeen months after her acquittal.) In addition, she sums up Peter with great accuracy when she calls him "a sort of latter-day knight errant searching for opportunities to . . . rescue damsels in distress."

The second is that even though the Harriet of the film weeps more freely than her counterpart in the novel, her tears are no sign that she lacks self-esteem. In fact, she places a high but certainly reasonable value on herself, informing Peter that she does like him, but developing further the knight errant metaphor by disassociating herself from the Andromedas of the world and telling him that mutual love, not just a rescue from a monster, must be the basis of the kind of relationship he is proposing. But even though she echoes the novel's Harriet in saying that it wouldn't be fair to Peter if she married him, the film's Harriet moves beyond self-esteem to self-absorption through her failure to think of the effect on Peter of her equating his offer of marriage with "another affair."

The Peter we encounter in this scene is different too—different from the Peter of the novel and from the Peter of earlier in the film. Rather than revealing how deeply Harriet's remarks have hurt him, he switches back to his role as "silly ass about town" and caps Harriet's comment on his romanticism with a teasing reference to her own romantic dreams of Greece and Venice. Peter's response is certainly understandable, but neither it nor his closing remark that "at least . . . [he] can still make . . . [Harriet] laugh" shows the added depth and honesty he displayed in earlier scenes. And, in fact, both comments fall short of the response Peter offers in the novel: not a glib one-liner but the best that can be expected of him at this point in his life, "I won't worry you. Not fair. Abusing my privilege and so on" (XXI). In the final scene of the novel, the emphasis is on the principles upon which Peter and Harriet's relationship rests. Harriet—accompanied by Eiluned Price and Sylvia Marriott—leaves the courtroom and looks about, expecting to see Peter. But Peter is not there. To understand what is happening we may look at the explanation Eiluned provides. Having realized that his generosity has cast him as King Cophetua and placed Harriet in the position of the beggar maid, Peter stays away. To do otherwise would not be "fair," to use his own word from the last of his scenes with Harriet. Harriet's surprise at Peter's absence is another sign of her own as yet incomplete understanding of Peter, of herself, and of their relationship. Here, at least in embryonic form, is the thematic material for the remainder of the tetralogy.

The film is unconcerned with these matters: Harriet leaves court alone; Peter comes to her, and Harriet rejects Peter outright. Unlike the Peter of the novel, the film's Peter cannot anticipate that his presence will be painful to Harriet. Given that Harriet has admitted that she likes him and that their last meeting ended in laughter, Peter has no reason to avoid meeting Harriet and every reason to wish her well. In turn, Harriet has no reason to treat Peter as she does. She has not told him or even asked him to stay away, nor has Peter promised to do so; yet Harriet looks directly at him, turns, and without a word or even a second glance walks away, leaving him to stare after her in pained betrayal. The added strength which the film has given her leads to an impetuous act of gratuitous cruelty, while the absence of Eiluned and Sylvia emphasizes Harriet's independence as the governing principle behind all she does. The final scene is powerful and successfully completes the film's picture of a more independent, less sensitive Harriet governed by emotion, not reason, and of a Peter unsure of himself and of how to construct a relationship with Harriet—a pattern which continues through the rest of the series.

The novel and film versions of *Have His Carcase* differ radically in fictional chronology. Probably because she was uncertain about exactly what to do with the Harriet-Peter relationship, Sayers kept Harriet out of her next novel, *Five Red Herrings* (1931); so almost a year and a half elapse between Harriet's acquittal in January of 1930 and the initial events of *Have His Carcase* on June 18, 1931. During these 17 months Harriet has started to come to terms with the events of *Strong Poison*; Peter has begun to construct what Sayers terms a "delicate structure of confidence" (*HHC* XIII) between Harriet and himself; and both have done some thinking about how things stand between them. As has been mentioned, the film adaptation of *Have His Carcase* allows no such breathing room and begins only a few weeks after Harriet's acquittal—which the film of *Strong Poison* moves from January 1930 to July of the same year, probably to avoid having to shoot winter scenes for *Strong Poison* and summer ones for *Have His Carcase*. The events of *Strong Poison* still dominate. Viewers are shown the final scene of *Strong Poison* by way of introduction to the new film, and a few minutes into the first episode, Harriet falls asleep and dreams of the scene in *Strong Poison* when she told Peter that she would not marry him.

Though the film of *Have His Carcase* is an excellent example of how to change a complex Golden Age plot to meet the needs of a visual format, its picture of Harriet and Peter's relationship is much thinner than the original's. The novel's principal goals are to deepen Peter's and Harriet's characters and to suggest the foundation on which they can construct a lasting relationship. Acting as Peter's partner in investigating the death of Paul Alexis helps Harriet take important steps toward overcoming her feelings of inferiority. But throughout the novel she continues her own work as a detective novelist, struggling to follow her publisher's suggestion that she add a love story to her novel-in-progress, *The Fountain Pen Mystery*, and, like Sayers herself, finding the topic cutting too close to the bone. The film, however, increases the role Harriet plays in investigating and solving the mystery of Paul Alexis's murder to the point that she completely neglects work on her new novel in order to detect. She participates in meetings which in the novel involve only Peter and the local police, joins Peter and sometimes Bunter in new scenes which telescope whole chapters of the novel into a few lines of dialogue, and ultimately sees the significance of the final clue only a second after Peter does so. But her activity ultimately diminishes her; and as the film hurries along her romance with Peter, it actually makes her even more dependent upon him.

Making Harriet more central, more active, and, at first glance, more independent accords well with the reshaping of her character that goes on in the film of *Strong Poison*, but as a result of the changes and the compression of 17 months into a few weeks, Harriet and Peter's first meeting in *Have His Carcase* is almost impossibly nonchalant and amicable. Driven by love, Peter can plausibly swallow his pride and come to Harriet; but it is almost inconceivable that Harriet, who in a line not found in the novel has reminded the audience as well as the police that she owes Lord Peter "a great deal," can welcome Peter as casually as she does and, what is more, go through the entire novel without apologizing for or even alluding to the harshness of their parting in *Strong Poison*.

Once viewers get by this incongruity, Harriet and Peter's relationship attains a certain internal consistency, though not a great deal of depth. Peter lets Harriet know his feelings and renews his marriage proposal several times; Harriet wants to go her own way yet feels an unexplained attraction for Peter. After a quarrel, Harriet tells Peter to leave her alone; he does so, but she seeks him out as soon as she needs help. And, in stark contrast to Harriet's treatment of Peter at the end of *Strong Poison*, the film of *Have His Carcase* ends with Peter and Harriet walking hand in hand away from the rock on which Harriet had found Paul's body.

But while the film brings Peter and Harriet closer together than the novel, it also puts her into a different position than she occupies in Sayers's novel, presenting her as having to choose between being her own person and accepting dependence by marrying Peter. The novel's Harriet undeniably sees herself facing the same dilemma; but the film's Harriet talks about it more and—unlike the novel's— accepts the role of Watson to Peter's Holmes rather than following her true career as a writer. And in the novel both Sayers as narrator and Peter furnish grounds for a different and, given what she will learn in *Gaudy Night*, more accurate assessment of Harriet's situation.

An excellent illustration of the difference between the two versions comes in their accounts of the quarrel Peter and Harriet have after she reports that the police have investigated the possibility that she murdered Paul Alexis. The film draws most of its dialogue from the novel, but the film's Harriet follows the novel's "Stop. Let go. I won't be bullied" (XIII) by blurting out an impetuous, "Please go away, Peter. Leave me alone." Thus, after she has discovered that Haviland Martin and Henry Weldon are one man, Harriet cannot simply tell Peter of her discovery but must come hat in hand to ask his help in sorting things out. The reconciliation scene is meant to be touching, but it reinforces the notion that Harriet must choose between living independently and submitting to Peter.

While Sayers had not worked out every detail of Harriet and Peter's relationship, the novel's version of this scene shows that the film has created a false dichotomy. In a key section not included in the movie Peter tells Harriet, "I know you don't want either to give or to take. You've tried being the giver, and you've found that the giver is always fooled. And you won't be the taker, because that's very difficult, and because you know that the taker always ends by hating the giver" (XIII). On first reading, Peter seems to be saying that it is impossible for Harriet to have any sort of relationship whatsoever. In fact, Peter (who in Sayers's hands is indeed starting to resemble a human being) is being much more subtle and for the first time is suggesting to Harriet a type of relationship she has not considered, one based not on giving and taking but on mutuality and sharing (and one which the film reduces to "a free and equal partnership . . . [through which] we will endeavor to solve this singularly fascinating murder"). And it is precisely this sort of relationship which he has been trying to establish; for, in another passage omitted by the film, Harriet forces him to admit in response to a direct question that he came to her precisely so that she "might not have to send for . . . [him]" (XIII).

As with *Strong Poison*, the final scenes of the novel and the film display the essential difference between the two works. Despite, or perhaps because of, Peter's increased sensitivity, Sayers was not prepared to bring Peter and Harriet together at the conclusion of *Have His Carcase*; Harriet remains too "scathed and embittered" (XIII) for that. So, together but still distant, the two leave Wilvercombe to dine in Piccadilly.

The film, however, rushes things along, and in its hurry further conventionalizes its account of Harriet and Peter. As has been mentioned, the film ends with Harriet and Peter walking hand in hand, a change designed to leave the viewer confident that the shallow and poorly motivated relationship that the series has established between its protagonists will turn out right. But more telling than this reinterpretation of Harriet and Peter as moonstruck adolescents are Peter and Harriet's closing words—practically throw-aways, so casually are they presented, yet clearly a synopsis of their situation: "The next time you find yourself in trouble, you might conquer your independent spirit and send for me," demands Peter; "I might," responds Harriet, accepting without demur his insufferable premise that she cannot seek his help without sacrificing her independence and indicating by her manner and her tone that she will do just that.

To bring Peter's courtship of Harriet to the same conclusion, her acceptance of his proposal, Sayers and the miniseries followed two very different routes. Sayers needed three years (from the publication of *Have His Carcase* in April 1932 to the appearance of *Gaudy Night* in November 1935) and two novels in which Harriet is not mentioned (*Murder Must Advertise* [1933] and *The Nine Tailors* [1934]) to take Peter and Harriet from Wilvercombe, which the two leave on July 8, 1931, to New College Lane on the night of May 19, 1935, when Harriet's "Placet" concludes a novel in which detective plot, love story, and theme are intertwined and inseparable. The film compresses events into a much smaller span of time. No months or years are mentioned, but the suggestion is that the start of *Gaudy Night* closely follows the end of *Have His Carcase*, for the details of events recounted in this novel and even in *Strong Poison* are fresh in Harriet's own mind and in the minds of everyone she encounters at Oxford. In addition, one week—not nine months—intervenes between Harriet's first trip to Oxford to attend the Shrewsbury College Gaudy and her return to investigate the doings of the college's "poltergeist"; and her investigation takes less than a week, rather than two and a half months.

Given the wide range of disagreement about the worth of *Gaudy Night*, it is useful to recall Sayers's own analysis of what she regarded as her best novel. First, she analyzes Harriet and Peter's love as a balance of two equally important factors: emotional attraction and a mutual respect for "intellectual integrity . . . the one great permanent value in an emotionally unstable world" ("Gaudy Night" 82). While Sayers's analysis deals only with the presentation of this theme in *Gaudy Night*, emotional attraction is the principal force behind Peter's actions in *Strong Poison* as well and appears repeatedly, for the first time on Harriet's side, in *Have His Carcase*.

The intellectual strand is harder to trace, but Sayers herself wrote that while she had wanted to say something about the topic all her life, she had done so only "in a confused way" ("Gaudy Night" 82) before *Gaudy Night*. In *Strong Poison* the importance of intellectual honesty is evident in Harriet's anger at Philip Boyes's tricking her into compromising her own principles; in Peter's ability and the judge's inability to understand Harriet's position; and in Peter's own comment that if he accepted Harriet's offer to be his mistress, others could forget that they were not married but he could not. And one can see it also in *Have His Carcase* when Peter tells Harriet that he does not want love under false pretenses but instead desires "common honesty" (XIII), exactly what had been denied Harriet in her relationship with Philip Boyes.

Second, Sayers analyzes *Gaudy Night* as a means of providing "the intellectual platform, [on which] alone of all others Harriet could stand free and equal with Peter" ("Gaudy Night" 82) and "come to him as a free agent, if she came at all" (87). In the intellectual life of Oxford Harriet locates the "means of freeing herself from the emotional obsession he [Peter] produced in her, and yet . . . [thinks she sees] that the celibate intellectual life rendered one liable to insanity in its ugliest forms" (85). Though given repeated chances to win Harriet by forcing her into "an emotional surrender from which there could be no subsequent return" (86), Peter refuses, seeing that if "Harriet accepted him under any sort of misapprehension, or through any insincerity on his part, they would be plunged into a situation even more false and intolerable than that from which they started" (86-87).

In the film, however, Harriet does not come to see that she and Peter can achieve a delicate, demanding, but enriching balance of head and heart, but acts out instead woman's traditional role by making a purely emotional decision and affirming her own second-class role. The film begins with Harriet resolved to tell Peter "to chuck it"; but she soon changes her mind, refusing to have their lives controlled by anonymous letter writers. And this same high level of independence continues to characterize Harriet while she is in Oxford attending the Shrewsbury College Gaudy. But the film quickly involves Harriet with the same dichotomy between marriage and freedom as in *Have His Carcase*.

In the novels, Harriet suffers from two types of mutually reinforcing inferiority: one because Peter saved her from the gallows and a second because her life with Boyes had robbed her of a sense of her own value. Peter literally gives her life back to Harriet by allowing her to risk it. Knowing that Harriet has been the target of one failed ambush, Peter warns her to expect another attack, gives her a lesson in self-defense, and buys her a dog collar to wear at night as protection against "thugs and throat-slitters" (XIX). Then he steps aside and lets Harriet assume full responsibility for herself. The film follows a different course. While the television Harriet shows no signs of lacking a sense of self-esteem, she is if anything more vigorous in reminding Peter and others that she owes him her life. When danger arises, Peter tells Harriet the obvious—that a threat which mentions her by name is particularly serious—and advises her to "Take care." No explicit connections are made, so unless Harriet has resolved the issue internally and not told anyone, including Peter, about it, the issue is simply allowed to die.

In fact, by the end of the film Harriet has every reason to feel even more inferior to Peter. Though she investigates more and detects more in *Gaudy Night* than in *Have His Carcase* (and in both films enjoys more success as an investigator than in the novels), her performance is still second-rate compared to Peter's; and though nominally a writer, Harriet has no role, no job other than detective. As we have seen, in the film of *Have His Carcase* she abandons work on *The Fountain Pen Mystery* in favor of crossword puzzles. In *Gaudy Night* she has no project of her own to work on; even the suggestion that she disguise her real purpose by helping Miss Lydgate with the proofs of her book comes from the Warden and the Dean.

In the novel, on the other hand, even though Harriet determines that her true work is in the active not the contemplative world, she also finds that the intellectual life appeals to one part of her nature. Like Peter, she holds a First Class degree (in the film, his is mentioned; hers is not), and she herself proposes that her work with Miss Lydgate serve as the cover for her real reason for staying in Oxford. More importantly, after Harriet puts it about that she is "spending a couple of weeks in College, while engaged in research at the Bodleian on the life and works of Sheridan Le Fanu" (VII), she gives as much time to her research as conditions permit and experiences an "acute homesickness for Oxford and the *Study of Le Fanu*" (XI) when she spends a few days back in London.

Most crucially, even during her search for the Shrewsbury College Poltergeist, the novel's Harriet continues to work on her newest novel, *Death 'twixt Wind and Water*. The significance of this decision becomes clear when, at the end of their time punting on the river, she and Peter discuss the novel and its central figure, Wilfrid. To her surprise, Peter takes her work seriously, tells her that she has not yet written the book she is capable of writing, and advises her to write about human beings, not cardboard figures. By acting on Peter's advice to the extent that by the end of *Gaudy Night* she can tell him that though Wilfrid needs more work, he is "almost human" (XXIII), Harriet establishes for herself that she does not need what for her would be a retreat into academe to be on an equal footing with Peter. Harriet recognizes that she can achieve this by doing her "proper job" (II) of writing the best detective novels possible and "really *working* at Wilfrid" (XXIII); and Peter acknowledges the worth of Harriet's work when he stammers, "If you have let me come as far as your work and your life . . . Here! I think I'd better remove myself before I do anything foolish" (XXIII).

Though the film does not furnish Harriet with an intellectual platform on which her position is equal to Peter's, it also does not leave her an Andromeda upon the rock. Those who have read the novel will be able to create a case for the film's Harriet being the sort of woman that Peter would want to propose to; but such a case, flimsy at best, is impossible for those who know only the film. In the course of *Gaudy Night* both Harriets learn why their respective Peters love them. In the novel, Peter urges Harriet to exercise her "talent for keeping to the point and speaking the truth" since that is "what I love you for" (XVII). In the film, Harriet accepts Peter's invitation to go punting with "I never resist a challenge," to which Peter replies "That's why I love you." The messages are important not just for what they reveal about Peter but for what they say about Harriet and her reasons for not marrying Peter.

In addition to recognizing that inferiority and gratitude do not form a satisfactory basis for a marriage, the novel's Harriet has resolved that never again will she compromise her principles as she did with Philip Boyes. Of primary concern to her is the danger that if she makes a commitment to Peter she will lose her life as a writer; "Could there ever be an alliance between the intellect and the flesh?" she asks herself (XXI). Because of Peter's honesty in assuring her that a life without personal relationships does not automatically qualify one for a "Freudian case-book" (XV) and in pursuing his investigation even when he recognizes that it will lead to her seeing the worst that love is capable of, Harriet accepts the truth of Miss de Vine's analysis that Peter will "never make up your mind for you. You'll have to make your own decisions. You needn't be afraid of losing your independence; he will always force it back on you" (XXII). Their relationship which, in Peter's musical metaphor, "isn't a matter of an autocratic virtuoso and a meek accompanist" but of "two . . . musicians" (XXIII) will be a demanding and dynamic one, "the repose of very delicate balance" (XXII) Miss de Vine calls it. In choosing it Harriet remains true to herself and demonstrates in her personal life the intellectual integrity which Peter regards as her defining quality.

While the film mentions the importance of intellectual integrity in connection with the mystery plot, a similar connection to Harriet's own life is made only in a scene in the first episode when Miss de Vine advises her to value anyone who likes her because of her honesty. No one else talks about the topic, and it is, in fact, cut from the key discussion that Harriet has with Miss de Vine in the third episode, immediately before Harriet accepts Peter's proposal. As in the novel, Harriet tells Miss de Vine, "if I once gave way to Peter, I should go up like straw" and in reply to Miss de Vine's

"How often has he used that weapon against you?" answers "Never" (XXII). But Miss de Vine's insights are cut short in the film. In the novel, Miss de Vine reminds Harriet that she has "had the luck to come up against a very unselfish and a very honest man. He has done what you asked him without caring what it cost him and without shirking the issue. He hasn't tried to disguise the facts or bias your judgement" (XXII). But in the film Miss de Vine simply asks Harriet what she is afraid of, and Harriet jumps ahead to "I shouldn't be at all a comfortable person for him to live with. I've got a devilish temper" (XXII), maintaining the emotional basis which her unwillingness to marry Peter has had all along. Most importantly, not until the final scene do Harriet and Peter talk about intellectual integrity, and the whole notion is badly undercut by an earlier scene not found in the novel in which Peter tells Harriet that it would be nice if she would dissemble occasionally to spare his feelings.

As has been said, the film uses parts of the novel to prepare for Harriet's acceptance of Peter's proposal; but once the mystery story has been told, very little time remains to develop the relationship between the two. Harriet and Peter spend too little time together and talk too little about their relationship to develop anything more substantial than the whirlwind romance necessitated by the compression of five and a third years into a matter of months. Even the treatment given this theme in the final scene of the series, the one in which Harriet accepts Peter's marriage proposal, does nothing to change this basis. The film echoes the novel in commenting on the way that Oxford alters a person's values. But while praise for the University's commitment to truth accords satisfactorily with what has been demonstrated in earlier parts of the film, lines not taken from the novel have to be added in an eleventh-hour attempt to connect this commitment to Harriet and Peter's personal situation. And the connection is made even more tenuous when, following Peter's declaration that he has not proposed to her in Oxford because he feared—rather than the novel's far more telling "knew" (XXIII)—that whatever answer she gave him would be final, Harriet tells Peter that he would in fact be taking "a risk" in proposing to her.

Harriet's choice of "risk" provides an almost ideal summary of the situation as the film presents it. Taking up Peter's earlier statement that he is attracted to Harriet because she is not afraid of a challenge, Harriet in effect challenges Peter to try his luck. When he responds with "Will you marry me?" she accepts with "Dear

Idiot" and a kiss. Not having overcome any of the objections she has voiced, Harriet succumbs to her emotions, won over by Peter's willingness to let everything ride on one throw of the romantic dice. In fact, given the way she orchestrates the scene, leading Peter to ask the all-or-nothing question whose answer he cannot possibly know but which she is sure of, Peter's pursuit ends not so much in Harriet's capture as in her surrender to her emotions and to the demands of a formula.

In her famous Introduction to *Great Short Stories of Detection, Mystery, and Horror*, published two years before *Strong Poison*, Dorothy L. Sayers devoted a major section to what she called a "fettering convention, from which detective fiction is only very slowly freeing itself . . . that of the 'love interest'" (38). One can almost see Sayers returning to this essay, reading her comments about Wilkie Collins's *The Moonstone* and E.C. Bentley's *Trent's Last Case*, two of the extremely rare "instances in which the love-story is an integral part of the plot" (39), and saying to herself, "Right. My story must be 'handled artistically and with persuasive emotion'; my characters' conduct must be 'completely natural and right, and . . . [they must be] so finely conceived as to be entirely convincing" (39). Sayers heeded her own counsel and surpassed her models. But the miniseries fell into the very trap Sayers had anticipated when she wrote, "the whole difficulty about allowing real human beings into a detective-story . . . [is that] the detective interest gets hold of them and makes their emotions look like pasteboard" (40). For it is these pasteboard emotions which drive the characters of the series to a thoughtless reenactment of the insidious stereotype which demands that every Jack have his Jill and that every Jill's one and only goal be marriage.

NOTES

[1]*Strong Poison* recounts how Peter saves Harriet from the gallows by identifying the real murderer of her former lover. In *Have His Carcase*, Peter and Harriet identify the murderer of Paul Alexis; in *Gaudy Night* Harriet and Peter again collaborate on an investigation, and on the last page Harriet accepts Peter's proposal of marriage. In *Busman's Honeymoon* Sayers describes Harriet and Peter's wedding, their honeymoon, and the first three months of their married life.

[2]Because there is no standard edition of Dorothy L. Sayers's novels, references will be to chapters rather than to pages.

WORKS CITED

Auerbach, Nina. *Communities of Women*. Cambridge: Harvard UP, 1978.

Gaudy Night. Dir. Michael Simpson. Prod. Michael Chapman. Writ. Philip Broadley. BBC2. 13, 20, 27 May 1987. *MYSTERY!* PBS. WGBH, Boston. 19, 26 Nov. and 3 Dec. 1987.

Have His Carcase. Dir. Christopher Hodson. Prod. Michael Chapman. Writ. Rosemary Anne Sisson. BBC2. 15, 22, 29 Apr. and 6 May 1987. *MYSTERY!* PBS. WGBH, Boston. 22, 29 Oct. and 5, 12 Nov. 1987.

Kenney, Catherine. *The Remarkable Case of Dorothy L. Sayers*. Kent, Ohio: Kent State UP, 1990.

Leonardi, Susan J. *Dangerous by Degrees*. New Brunswick: Rutgers UP, 1989.

Sayers, Dorothy L. *Gaudy Night*. London: Gollancz, 1935.

____. "Gaudy Night." *Titles to Fame*. Ed. Denys K. Roberts. London: Nelson, 1937. 75-95.

____. *Have His Carcase*. London: Gollancz, 1932.

____. Introduction. *Great Short Stories of Detection, Mystery, and Horror*. Ed. Dorothy L. Sayers. London: Gollancz, 1928. 9-47.

____. Introduction. *Tales of Detection*. Ed. Dorothy L. Sayers. London: Dent, 1936. vii-xiv.

____. "The Present Status of the Mystery Story." *The London Mercury* Nov. 1930: 47-52.

____. *Strong Poison*. London: Gollancz, 1930.

Strong Poison. Dir. Christopher Hodson. Prod. Michael Chapman. Writ. Philip Broadley. BBC2. 25 Mar. and 1, 8 Apr. 1987. *MYSTERY!* PBS. WGBH, Boston. 1, 8, 15 Oct. 1987.

Hard-boiled or Ham-It-Up?
The Thin Man Movies

Frederick Isaac

The Thin Man (1934) is an effective, though simplified, cinematic adaptation of Dashiell Hammett's novel. The five subsequent Thin Man films successfully follow the formula of the "Screwball Mystery," whose goal is to identify a dangerous killer while taking itself as lightly as possible. Considered as a group, the films also accurately mirror the social changes going on in the United States between 1934 and 1947.

The Thin Man is not Dashiell Hammett's best-known work. That honor goes to The Maltese Falcon. However, it may be argued that in The Thin Man Hammett used the widest array of characters and created the wildest and most unpredictable situations in his entire oeuvre. In addition, and best of all, it is the source of the detecting couple Nick and Nora Charles. After seeing one or more of the six movies featuring William Powell and Myrna Loy as Nick and Nora, the mystery reader may well ask what sort of films they are. Are they mysteries like those taken from the work of such writers as Agatha Christie or Rex Stout? Did they presage the *noir* style of the 1940s, with its gloomy cityscapes and hunter-hunted themes? Or were they meant not to be mysteries at all, but merely vehicles for screwball comic romances, taking advantage of the styles established by Busby Berkeley and Preston Sturges? In fact, these films alternate elements of both mystery and comedy, often to surprising ends. I will first take a brief look at the novel itself. Then I will focus more closely on the movies from several perspectives: the role of the stars; plot and character components; and the parts comedy and mystery play in the creation of the lasting Thin Man image. These varied perspectives will demonstrate that by blending comedy and suspense these movies created a fusion of styles and forms that has rarely been matched in the intervening years.

Written in 1933 during the Great Depression, The Thin Man was an immediate success. Three reasons may be cited for its enormous and lasting popularity. First, its characters, especially

49

Nick and Nora Charles, are portrayed as children of the Twenties who live the high life and disregard the conventional social standards. The novel is filled with action, and with dialogue not supposed to be heard in polite society. In the famous scene in their bedroom, Nick punches Nora (8); later, Nick says of one character that "she hates men more than any woman I've ever known who wasn't a lesbian" (24); and in her most famous quote Nora says: "Tell me, Nick. Tell me the truth: when you were wrestling with Mimi, didn't you have an erection?" (25).[1] Nick and Nora live their own lives, free of both the Depression and the new, more stringent morality that was on the horizon. Their adventure is filled with drama and comedy, mixing high society life and gangsters in equal measure. The book's ability to balance such disparate elements is one of its continuing charms.

Second, the novel's contempt for the just-ended Prohibition era appealed to readers. Rather than presenting Nick and Nora as upstanding citizens, *The Thin Man* goes out of its way to show them moving easily between saloons and smart-set society, drinking their way through life. The booze flows through the whole story like a mountain stream; there is practically no chapter where someone isn't making, serving, or holding one or more drinks. Even today, almost 60 years later, one of the most precise characterizations that can be made of Nick and Nora is that they are "lushes." Even the scene in which Nick figures out the solution takes place in Studsy Burke's Pigiron Club, a setting prominently mentioned elsewhere in the book.

Finally, *The Thin Man* toys with the conventions of both the traditional whodunit mystery and the hard-boiled style Hammett helped create and popularize. To begin with, the entire book involves a hunt for a missing man instead of the more typical murder investigation: Nick searches for Clyde Wynant rather than for a killer. Even when Nick uncovers the reason for the mystery, he does not investigate further, but simply tells the police what he thinks has happened and why. As a result, Hammett turns the traditional mystery askew, making mincemeat of both fans and commentators trying to categorize the novel.

The legendary popularity of *The Thin Man* began even before the book's publication. *Redbook* was so enthusiastic that in December 1933, a month before the novel's official release, it published a condensed and cleaned-up version. When *The Thin Man* was issued by Alfred Knopf, it captured the public imagination with its high-living heroes and its bewildering plot twists. The book sold 20,000 copies in the first three weeks, and another 10,000 during the remainder of 1934. All the hype and the curiosity led, Diane Johnson points out, to a quick decision by Metro-Goldwyn-Mayer to create a film version, which was shot in eighteen days and released in June 1934 (113).[2]

Every serious mystery fan is aware that the transformation from print to film is often a leap of faith; even the most basic plot elements have been twisted into completely unrecognizable shapes by movie makers. It is, therefore, something of a marvel that *The Thin Man* is a reasonably faithful facsimile of the book. Some characters are missing, many scenes are dropped, the suggestive language is cleaned up, and the ending is more traditional than Hammett's original. Nonetheless, the major themes remain clear. This imitation of a popular original was, in fact, probably one reason that the film was nominated for four Academy Awards in 1934.[3]

In the novel, Nick Charles is 31 and Nora, his heiress wife, is 26. Rather than finding a pair of young actors to play the roles, Metro-Goldwyn-Mayer reached into its stable and pulled off a great coup. William Powell was 42 in 1934, and best known for his portrayal of the superior and distant Philo Vance in four movies for Paramount. To play the high-spirited, sharp-tongued Nora, the studio found a 29-year-old with a dazzling smile and flashing eyes, and instantly turned Myrna Loy into a classic character actress.

Even more fortunate for MGM, the stars became a real team. They liked each other, befriended each other, and exuded the kind of enjoyment that communicates across the screen and over the years. While some credit for this must be given to the screenwriters and directors, especially W.S. Van Dyke (who directed the first four movies), the pair's ability to hold audiences through their rapport remains one of the series' most endearing qualities. Examples of the pair's relationship abound throughout the series, beginning with their first appearance together in *The Thin Man*. It is true that movies are written, and not merely "played" by the actors; but it is equally clear that in this instance the stars quickly established an off-screen relationship that found its way into the films. While it is impossible to identify particular elements or lines introduced by William Powell or Myrna Loy, it is equally unthinkable that they had no part in the ongoing development of the roles. In the end, Nick and Nora Charles are not only Hammett's creations and those of the screenwriters; they were developed and made fully memorable by William Powell and Myrna Loy.[4] The constant challenge in Nora's eyes when Nick wants to go sleuthing without her (once he locks her in a closet, and on another occasion he sends her away in a cab in order to go alone) and the pair's constant sniping about the cases would have been seen as unreasonable if the actors had not made it clear that their fundamental regard for each other is unaffected. Because Powell and Loy were personally friendly, the characters gained from the off-camera relationship.

As we have seen, Hammett's book challenged the reader's expectations of the mystery genre in several ways. The film version, though, was much more consistent with audience expectations. Because movies of the time were plot—and especially solution—driven, *The Thin Man* and its successors eliminated much of Nick and Nora's wild social life. To comply with the need to explain how the mystery began, the film added a prologue, set in Clyde Wynant's warehouse prior to his disappearance, before introducing Nick and Nora. Finally, to comply with the required need for a dramatic climax, the movie created a wonderful and wacky dinner party at which all the suspects appear, and at which Nick gives the solution.

The Thin Man movies did not have enormous casts. *The Thin Man*, which is taken more or less directly from the book, adds Clyde Wynant, but retains his ex-wife Mimi, his daughter Dorothy and son Gilbert, and Mimi's new husband, Chris Jorgenson. All the gangsters also remain, but the subplots involving Nick and Nora's New York friends are dropped. However, the number of significant characters is, in the end, the same as in the book, and enough people get involved in the action that suspicion can be distributed widely among them. Each of the other five films (all of which include murders) has five or six suspects, each of whom tests the heroes' powers of reasoning, but the number of significant speaking roles remains small, usually six or eight.

Many of these characters are intriguing in their own right, adding to the tension and drama; most striking about them is how few are entirely what they seem. (Jessie Ralph as the ultra-proper Aunt Katherine in *After the Thin Man* [1936] and C. Aubrey Smith as Col. MacFay in *Another Thin Man* [1939] are in that category.) It is seldom a good idea to take other characters on their word. Only in the fourth movie, *The Shadow of the Thin Man* (1941), does a romantic couple (played by Barry Nelson and Donna Reed) get from beginning to end without withholding an important secret. If one were to bet on a couple's being what they seem, it is safe to say, as five-year-old Nicky, Jr., does in *Shadow of the Thin Man*, "Son of a Gun at 40-to-1."[5] Even the connections between characters aren't always obvious. Beginning with *After the Thin Man*, every film includes at least one hidden or misidentified relationship, adding to the confusion and the joy of watching Nick and Nora Charles in action. The viewer learns never to count on anything. The person who the audience thinks is guilty may be the actual criminal; but, even then, Nick will probably uncover a secret about him or her just before the final revelation.

The police, on the other hand, are exceptionally bland, rarely moving beyond the stereotypical, and gradually become less and less important to the solution of the crime, while Nick and Nora are increasingly recognized as lightning rods for murder. In the novel, Lt. John Guild befriends Nick and Nora in a meeting after Morelli shoots Nick in Chapter 8's famous bedroom scene. The two men meet a few more times, and Nick finally tells Guild his suspicions. The book ends quietly at that point, with no big climax or shootout. In the film version, Guild (played by Nat Pendleton) plays a rather less intelligent cop, more like Fearless Fosdick than Dick Tracy. Because he is uncertain how to deal with the situation, Guild lets Nick have his way on everything, as if happy to be shown up.[6] Guild also appears in the third film, *Another Thin Man*, but has little more than a cameo presence and makes no significant impact; in that film, Otto Kruger, as Van Slack, the no-nonsense Long Island District Attorney, shares the spotlight with Nick and Nora. In the second and fourth films, set in San Francisco, Nick deals with Inspector Abrams of the San Francisco Police, played by Sam Levene. Abrams is dumb to the point of exasperation, and is also loud. The only time Abrams shuts up is in *The Shadow of the Thin Man* when Nick surprises him with some evidence that the cops ought to have found in their initial search.

The police are even less in evidence in the final two films. In *The Thin Man Goes Home* (1944), the most significant scene involving the local police occurs when Nora leads the stupid small-town police chief on a long walk, so Nick can do some serious investigating. The climactic final sequence takes place with state police, not the locals, in charge. In the final film, *The Song of the Thin Man* (1947), realistic police are completely absent; the climactic scene aboard the party boat reverts to a standard 1930s style: the police, disguised as the staff at a high society party, are wearing guns and big shoes and haven't been taught to wait on tables. While this ludicrous representation is no worse than the way most cops were portrayed throughout the era, it is still quite far from the novel's presentation of John Guild, the honest and hardworking (though ineffectual) cop.

Just as the police are little more than an atmospheric stereotype in the Thin Man films, so too the settings function merely as stage props and create little sense of place. The problem is particularly noticeable in the five films set in major cities. New York, the site of *The Thin Man*, is also the ostensible location of the third and sixth films, *Another Thin Man* and *The Song of the Thin Man*. The second and fourth movies, *After the Thin Man* and *The Shadow of the Thin Man*, take place in a highly stylized San Francisco. The fifth, *The Thin Man Goes Home*, is unexpectedly placed in bucolic Sycamore Springs, Nick Charles's hometown. The novel was set in a very real New York, where Hammett was living with Lillian Hellman. From the very first line, which locates the speakeasy on 52nd Street, there are references to the theaters, Radio City (one of the new wonders of the city, recently opened and catering to a society crowd), and even to less desirable locations like Nunheim's apartment next to the 6th Avenue El. In contrast, the film's attempts to establish the location, either visually or in dialogue, are less successful. Only once is there an exterior set. When Nick and John Guild go to see Nunheim and Nora wants to follow them, Nick puts her in a taxi, closes the door, and tells the driver, "Grant's Tomb."

Similarly, the second and third New York movies give little if any substance to the great metropolis. In *Another Thin Man* Nick and Nora go to see Col. MacFay on Long Island, which at the time had numerous mansions, and visit the apartment of the mysterious Linda Mills. Despite these references, nothing visual commits the audience to the city. *The Song of the Thin Man* opens with a singing and dancing sequence on an ocean-liner-sized party boat, and the focus later shifts to late-night jazz clubs. Though the tone is not as grim as that of *After the Thin Man*, Nick and Nora see practically nothing by daylight. During one late-night jaunt, Nora says, "It's nice to know people still go to bed. Mr. Charles and I used to go to bed," and, later in the same sequence, observes, "I should have worn a sleeping bag."

After the Thin Man begins as Nick and Nora arrive home in San Francisco from their successful case in the East. But aside from a single panoramic shot over the city (probably from the front of the Museum of the Legion of Honor), the movie is composed of dark interiors and even more gloomy outside scenes shot in the "fog" of a New Year's Eve and Day. The choice is quite appropriate, for *After* the Thin Man is by far the darkest of the movies in tone, and the one with the fewest humorous scenes. The Shadow of the Thin Man, a much sunnier film, includes a couple of panoramas of the City by the Bay and makes a few other references to the city, including its seafood industry. But despite these gestures, Shadow of the Thin Man is only moderately successful in establishing San Francisco in any meaningful way.

In contrast to their nondescript depiction of New York and San Francisco, each of the films vibrantly portrays the social changes taking place in American society during the decades of their creation. In the course of the series Nick and Nora grow a bit older, but they remain rich and comfortable. Each episode in their saga, however, reflects something of what was occurring in the nation and the world. By using the underworld of gambling and horse races in The Shadow of the Thin Man and late nights and cool jazz in The Song of the Thin Man the series deliberately attempted to incorporate changes in the life-styles. And any observant viewer can easily see that the World War II America depicted in The Thin Man Goes Home is profoundly different from what it was in the post-Prohibition years of the first two movies.

In addition, changes in personnel affected the tone of the films. After making four films, the team that had made The Thin Man had broken up. The last member of the original group to depart (other than William Powell and Myrna Loy who appear in all six films) was the director. W.S. "One Take" Van Dyke had been a prime contributor to the atmosphere of the series from the very beginning; his death in 1942 is a principal reason the last two films look and feel different from the earlier ones. The mystery of The Thin Man Goes Home (about which more later) contrasts almost absolutely with the idyllic small-town setting and nostalgic screwball comedy present in the domestic scenes: Nick hits his head on a drop-leaf table; Nora has trouble opening a lounge chair; after Nick "fixes" it, the chair collapses when she sits down; while Nick goes in search of clues, Nora joins a jitterbug session and is tossed around by a serviceman on leave. The two elements converge only once, when Nora, Nick's old pal Brogan (whose presence in Sycamore Springs is never explained), and one of the villains stroll through the town. Nora is so intent on following her own quarry that she never suspects that she herself is being tailed. The scene is especially unnerving because the audience quickly realizes that Nora is in real danger. To further his own investigation, Nick has unknowingly put her in jeopardy. This movie has many problems, but missed its mark principally because it tried to do too many things—in particular the "Home Front" sub-plot—at the same time.

More successful is the final film, *The Song of the Thin Man*, which makes a major alteration in the crime-fighting relationship between Nick and Nora. In the other films, Nora is almost always overlooked or neglected in the "serious" business of detection. This time, however, she becomes more of an initiator and less of a distraction. Her scene in the mental hospital with the obviously troubled Buddy is touching, and is noteworthy for being the only time Nora knowingly places herself in jeopardy, a development reflecting a recognition of the change in her position, and by extension that of women in general, during and after World War II.

But while the films present memorable characters and reflect well the temper of their times, they frequently fall short as mysteries. Compared to the novel, *The Thin Man* limits both the complexity of the mystery surrounding Clyde Wynant's disappearance and Nick's activities as a detective, concentrating instead on wonderful set pieces like Nick and Nora's Christmas party and the climactic dinner party at which the murderer is identified. The mystery is, in fact, simplified so much that Nick's investigation bears little resemblance to what he does in the novel. But while Nick's explanation depends to a great degree on several chains of inference and on clues he has concealed until the last minute, the film is simply reflecting the novel in this regard and actually makes more information available to the viewer than the novel does to the reader. However, because of what is revealed through the prologue and the murderer's confirmation of Nick's accusations, the film loses the sense of uncertainty created by a novel whose last words are Nora's comment, "it's all pretty unsatisfactory."

Beginning with the second movie, *After the Thin Man*, the murderers and their motives become increasingly more difficult to identify, and Nick's solutions increasingly arbitrary and impossible to anticipate. In their complexity and desire to surprise all but a lucky few members of the audience, the films pay only lip service to the notion that the audience should possess as much information as the detective. In several cases, a significant amount of the information Nick presents in the climactic "gathering of the suspects" scenes has not been presented previously. The result for even the careful viewer is often astonishment at the clues themselves, rather than satisfaction at the creative way known pieces have been joined and red herrings disposed of. The effect is of a puzzle, but one for which the detective (or the screenwriter) has hidden some pieces from the other players.

A more serious difficulty is that, while Nick's solutions are usually buttressed with convincing arguments, the earlier stages of his investigation are based only on a very few clues, considerable intuition, and large amounts of extrapolation. While this is true to some extent in all Hammett's novels, the problem is more pointed in the movies. In the third film, *Another Thin Man*, a casual comment to Nick hints at the existence of a mysterious woman, who ultimately becomes the key to the whole mystery. In *The Song of the Thin Man* Nora notices a piece of jewelry which ultimately leads to the capture of the villain. These are the most blatant examples of Nick's (or the writers') creating whole solutions from minor details, but the pattern is, in fact, fairly consistent through the series. Similar plot problems also occur in the third and fifth movies, *Another Thin Man* and *The Thin Man Goes Home*. In *Another Thin Man*, after several interactions between Nick and the gang that had been threatening Nora's advisor, Col. MacFay, the audience is willing to believe that none of them is the murderer. But, in fact, the killer turns out to be someone who cannot be guilty unless Nick has made a major blunder. One short scene, quickly forgotten, creates the problem. Either the events of the scene are true, and the individual cannot be the killer; or the person *is* the killer, and the scene contains an obvious lie that Nick does not confront. As a mystery, *The Thin Man Goes Home* is even weaker; there is practically no serious investigation by anyone, at any time. The audience sees what Nick does, where he goes, whom he talks to, but most of his activity leads nowhere and is never followed up. The movie ends with a long series of revelations by Nick about the town of Sycamore Springs, its people, and its situation (including the existence of a major defense plant) which have been mentioned only in passing and have never been elaborated on screen. Because the solution brings out evidence never before mentioned and answers are given to questions that have not previously been asked, the audience is not certain whether or not to credit Nick for solving the murders. Ultimately the climactic scene rings hollow, and the whole film, never on firm ground, collapses.

Another reason that the detective element of the Thin Man films occasionally seems weak lies in what is probably most distinctive about them: their effort to meld the serious business of detection with a mix of romantic and screwball comedy. *The Thin Man* itself contains a number of jokes, some taken from the book and others added by the screenwriters. Throughout *The Thin Man* Powell and Loy expand on the fun-loving relationship of Hammett's characters to connect with each other and with the audience. In their second scene together, Powell performs a set-piece vaudeville trick on Loy behind the back of another actor but in full view of the camera.[7] Later in the film, when Nick and Nora decide to take on the case, he calls her "Doctor Watson," and the two skip off toward the bedroom to dress for their hunt, as pleased with themselves as a pair of mischievous six-year-olds.

In addition to their physical clowning for the camera Powell and Loy make numerous verbal jokes. After the famous "knockout" scene (taken almost directly from Chapter 8 of the novel), Nick and Nora are being questioned in their bedroom. When one of the cops finds a gun hidden among Nora's clothes, Lt. Guild asks, "Haven't you heard of the Sullivan Law [New York's gun registration ordinance]?" Without batting an eyelash, Nora quips back, "That's all right, we're married." Reading reports in the newspapers later that day, Nora tells Nick, "It says you've been shot five times in the tabloids." He quips, "It's not true, he didn't come anywhere near my tabloids."

Having presented Nick and Nora as the ultimate fun-loving couple in their first appearance, the studio attempted to make the most of it in the other films. Except for the almost unrelievedly bleak second film, *After the Thin Man*, comic scenes and bits of comic dialogue appear in every film, succeeding best in the third and fourth movies, *Another Thin Man* and *The Shadow of the Thin Man*. In the opening scene of *Another Thin Man*, Nora tells Nick that Operator 15 has been trying to contact him. "Certainly not, she knows better than that," he replies. She retorts, "I don't know why I always take it for granted you're kidding." Later when Nick and Nora are arguing about the veracity of other characters, Nora shakes her head and shoulders angrily as she says, "My father was just as honest as yours." Nick, in one of Powell's best moments in the whole series, mimics her movements and responds, "Someday you'll learn what a hot recommendation *that* is."

Another Thin Man may well contain the series' best combination of comic and mystery elements. Late in the movie Nick and Nora arrive separately at the West Indies Club; when he spots her surrounded by admirers, he enters the circle and says, "Now, Mommy, you know better than to come to a place like this your first day out of bed. What if the health inspectors find out? They'll put you right back in quarantine." Nora replies: "I won't stay in quarantine! I don't care who catches it!" Almost as if they had never been there, the ten men crowded around Nora vanish into the woodwork. The following scene includes several more snappy comments by both Nick and Nora, the arrival of one of their enemies, crucial information about a mysterious woman, and a fight. After all this action, Nick and Nora leave arm-in-arm, as if nothing has occurred.

In *The Shadow of the Thin Man* Nick and Nora find themselves in several similar situations. When Nick goes to the racetrack late at night looking for a clue, he hears a noise. Drawing his pistol, he rounds a corner, sees someone, and says, "Stick 'em up or I'll blow you in two!" A frightened Nora answers, "Don't shoot, Nicky, it's me!" to which Nick gallantly replies, "Why, Mrs. Charles." A later sequence, in a restaurant, is this film's best combination of detection (Nick talks to one of the gangsters), action (a brawl including both customers and waiters), and humor. At its conclusion, Nora turns to their dinner guests and says, deadpan: "And with the *two* dollar dinner you get machine guns."

The Shadow of the Thin Man also gained interest, and perhaps some family attendance, by including some hilarious scenes between William Powell and Dicky Hall as father and son. Although these set-pieces are all outside the plot, they contain some excellent by-play. They also indicate some of the studio's difficulties in trying to merge the high-living Nick and Nora with the needs of the pre-World War II decency code and family values. When one views *Shadow* 50 years later, it is clear that the attempts were only occasionally successful. Despite the inconsistencies, however, these vignettes of family life clearly served their purpose in sanitizing Nick and Nora as they aged.

Is it appropriate to interject comedy in the serious business of murder? According to S.S. Van Dine's Rule 16, "A detective novel should contain no . . . 'atmospheric preoccupations'" (191-92). Such additions, Van Dine continues, detract from the significance of the criminal investigation. Clearly, Dashiell Hammett disagreed, feeling that the detective story needed some light touches alongside the grim business of murder and investigation. All five of his novels have comic moments, from single lines to longer digressions. Nonetheless, there is no question that *The Thin Man* is a mystery first, a comedy of manners second. Throughout the book, whenever Nick and Nora try to return to their carefree life of parties, games, and booze, they are interrupted by Dorothy Wynant, her mother Mimi, or Lt. Guild, all of whom want them back on the case.

As has been noted, the Thin Man movies also sought to entertain and lighten their mood by combining humor and detection. While their mixture frequently succeeds, the blend also diminishes the tension and danger of the scenes. Moreover, the series frequently plays on the audience's sense of humor rather than its interest in the investigation at hand, using both verbal and visual jokes to distract the audience from the lack of clues and give Nick's final revelations more impact. If viewers were more entertained by the humor of scenes like the one at the West Indies Club than bothered by the problems it raises regarding the solution of the crime, the writers and producers were probably happy.

Judged in terms of logical and sustained detection, *The Thin Man*, closely adapted as it is from Hammett's novel, is by far the best mystery in the series. Aside from *The Thin Man*, Nick and Nora do their most extensive detective work in their final film, *The Song of the Thin Man*, in which they search for the killer of a dance-band leader. To discover this person, they must find one of the musicians, who has disappeared. In their quest they take on an assistant, another member of the band ("Clinker" Krause, played by Keenan Wynn), who was a friend of the missing Buddy Hollis. The trio's investigation includes almost all the needed clues; a trek through the then-new world of modern jazz; one segment at an after-hours private party (when an important clue is destroyed); and another in a Greenwich Village-like dive. These scenes are played almost entirely without humor, except for a few one-liners; and while the movie has its share of jokes, they never take the audience too far from the ultimate problem.[8]

So what were they, these six films featuring a likable, slightly raffish married couple in the midst of friendly crooks, evil murderers masquerading as upstanding citizens, and buckets of blood? First, they were not traditional mysteries, though they used most of the trappings of the genre. They contain too much fun, too many witty lines, and too interesting a side-life for even minor characters. On the other hand, despite the jokes, they are far too serious to qualify without demurral as comedies. Even in their most antic moments, these movies keep the ideas of crime and retribution firmly in mind. And the bleak *After the Thin Man*, which starts and ends with love gone sour and whose choice of villain may have been truly shocking to 1930s viewers used to having only unlikable characters turn out to be guilty, sometimes approaches the darkness of the *noir* film.

The result, therefore, was something in the middle. Nick and Nora's adventures are not as consistently serious as the *noir* cinema of the period, but the films are still far from the utter silliness of the Busby Berkeley or Astaire-Rogers musicals: Their presentation of murder and mayhem can never be taken lightly. Whether the viewer thinks of the hero and heroine or of the plots, the other is never far away. Further, despite the distance between the comic and criminal elements, they are seldom separated. The most hilarious scenes usually have some element of plot connected or interwoven, while the idea of death is usually mitigated by quips or by a sudden change of mood in the following scene.

In the end, the series depends on its own unpredictability. Under the mystery genre's rules, the discovery of bodies requires a solution to the "who" question; but these movies were not shy about adding an element of joy, inviting the audience to join the heroes on the chase. And while Busby Berkeley's "Gold Diggers" musicals became cloying because of the lack of plot, Nick and Nora give viewers meaningful reasons to spend time with them, their friends, and their nemeses.

The result is what might best be described as the "Screwball Mystery," a sub-genre that has as its principal goal the capture of a dangerous killer, but which takes itself as lightly as possible. At the same time, those connected with the films, especially W.S. Van Dyke, William Powell, and Myrna Loy, seem to have taken to their roles with abandon, as if it was the chance of their lifetimes to make their marks on the movie world. Make no mistake, the Thin Man films are far from perfect; but what they lack in gloss they make up in fun. Even 60 years later, the gleam in Myrna Loy's eye is bright and the crease in Bill Powell's pants is crisp. Together, they are still among the best of the husband-and-wife detecting pairs. Just as in their own time, Nick and Nora remain just too much fun to let go.

NOTES

[1]Citations from the novel will be to chapters, rather than pages. Some of Hammett's racier language was censored when the novel was excerpted in *Redbook*. While the hardback version returned to the original text, the paperback edition was expurgated; and the two forms have never been reconciled. From 1935 until the present, there have, therefore, existed two renditions. See, for example, the end of Chapter 26 (133 of the Random House paperback), where Nora's remark becomes "didn't you get excited?"

[2]The quick shooting schedule was required in part because Myrna Loy, the studio's choice to play Nora, had already been scheduled for another film set to begin production. In another stroke of good fortune, the director, W.S. Van Dyke, was well-known for bringing films in quickly. It could not have been lost on the studio, though, that it was to their advantage to get such a hot property out to theaters as quickly as possible.

[3]Best Movie; Best Actor: William Powell; Best Director: W.S. Van Dyke; and Best Adaptation. For a complete filmography, including all speaking parts and all major production figures, see Pitts, 270-71. The movie won no awards; the Oscars were swept that year by *It Happened One Night*. Interestingly, the two films deal very directly with current mores. While William Powell and Myrna Loy as Nick and Nora reminded viewers of Prohibition and the high life, Clark Gable and Claudette Colbert (playing a society reporter and a runaway heiress who fall in love) represent the coming era, particularly the creation and enforcement of sexual restrictions mandated by the recently established Hays Office and its decency code.

[4]The actors were not locked into their roles; rather, the characters became identified with the actors who brought them to life. William Powell, for example, was nominated for an Academy Award for his role in Clarence Day's *Life with Father*; Myrna Loy gained additional fame for such movies as *The Best Years of Our Lives*, *Mr. Blandings Builds his Dream House*, and *The Red Pony*. Contrast this, for example, with Basil Rathbone, whose portrayal of Sherlock Holmes has entirely over-shadowed his portrayal of villains such as the Sheriff of Nottingham opposite Errol Flynn in *The Adventures of Robin Hood*.

[5]This memorable quote occurs in the first sequence of the film. Nora's response is typical, "When you grow up you'll be able to say, 'My father was a tout.'"

[6]This is entirely typical of both detective-fiction and movie cops. In fact, the role of Guild in the film may have been adapted from the Philo Vance movies. In those films (and the books they came from) the cops and the District Attorney literally stand aside while Vance uncovers the criminal and frequently metes out the appropriate punishment.

[7]This scene comes from Chapter 2, when Herbert Macaulay, the missing man's lawyer, comes to call on Nick. While the movie retained most of the text of the novel, it appears to have left the sight-gags to the actors.

[8]One is too good not to quote. As they search for Buddy, Clinker gets a good idea, and Nick tells him, "You have the nose of a bloodhound." Nora follows by patting him on the back and saying, "Don't worry, the rest of your face looks fine."

WORKS CITED

After the Thin Man. Dir. W.S. Van Dyke. Prod. Hunt Stromberg. Writ. Albert Hackett and Frances Goodrich. With William Powell, Myrna Loy, James Stewart, Jessie Ralph, and Sam Levene. Metro-Goldwyn-Mayer, 1936.

Another Thin Man. Dir. W.S. Van Dyke. Prod. Hunt Stromberg. Writ. Albert Hackett and Frances Goodrich. With William Powell, Myrna Loy, C. Aubrey Smith, Otto Kruger, and Nat Pendleton. Metro-Goldwyn-Mayer, 1939.

Hammett, Dashiell. *The Thin Man.* 1934. New York: Alfred A. Knopf, 1962.

____. *The Thin Man.* 1934. New York: Random House, 1972.

Johnson, Diane. *Dashiell Hammett: A Life.* New York: Random House, 1983.

Pitts, Michael R. *Famous Movie Detectives.* Metuchen, NJ: Scarecrow, 1979.

Shadow of the Thin Man. Dir. W.S. Van Dyke. Prod. Hunt Stromberg. Writ. Irving Brecher and Harry Kurnitz. With William Powell, Myrna Loy, Barry Nelson, Donna Reed, Dicky Hall, and Sam Levene. Metro-Goldwyn-Mayer. 1941.

Song of the Thin Man. Dir. Edward Buzzell. Prod. Nat Perrin. Writ. Steven Fisher, Nat Perrin, James O'Hanlon, and Harry Crane. With William Powell, Myrna Loy, Keenan Wynn, Gloria Grahame, and Jayne Meadows. Metro-Goldwyn-Mayer, 1947.

The Thin Man. Dir. W.S. Van Dyke. Prod. Hunt Stromberg. Writ. Albert Hackett and Frances Goodrich. With William Powell, Myrna Loy, Maureen O'Sullivan, Nat Pendleton, and Cesar Romero. Metro-Goldwyn-Mayer, 1934.

The Thin Man Goes Home. Dir. Richard Thorpe. Prod. Everett Riskin. Writ. Robert Riskin, Dwight Taylor, and Harry Kurnitz. With William Powell, Myrna Loy, Harry Davenport, Gloria DeHaven, and Donald Meek. Metro-Goldwyn-Mayer, 1944.

Van Dine, S.S. "Twenty Rules for Writing Detective Stories." *The Art of the Mystery Story.* Ed. Howard Haycraft. New York: Grosset and Dunlap, 1946. 189-93.

From Nuisance to Nemesis:
Visual Representations
of Miss Marple on Film and Television

Iska Alter

Though Margaret Rutherford's performance in four films produced during the 1960s has defined Miss Marple for a generation and a half of theater-goers, her comic interpretation does not do justice to Christie's creation. As critics have come to perceive new depths and new complexities in both Christie and Marple, it has become clear that Angela Lansbury, Helen Hayes, and Joan Hickson more accurately reflect the Jane Marple of the novel—with Hickson most fully capturing the essence of St. Mary Mead's most famous resident.

Until the recent work of such scholars as Gillian Gill, Marian Shaw, and Sabine Vanacker suggested otherwise, it has been the rule to view elderly spinster Jane Marple, "everybody's universal great-aunt" (*Hotel* 121), with the same polite dismissal as do the unwary participants in the criminal mayhem that occurs in the dozen novels and 22 short stories in which she appears. Most critics support the judgment of Jane's nephew, the novelist Raymond West, that, although Jane often assumes a persona of benignant, blue-eyed innocence to mislead into error the murderers she must bring to justice, a dithering fussiness is the essential fact of her character.

By emphasizing her old-maidenly inexperience, no doubt the result of her continued residence in the ordered, traditional world of St. Mary Mead, her out-of-date notions of femininity, her apparent confusions, and her verbal incoherencies, these same critics reduce Miss Marple to near-comic status, a detector whose powers are conditional, perhaps even gratuitous. That she solves crimes is merely an accident of woman's intuition, a magical leap of insight unrelated to reasoned analysis, the province of Agatha Christie's male detective, the ratiocinative Hercule Poirot, to be preferred "not only because he is an altogether livelier character, but also because his insights are more rational and less inspirational than Miss

Marple's" (Symons 33). In short, for a considerable number of commentators and well-entertained readers, Jane Marple remains a slightly dotty old lady from an idyllic English village, tripping over corpses, killers, and answers.

However, a close (re-)reading of the Marple texts, encouraged by the revisionary critical attention paid to Christie as a primary negotiator of the form's generic contact with its audience, reveals Jane Marple to be a subversive, unsettling figure. From the beginning of her detecting career, Jane Marple's gentle demeanor has masked a consistent and disquieting cynicism about the rhetoric of behavior, action, and motive: "I'm afraid that observing human nature for so long as I have done, one gets not to expect very much from it. I dare say idle tittle-tattle is very wrong and unkind, but it is so often true, isn't it?" (*Vicarage* 187). Her skeptical appraisals of individual conduct are informed by an acute, almost physical sense of the irremediable existence of evil: "I have at several times in my life been apprehensive, have recognized that there was evil in the neighborhood, the surroundings, that the environment of someone who was evil was near me. . . . It's rather . . . like being born with a very keen sense of smell" (*Nemesis* 122); and her pessimistic metaphysics are the product of "a mind that plumbed the depths of human iniquity" (*Body* 101). Over time, her knowledge of the poisoned wellsprings that nourish society becomes increasingly associated with the uncanny, with the oracular, and, at last, with myth. As she describes her vision of Macbeth's three witches, she might well be describing the nature of her own magic:

> You know, Raymond, my dear, if *I* were ever producing this splendid play, I would make the three witches *quite* different. I would have them three ordinary, normal old women. Old Scottish women. They wouldn't dance or caper. They would look at each other rather slyly and you would feel a sort of menace just behind the ordinariness of them. (*Nemesis* 83-84)

By 1953 and *A Pocket Full of Rye*, Miss Marple's seemingly occult uncanniness is transformed into archetype, her role expanding into retributive Nemesis—"[Inspector Neele] was thinking to himself that Miss Marple was very unlike the popular idea of an avenging fury. And yet . . . that perhaps was exactly what she was" (113)—an identity that comes to dominate the character of the spinster sleuth until the final novel of the series.

Nor is it possible any longer to denigrate as mere inspiration the process of analogical thinking that permits Jane Marple to construct the patterns of conduct and character that ultimately provide the solutions to the mysteries with which she is confronted. Her solutions, she realizes, are "really what people call intuition and make such a fuss about. Intuition is like reading a word without having to spell it out. A child can't do that, because it has had so little experience. But a grown-up person knows the word because he's seen it often before" (*Vicarage* 241). This "special knowledge," one sign of adult reasoning, is eventually absorbed into the oracular voice that is a component of Marple's later prophetic personality.

Given the changing terms of interpretation, it is also no longer quite so easy to see the small, closed community of St. Mary Mead which Miss Marple inhabits (or the ones she visits) through the idyllic haze of nostalgia. As early as *The Murder at the Vicarage*, she has no illusions about the quality of her environment:

> "I regard St. Mary Mead," he said authoritatively, "as a stagnant pool." . . .
> "That is really not a very good simile, dear Raymond," said Miss Marple briskly. "Nothing, I believe, is so full of life under the microscope as a drop of water from a stagnant pool. . . ." (309)

Far from being the unchanging embodiment of some golden past, the English village is a site of very modern murder, the ironic barometer measuring accurately the extent of social disintegration and personal wickedness—"'one does see so much evil in a village,' murmured Miss Marple in an explanatory voice" (*Body* 153).

Although Shaw and Vanacker have a point in suggesting that the problem of dramatizing Miss Marple effectively is functional, stemming "from the difficulty of portraying old age in comedy" (90), any examination of Miss Marple's visual representations must give primary emphasis to these shifting explanations of her character, her activities, and her habitations. Even the least favorable interpretation of Jane Marple demands another sort of performance strategy than that provided by the crude vigor of Margaret Rutherford's ebullient comic energy. The selections of Angela Lansbury, Helen Hayes, and Joan Hickson, whose varied theatrical ranges are not contingent on stereotype or caricature, as successive visual representations of the new, darker version of Christie's venerable amateur follow from these alternate readings, though only Hickson fully embodies the Jane Marple of the novels.

Margaret Rutherford, the first important cinematic depiction of Jane Marple, reflects both the trivialization of Jane Marple and, notwithstanding her great popularity, the derogation of Agatha Christie as a serious writer of mysteries. Regarded as inappropriately cast by Christie, who commented that Rutherford "always looked like a bloodhound" (qtd. in Riley and McAllister 202), Rutherford— through her bumptious physical presence, her idiosyncratic gestural vocabulary (a combination of Madame Arcati, Miss Prism, and a St. Trinian's pedagogue), and her own initial unwillingness to accept the elderly sleuth's preoccupation with murder ("not the sort of thing I could get close to" [qtd. in Tennenbaum 251]) seriously subverted Jane Marple's fundamental hardness and distorted Christie's plots. That this misconstruction occurred may be the result of social attitudes about a particular form of the genre ("What," the stereotype asked, "could the English village mystery bring to the post-World War II community of readers except laughter?") as well as about the genteel tradition of women writers of crime fiction in what increasingly had become a "hard-boiled" profession. Under such circumstances, it hardly could surprise that Miss Marple would resemble more a pugnacious Newfoundland than the sly, cynical, and knowing figure Christie actually envisioned.

With the appearance on screen of Angela Lansbury and Helen Hayes as Jane Marple during the 1980s, both more physically suited to the role and both possessing reputations as serious actresses with fewer associations with aggressive comedy, the film and television re-creations of Miss Marple and Christie's textual invention moved closer together. Yet they also are finally unsatisfactory: Lansbury's portrayal appears uncomfortably strained and artificial, while Hayes's rendition is too flirtatiously American, more exurban Connecticut than St. Mary Mead. In addition, during this period, Agatha Christie's reputation was undergoing considered re-evaluation, and her place as an investigator of and innovator within the genre had become more clearly articulated. Further, changing perceptions of fictive women detectives, whether they be Kinsey Millhone or Jane Marple, made it possible to challenge the dominion of Rutherford's "dear spinster lady, very much like myself to look at" (qtd. in Tennenbaum 251). Thus, it is only with Joan Hickson's subtle, almost effortless metamorphosis into the Nemesis of St. Mary Mead that we are permitted to realize, then acknowledge, the shrewd authority of the woman who knows and understands the power of evil, and who will do anything she must, in spite of age and class, to strike through into the transgressive heart of her society.

Until Joan Hickson's revisionist portrayal, and in spite of authorial disapproval and actorly reluctance, Margaret Rutherford was (and perhaps remains) for readers and viewers alike the quintessential Miss Marple in four films from British MGM: *Murder She Said* (1962), *Murder at the Gallop* (1963), *Murder Most Foul* (1964), and *Murder Ahoy!* (1964). The decision to cast Miss Rutherford as the geriatric neo-Victorian detector, whom Christie described as "an attractive old lady, tall and thin, with pink cheeks and blue eyes, and a gentle, rather fussy manner" (*Sleeping* 18), ensured that the productions would be comedies, not just because of Rutherford's history as a theatrical comedienne, but, even more basically, because her very appearance—the battleship bulk, the hound-like face, the juicy voice—inevitably generate laughter, independent of any role she undertakes. In fact, it becomes a necessity of plot and performance that, no matter what the literary origins of the narrative might require, this outsized feminine body be used as an instrument of cinematic humor. Thus, although Miss Marple's age and Christie's texts increasingly demand the opposite, Rutherford cannot be sedentary or still; she must provide the camera opportunity to focus on her ludicrous physicality. She is an expert golfer (*Murder She Said*); a prize-winning horsewoman—riding side-saddle, of course (*Murder at the Gallop*); a champion shot (*Murder Most Foul*); and an excellent sailor (*Murder Ahoy!*). We chuckle at this Miss Marple's attempt to scale a wall on the shoulders of her slight companion, Jim Stringer (played by Rutherford's husband Stringer Davis); we snicker as she does the twist with the ever-present Mr. Stringer as her partner; we guffaw at her recitation of "The Shooting of Dan McGrew." However, such antic behavior in the face of violent death transforms murder into comic grotesquerie and by dissolving the potential horror into the actual giggle makes it virtually impossible to believe in the moral seriousness of the crime as Christie insists we must.

Because Rutherford's imposing presence literally fills the screen, dominating the playing landscape as well as undermining subsidiary characters' power to act, she becomes the primary source of performative energy in every film, determining the narrative behavior of others. Novelistic multiple plots which serve to remind readers that evil is a snare that can entrap anyone are reduced by screenwriters David Pursall, Jack Seddon, and James Cavanaugh to single, simplified, easy-to-follow storylines in which Rutherford's choices control the development of the mystery and the dynamics of its solution.

Given the consequences of Rutherford's particular physicality and the combative comic style that derives from it, is it any wonder that her Miss Marple works alone, isolated from a sustaining community, serving as the central figure who compels the narrative situation into being as witness to the crime, discoverer of the body, or disbeliever in the institutional solutions, and then managing the situational puzzles to their successful conclusions? In *Murder She Said* (based on *4:50 from Paddington*), both Elspeth McGillicuddy and Lucy Eyelesbarrow have been eliminated from the proceedings and their functions absorbed by Rutherford. Her discovery of and suspicions about the mysterious death at Enderby Hall in *Murder at the Gallop* (Richard Abernethie is quite dead before the story begins in *Funerals Are Fatal*, the distant fictional ancestor of the film, which features Hercule Poirot) initiates the events that bring Jane Marple to Hector Enderby's riding academy *cum* hotel. And she is the lone immovable juror unpersuaded by Inspector Craddock's easy answer to Mrs. McGinty's death in *Murder Most Foul* (derived from a second Hercule Poirot novel, *Mrs. McGinty's Dead*).

Although these alterations, like many others, are designed to emphasize Rutherford's position as the principal organizing force in the cinematic revisions of Christie's text, she is nevertheless given a feminized if steadfast male companion, Jim Stringer/Stringer Davis, whose role is akin to that of the nurturing secretary in the conventional hard-boiled detective story, apparently echoing Davis's off-screen conduct as Rutherford's husband.

> He saw to it that she was always well supplied with her favorite ginger chocolates or peppermint creams. He made sure that her lunch—soup, cheese, and biscuits—was sent to her dressing room. Then, he would spend some time personally answering her fan mail because it was his wife's opinion that those who cared enough to write deserved a reply. . . . The magic of this special relationship is evident in their scenes together in the series. (Tennenbaum 251)

While Cadogan and Craig assert that Rutherford's characterization of Miss Marple is "the stock, unacknowledged lesbian figure of popular fiction" (171), the extra-textual relationship between the bluff, manly Miss Marple and the gentle, effete Jim Stringer (as well as the marriage proposals she receives from Mr. Crackenthorpe [*Murder She Said*] and Hector Enderby [*Murder at the Gallop*]) is, more importantly, a curiously ambiguous effort at normalizing or, at the very least, containing Rutherford's aggressively unfeminine independence.

Because the effect of this reconfigured gender alliance is problematic, Rutherford remains a singular eminence. There is no equivocation in her actions, no uncertainty in her speech, no doubts about her judgments. But there also is no sense that the character is situated within the fully articulated social context of an English village, or is aware of the complex web of human connection created by long existence in such an environment, the understanding of which surely confers upon the fictional Miss Marple her near-magical power as a detector. On the contrary, the analytical skills exhibited by Rutherford are those of an eccentric, marginalized figure. She unravels mysteries not because she is familiar with the patterns of a closed community, but because she brings to them the perspective of an outsider. It can be no accident, therefore, that *Murder at the Gallop* and *Murder Most Foul* are strained adaptations of cases involving Hercule Poirot—the literal alien who achieves his successes by exploiting his differences.

In the end, none of Christie's detective fictions seems a satisfactory vehicle for Rutherford's broad, rambunctious exaggerations. The series dwindles to a halt with *Murder Ahoy!*, an original but particularly clumsy blend of the usual comedy and crime, amid critical disdain—"It is . . . a simple matter of lots of dialogue, only a bit of which is truly funny, and a modicum of action, which is rarely exciting, intriguing, or comic" (Weiler)—and Christie's sense of betrayal—"to have one's characters incorporated in somebody else's film seems to me monstrous and highly unethical" (qtd. in Morgan 336).

The interpretive choices that established the comic design of the cinematic narrative and re-created Miss Marple in the ample image of Margaret Rutherford also determined the manner and mannerisms which governed the behavior of the secondary casts of characters. In a pattern assumed by the entire series, explaining the mystery and orchestrating its solution become less important than displaying the eccentricities of those whose maneuvers generate the mystery. In the novels, the eccentrics, the outsiders, the disturbed, and the dangerous as well as the commonplace and the ordinary act within the elaborate and complex anthropology of an English village or other similarly closed community in which Christie's homicides occur. And even though Christie's satiric skill often goes unmarked and her social commentary unrecognized, such a setting contains, accepts, punishes, and finds uses for the odd and the idiosyncratic.

However, the Rutherford films strip away the social content that the author has taken pains to construct until all that remains to engage the viewer are foibles, quirks, and tics. While this reductive process makes comedy, it disallows any serious representation of motive, transforming crimes into simple, soluble puzzles.

Agatha Christie finally admitted a certain grudging respect for Rutherford's performances, calling her "a fine actress" though "she bears no resemblance to . . . [my] own idea of Miss Marple" (qtd. in Osborne 184); and she eventually dedicated *The Mirror Crack'd from Side to Side* to Margaret Rutherford "in admiration." But beginning with the most successful—*Murder She Said* (of which Christie remarked, "there's no sustained interest . . . and *no* kind of suspense" [qtd. in Morgan 328])—through *Murder at the Gallop* and *Murder Most Foul*, films which substituted Marple for Poirot as if detectives were interchangeable parts (and about which Christie said, "I get an unregenerate pleasure when I think they're not being a success" [qtd. in Osborne 203]), to the already noted dishonesty of *Murder Ahoy!*, Christie always regretted the Rutherford series:

> I kept off films for years because I thought they'd give me too many heartaches. Then I sold the rights to MGM, hoping they'd use them for television. But they chose film. It was too awful! They did things like taking a Poirot and putting Miss Marple in it! And all the climaxes were so poor, you could see them coming! . . .They wrote their own script for the last one—nothing to do with me at all—*Murder Ahoy!* One of the silliest things you ever saw! It got very bad reviews, I'm delighted to say. (qtd. in Osborne 203)

It would be 16 years—half a generation—before Miss Marple would reappear on the silver screen, this time incarnated by Angela Lansbury (*The Mirror Crack'd* [1980]), then somewhat later on television by Helen Hayes (*Caribbean Murders* [1983] and *Murder with Mirrors* [1985]), and only after the million-dollar successes of *Murder on the Orient Express* (1974) and *Death on the Nile* (1978) had assured moviedom it could expect a profit from a Christie detective. By the early 1980s Dame Margaret Rutherford and Dame Agatha Christie were dead; and Christie's heretofore patronized status as merely an excessively popular writer with a singular talent for ingenious plot construction was undergoing critical re-examination as, more generally, was the place of the woman writer and the cultural significance of the female detective within the changing expectations about the genre.

But it would not be until 1984 (1986 in the United States) that the BBC first offered viewers British character actress Joan Hickson as the once and future Jane Marple, whose shrewd accuracy of judgment, hard-headed unsentimentality, and nose for evil she so completely embodies.

The selection of Angela Lansbury and Helen Hayes indicates the change in attitude toward Miss Marple, Agatha Christie, and the genre both represent. Neither Lansbury nor Hayes is fundamentally a comic actress, although each has performed in comedy (often in darker comedies of manners, a particularly apt preparation for Christie's spinster sleuth), and such humor as does appear in these new Marple adaptations seems to emerge naturally from the interplay of situation and character rather than from caricature. Both actresses have had careers conspicuous for their range and variability, and both, to a greater (Lansbury) or lesser (Hayes) degree, take Jane Marple and her vocation seriously. Hayes's version of the character, whose abilities the actress attributed to blandness (Fraser), and whose performance Shaw and Vanacker call "cuddly" (92), appears in a medium that may be more congenial to Christie's character than the enlarged movie screen (as noted elsewhere, Christie had sold the rights to MGM hoping for television productions). Nonetheless, it is Lansbury's more stringent portrayal in *The Mirror Crack'd* that provides the real transition to the satisfying BBC series.

Like its immediate predecessors from EMI Films—*Murder on the Orient Express* and *Death on the Nile*—*The Mirror Crack'd* seems to have been conceived for the purpose of giving middle-aging, if slightly overripe, movie stars (in this case, Rock Hudson, Elizabeth Taylor, Kim Novak, and Tony Curtis) a less taxing cinematic venue, what *Variety* termed "a nostalgic throwback to the genteel murder mystery pix of the '50's" (qtd. in Sanders and Lovallo 443), in which to strut their stuff. But unlike the earlier Marple films in which Margaret Rutherford is the only begetter of the investigative play, *The Mirror Crack'd* situates histrionic authority in the presumably diverting ironies of real Hollywood figures incorporating the fame/notoriety of their public images into their roles of warring former sex symbols, sleazy agents, and temperamental directors (embellishing to near-camp the satiric elements suggested in the original text). Indeed, many of the plot alterations in the transformation of novel into screenplay support this strategy: the development of Kim Novak's character in order to create a feud between Lola Brewster and Marina Gregg (played by

Elizabeth Taylor), a shift continued in the recent BBC version; the expansion of the scheming presence of Marty Fenn (Tony Curtis); the excision of several subplots including those involving Marina Gregg's adopted daughter and Giuseppe the blackmailing butler; and the imposition of a stagy final suicide to replace the source's morally ambiguous conclusion (after all, who wants to believe that Rock Hudson would deliberately murder Elizabeth Taylor no matter how noble the reason?).

Miss Marple cannot be allowed to overwhelm the central melodramatic collection of egos that drives the action (as Margaret Rutherford might have done and as Joan Hickson has no need to do), even while she must be astute and aggressive enough to solve its central murderous puzzle. Given such requirements, Angela Lansbury, well-known, certainly a skilled and even subtle performer, able to hold her own against ostentatious theatricality, yet not so flamboyant as to compete directly with deliberately contrived actorly excess, appears to be an inspired choice. Because she must be perceived as equal to the seductive glamour of displaced Hollywood residing at Gossington Hall, Lansbury's Jane Marple has been provided with some additional sophistication: she smokes; she drinks; her wardrobe, while still conservative, has been spruced up; and her home is far more elegant than an elderly lady of supposedly modest means should inhabit. She also has acquired a harder edge—sharper, more peremptory, perhaps even a trifle nasty in her treatment of others, quite without the brusque geniality associated with Margaret Rutherford or the unsentimental kindliness that will become a significant element in Joan Hickson's reading of the character.

Because the events of *The Mirror Crack'd* unfold in St. Mary Mead, both the village and Miss Marple's place within the fabric of communal life must be visualized on screen. As the Rutherford films also imply, the English village is a static phenomenon, seeming to exist unspoiled by the processes of historical change that the novel so carefully documents (even as it denies their power ultimately to affect unchanging human nature). St. Mary Mead, photographed in sunshine and in bright, clear color, becomes the veritable realization of Marina Gregg's nostalgic fantasies: a safe haven against the psychic dislocations and social outrages of contemporary experience. However, to maintain the symbolic value of this putative demi-paradise, any disruptive force threatening the moral ecology of this near-idyllic landscape (which, in this case, proves to be the actress herself) must somehow be isolated and expelled. So Marina Gregg and St. Mary Mead are left to their respective fates.

Although St. Mary Mead is presented as both a visual and an imagined sanctuary, it nevertheless possesses an established social order in which Marple plays a distinctive part. Her identity as busybody/seer (more busybody than seer in this production) is clearly articulated in the first scenes of the film as she rather too smartly and too dismissively reveals the ending of the parodic murder mystery, halted by the vicar's mechanical incompetence, we and a group of residents have been watching in the church basement. After she has left, a male member of the audience who already has seen the film attests that her solution is—as usual— correct. The community recognizes her exceptionalism, and she accepts their deference to her superior abilities as her due. This respectful local pattern of attention, acknowledgment, and approbation, to which even the police are a party, continues throughout the film. The regard shown by the authorities is further enhanced by making Chief-Inspector Dermot Craddock Marple's nephew (in Christie's novel he is Sir Henry Clithering's nephew and godson), transforming what is normally a professional connection into a familial relationship, and thereby naturalizing Marple's interaction with the constabulary (a change that recurs, and for much the same reason, in the BBC's version of *The Mirror Crack'd*). In fact, Marple is as much the village's pride as the exotic outsiders are its curiosity.

The Mirror Crack'd was only moderately successful. Financially, according to *Variety*, "it netted its distribution in the U.S. and Canada $5.5 million, which . . . is a very meager return" (qtd. in Sanders and Lovallo 443). Artistically, in spite of *Variety*'s review that called it "a worthy if more leisurely successor to *Murder on the Orient Express*" (qtd. in Sanders and Lovallo 443), the situation is no better. If the production works, it does so at the expense of Christie's original, employing distortion and imbalance to create a cinematic narrative that diverges significantly from the source.

While Lansbury's Miss Marple is certainly a more serious figure than Rutherford's, eliminating Rutherford's exaggerations and infusing the spinster with a requisite hardness previously lacking, her performance nevertheless seems stilted and uncomfortable. It is not simply that the actress is too young for the role, and that her makeup only emphasizes that fact. The added sophistication the director deemed necessary turns the desired hardness brittle, and there is precious little charm in the flirtatious mannerisms she employs with Chief-Inspector Craddock, nephew or not. Her abruptness engenders dislike rather than sympathy or even respect, and her arrogance drives her to inappropriate action—the fictive Miss Marple does not awaken the vicar in the middle of the night to uncover the last clue that solves the mystery. As serious a lapse as the (mis)representation of the detecting protagonist is the decision, finally, to make the crime and its mystery secondary to the exhibition (or exhibitionism) of the larger-than-life Hollywood personalities whose energies and excesses usurp the screen.

In the early mid-1980s, before the revisionary BBC productions presented Joan Hickson's singular impersonation of the canny, near-supernatural Miss Marple to American viewers, Helen Hayes attempted the elderly detective twice on national television. These films met with negligible success, even though Sue Grafton was one of the writers for *A Caribbean Mystery* (1983), and in *Murder with Mirrors* (1985) a gaunt but determined Bette Davis returned after a long illness to act with Helen Hayes for the first time in their careers. Hayes was attracted to Christie's novels ("I've read everything by Agatha Christie" [qtd. in Fraser]) and took her role seriously ("I'm very familiar with Miss Marple and I think I see her as Agatha Christie wanted me to" [qtd. in Fraser]). Nonetheless, these films remain less than memorable curiosities when compared to the vitality of the earlier film versions and the strengths of the later television representations.

Hayes offers a clear, if simplified, definition of Jane Marple that seeks to control the fluffy/fussy stereotypical qualities so often associated with the character, remarking that Miss Marple "doesn't look like a great sleuth or a great activist of any kind—she's bland—and I think that's the way she gets the job done" (qtd. in Fraser). But the productions themselves seem markedly at odds with, even subversive of, such an interpretation. The inappropriate suggestions of romantic interest on the part of Major Palgrave (now without the glass eye that is so significant a clue in the novel *A Caribbean Murder*) and Mr. Rafiel (not dying, but transformed instead into a lively, admiring beau) are not a source of comedy as are the proposals offered to Margaret Rutherford, but attempts to normalize a figure whose spinsterhood can be seen as a rejection of the conventional prescriptions directing the valued feminine life. And the theatrical concerns which critically inform both text and subtext of *They Do It with Mirrors* appear only to provide an excuse for Hayes to play briefly at Lady Macbeth and Portia. Shaw and

Vanacker are right to call the two films "variously grotesque and farcical" (93)—more important for the medium used than for their influence on the construction of a more textually sustained Marple persona. What is significant about these two dramatizations is that the inflationary power of the film's big screen has given way to the smaller-scale, almost domesticated, sensibility of television.

In 1984, with *The Body in the Library*, the BBC got Miss Marple right. Able, perhaps by virtue of miniaturization, to strike the most satisfying (one hesitates to say "nearly perfect") balance among authorial purpose, the constituents of the medium, the acting style mandated by such a medium, and the scriptwriter's adaptations, television seems to be (as Christie suspected) the most appropriate form in which to dramatize the author's domesticated, yet no less serious explorations about the discovery of guilt, the protection of the innocent who, as Christie put it, "must be able to live in peace and charity with their neighbors" (*Autobiography* 425), and the nature of evil.

The scaled-down requirements of visual presentation not only enforce a kind of histrionic discipline, but they also contain and therefore deepen the emotional circumstances that create murder and its aftermath, making even more ironic the tidy settings in which the crimes occur. The distorting mirror of the big screen which exploits the broad gestures of caricature and camp gives way to the control, normalization, or deflation of the exceptional as well as to demonstrations of how the small subtleties of the everyday mask the potentially explosive tensions hidden within the usual. Even the sketches which decorate the opening credits of the BBC films, firmly locating the audience inside the activities of a closed community, ask the audience to consider the dangerous hypocrisies that expose the conventions to disintegrative assault.

The inspired choice of Joan Hickson, herself an octogenarian, whose apparent frailty, "look[ing] as though she should be blown off the screen by a hint of violence" (Goodman), cannot diminish the Victorian uprightness (one of Christie's favorite words describing her elderly heroine) of posture and moral purpose that seems forever to exclude other actresses from the role. Perhaps because of the actress's age, this Miss Marple, unlike her predecessors, is permitted a quality of stillness through which her penetrating intelligence is made visible. Dressed in slightly shabby, nondescript suits, skirts, and cardigans, mostly of neutral colors, often accompanied by a saucer-shaped hat deceptively shading her face, Joan Hickson allows her Jane Marple to fade quietly into the background of scenes, the better to observe undisturbed and unknown, as she does in her encounter with the young Florence Small in *The Body in the Library*, a visual embodiment of the text's description of Miss Marple's ability to disappear into practiced anonymity: "In the corner of Superintendent Harper's office sat an elderly lady. The girls hardly noticed her. If they did they may have wondered who she was" (173).

The frequent closeups (necessary for a character who can no longer move swiftly or dramatically) reveal, as Shaw and Vanacker note, a "head-on-one-side, shrewd and evaluative gaze" (93). They also make clear, as the novels do not always, that the interrupted, pause-filled speech pattern that so easily sanctions the misperception of Miss Marple as a primly dithering spinster is rather a function of thought processes that outrun language. The precise, fluting voice softened by age chosen by Hickson to offer Miss Marple's unexpectedly cynical judgments about fallen humanity with calm and knowing assurance further emphasizes the ironic discrepancy between persona and utterance.

We watch Hickson manipulate the consciously assumed identity of a flustered, fluttery old lady, employing the stereotypical tools of gossip and curiosity to gain acceptance into unfamiliar societies and enter unfamiliar lives in order to explore the plot's central mystery. And the mastery over the gestures of domesticity, the chores of household and communal life, signifying the feminine, that mark Hickson's performative vocabulary is not simply portrayed as the necessary daily activity of a spinster's existence. The frequency with which she is shown knitting (a singular, Englished version of the three Fates weaving the patterns of human destiny); or concerned with gardens, gardeners, plants, and flower arranging, culminating, perhaps, in the house and garden tour that forms the spine of *Nemesis* (a reflection of her interest in questions of proper growth and nurturance); or pouring the comforting, curative cup of tea (a sign of the magical wise woman or healer) indicate the extent to which these acts have been naturalized as the instruments of masquerade allowing Hickson to disguise her powers of analysis and insight in order to disarm, deflect, or distract those whom she would bring to justice. Even when Hickson is absent from the screen for long stretches, the controlled strength of her performance and its concentrated energy still authorizes the viewer to feel her presence in the shadows of the action, as suspects argue about her function in their community, friends inquire about her crime-solving activities, and the police complain about her intrusions.

The changes made in Christie's narratives for the Rutherford films were designed to enhance Rutherford's comic primacy, now situated within a radically simplified mystery; and the alterations to *The Mirror Crack'd* served to refocus audience attention on the self-referential shenanigans of genuine, if overage, movie stars playing their fictive counterparts, thus subverting Marple's challenge to the expansive egos of the Hollywood community in exile. The modifications in the BBC versions seem, however, to emphasize the seriousness of Jane Marple's enterprise in detection. As a rule, much of the author's dialogue has been retained, as have the layered plots, but where possible the circumstances have been adjusted to render Hickson's work a moral imperative.

In *4:50 from Paddington*, for example, Dr. Quimper's misdiagnosis of Alfred Crackenthorpe's cancer (according to Emma Crackenthorpe, Quimper is a paragon for his support of National Health) and his brutal shooting of Harold more fully justify Miss Marple's verdict, "I am very, very glad . . . that they haven't abolished capital punishment yet because I do feel that if there is anyone who ought to hang, it's Quimper" (254), than the original elaborate poisonings of two very unsympathetic brothers. And in the television adaptation of *Nemesis* the transformation of Michael Rafiel from convicted near-sociopath to a homeless yet caring young man forced into living rough because of the ambiguous resolution of his supposed crime makes Hickson's journey into the dark, dangerous heart of possessive love all the more urgent.

Although there can hardly be any question that Margaret Rutherford, Angela Lansbury, Helen Hayes, and Joan Hickson represent markedly different interpretations of Christie's elderly detector, each shaped by considerations of medium, acting style, and attitudinal shifts of culture and criticism about detective fiction, a curious but powerful impression emerges after viewing so many images. In none of the characterizations is Jane Marple the easily dismissed embodiment of the fluffy, twittering spinster sleuth fortuitously rather than rationally solving crimes. Instead she remains, through all the variations, Nemesis—a shrewd, independent, relentless force for justice.

WORKS CITED

The Body in the Library. Dram. T.R. Bowen. Dir. Silvio Narizzano. MYSTERY! PBS. WGBH, Boston. 2, 9, 16 Jan. 1986.

A Caribbean Mystery. Dir. Robert Michael Lewis. With Helen Hayes, Maurice Evans, Bernard Hughes. CBS. WCBS, New York. 22 Oct. 1983.

Christie, Agatha. *An Autobiography.* 1977. New York: Berkley, 1991.

____. *At Bertram's Hotel.* 1965. New York: Harper, 1992.

____. *The Body in the Library.* 1942. New York: Harper, 1992.

____. *4:50 from Paddington.* 1957. New York: Pocket Books, 1958.

____. *Funerals Are Fatal.* 1953. New York: Harper, 1992.

____. *The Mirror Crack'd from Side to Side.* 1962. New York: Harper, 1992.

____. *Mrs. McGinty's Dead.* New York: Dodd, 1952.

____. *The Murder at the Vicarage.* 1930. New York: Dodd, 1977.

____. *Nemesis.* 1971. New York: Harper, 1992.

____. *A Pocket Full of Rye.* 1953. New York: Pocket Books, 1955.

____. *Sleeping Murder.* New York: Dodd, 1976.

____. *They Do It with Mirrors.* New York: Dodd, 1952.

Craig, Patricia, and Mary Cadogan. *The Lady Investigates: Women Detectives and Spies in Fiction.* 1981. New York: Oxford UP, 1986.

Death on the Nile. Dir. John Guillin. With Peter Ustinov, Mia Farrow, Bette Davis, Maggie Smith, David Niven, and Angela Lansbury. EMI. 1978.

4:50 from Paddington. Dram. T.R. Bowen. Dir. Martyn Friend. MYSTERY! PBS. WGBH, Boston. 9, 16 Mar. 1989.

Fraser, C. Gerald. "Television Week." *New York Times* 16 Oct. 1982: 84.

Gill, Gillian. *Agatha Christie: The Woman and Her Mysteries.* New York: Free, 1990.

Goodman, Walter. "A Sterling Gallery of Sleuths." *New York Times.* 13 Mar. 1988: Section 2, 31+.

The Mirror Cracked. Dir. Guy Hamilton. With Angela Lansbury, Geraldine Chaplin, Tony Curtis, Rock Hudson, Kim Novak, and Elizabeth Taylor. EMI. 1980.

Morgan, Janet. *Agatha Christie: A Biography.* New York: Knopf, 1984.

Murder Ahoy! Dir. George Pollock. With Margaret Rutherford and Stringer Davis. MGM. 1964.

Murder at the Gallop. Dir. George Pollock. With Margaret Rutherford, Robert Morley, and Stringer Davis. MGM. 1963.

Murder Most Foul. Dir. George Pollock. With Margaret Rutherford and Stringer Davis. MGM. 1964.

Murder on the Orient Express. Dir. Sidney Lumet. With Albert Finney, Lauren Bacall, Ingrid Bergman. EMI. 1974.

Murder She Said. Dir. George Pollock. With Margaret Rutherford and Stringer Davis. MGM. 1962.

Murder with Mirrors. Dir. Dick Lowry. With Helen Hayes, Bette Davis, John Mills, and Leo McKern. CBS. WCBS, New York. 20 Feb. 1985.

Nemesis. Dram. T.R. Bowen. Dir. David Tucker. MYSTERY! PBS. WGBH, Boston. 10, 17 Dec. 1987.

Osborne, Charles. *The Life and Crimes of Agatha Christie*. New York: Holt, 1982.

Riley, Dick, and Pam McAllister, eds. *The Bedside, Bathtub, & Armchair Companion to Agatha Christie*. New York: Ungar, 1979.

Sanders, Dennis, and Len Lovallo. *The Agatha Christie Companion*. New York: Avenel, 1984.

Shaw, Marion, and Sabine Vanacker. *Reflecting on Miss Marple*. London: Routledge, 1991.

Symons, Julian. "The Mistress of Complication." *Agatha Christie: First Lady of Crime*. Ed. H.R.F. Keating. New York: Holt, 1977. 25-38.

Tennenbaum, Michael. "Margaret Rutherford: The Universal Aunt." Riley and McAllister. 249-51.

Weiler, A.H. Rev. of *Murder Ahoy! New York Times* 23 Sept. 1964: 55.

De-feminizing *Laura*:
Novel to Film

Liahna Babener

Otto Preminger's film Laura *(1944) transforms* Vera Caspary's *novel of the same name (1943) into a spectacle of female objectification imaged forth to gratify the male gaze. The narrative is reconstructed to silence Laura's voice and deny her power. This alteration relocates the action in the masculine contest for sexual mastery over Laura who is both eroticized and made a vessel of womanly culpability.*

Few screen icons have commanded as tenacious a place in spectators' collective memory as has Otto Preminger's Laura, offered up as the incarnation of womanly allurement, and played beguilingly by Gene Tierney in the 1944 film of the same name. That classic *noir* romance, however, actually originated as what might arguably be called a feminist novel. Written in 1943, Vera Caspary's *Laura* establishes Laura Hunt as the protagonist, subject, and controlling sensibility of her own story, an emphatic contrast to the voiceless *femme fatale* that film viewers remember. Caspary centers her narrative around a young woman's passage into adult self-determination, and employs the mystery component—the unriddling of Laura's apparent murder—as a means to effect her escape from the proprietary manipulations of men, and ultimately as a device to critique patriarchal imperatives.

Blunting the feminist dimensions of the novel, however, Preminger remakes the story into the triumph of patriarchy, a spectacle of female objectification imaged forth to gratify the cinematic gaze. Reconstructing the narrative to silence Laura's voice and deny her discursive power, and relocating the action in the masculine contest for sexual mastery over Laura, the film advances a disturbing assault on the feminine. Laura is reconstituted from subject into object, transformed into the passive recipient of driving male desire; her own female desire, around which the novel is built, is commandeered and squelched in the film on behalf of the male characters who strive to control, possess, and ultimately

83

exterminate her. To legitimize her repression by men, Laura is both eroticized and made a vessel of womanly culpability, thus enlisting the spectator in the film's project to suppress the feminine and reinscribe traditional gender codes.

While it may be a stretch to call Caspary's novel an example of *l'ecriture feminine*, its story and structure collaborate to afford readers a proto-feminist commentary on the state of sexual politics in America at mid-century, capitalizing on the sharpened consciousness of an emergent female readership during wartime. Mirroring the cultural modification taking place in the nation as women assumed positions of economic and personal self-sufficiency in the absence of the usual domestic constraints, Caspary makes Laura Hunt's evolution from youthful dreamer to self-assured careerist the dramatic center of the tale.

The novel's story line, nominally a mystery, follows the unraveling of the enigma surrounding Laura's supposed death. Thought to have been murdered as the narrative opens, Laura is recollected for the reader by others whose perceptions of her are colored by their own self-interest. Mark McPherson, the detective assigned the case, envisions the victim as a kind of vestal relic, falling in love with his idealized image; and Waldo Lydecker, Laura's mentor and would-be lover, portrays her as naive and ingenuous, his own Galatea waiting her creator's command. But Laura surfaces, alive, at mid-point in the plot to assert her own point of view and counteract the false profile of herself built up from the men's romantic figurations. Against their collective fantasy, Laura establishes herself as the subject of her own drama, an accomplished professional who has risen to her position through grit and determination, as well as a sexual (as opposed to sexualized or de-sexed) woman whose libidinal life is actively realized.

Before her "death," Laura's success and generous nature have made her the target of usage by male hangers-on. Her fiancé, Shelby Carpenter, is a bounder whose profligacy she has bankrolled; Lydecker plays her protector and advocate, but he actually resents her accomplishments and tries to stifle her independence. Both men are jealous of her sexual vitality. On the eve of her ostensible murder, Laura is mulling over these unsatisfactory involvements, presumably resolving to shake off the sycophants who are consuming her.

Caspary makes Laura's endeavor to assess and resolve her life the focal point of the novel. As Jane Bakerman has argued, Caspary's fiction recurrently centers on "young working women trapped amid the expectations of society, their own romantic dreams, the seemingly vast opportunities of the marketplace, and the enticing new freedoms purportedly available to them" in the commercial world ("Caspary's Chicago" 81). Laura's climb up the success ladder, while it stands as testimony to her drive and ability, has taken a personal toll, leaving her vulnerable to masculine exploitation and embitterment. The underside of achievement for women is often emotional alienation and punitive retaliation; and as Caspary demonstrates, Laura's plight is that her public stature and sexual autonomy have invited the envy and anger of the men who surround her, now culminating in a killer's wrath.

Laura's disaffection with her failed romantic relationships, revealed in the section of the novel narrated by the protagonist herself, serves as an antidote to the men's sentimentalized vision of her. She sees through Carpenter's callow facade to his rancor over being "kept" by a woman, and she penetrates through Lydecker's munificent patronage to recognize his grasping fixation on her. Given her history of usage, she despairs of her subsequent attraction to McPherson, fearing from him the same sexual condescension she has endured from the others. The seeds of such masculine malice are implanted in McPherson; but ultimately, Caspary absolves him of those impulses, or rather shows us how he suppresses them to secure a complementary relationship with Laura. He comes to love the woman she is, rather than the rarified image he had conjured of her, and she in turn conquers her reticence in his favor.

Important here are several elements that underscore the feminist leanings of this novel: the strife between Laura and the men in her life is expressly set forth as gender combat (which, of course, enables us to interpret the murder as an act of masculine rage); Laura's effort to break out of her victimization pattern is made the overarching issue of the story; and, in unmasking the patriarchal motives of her erstwhile suitors and subjecting McPherson to her self-protective scrutiny, Laura assumes authority over her life—she constitutes herself as subject.

Indeed, Laura in effect acts as the operative who delivers herself from jeopardy. Jane Bakerman has noticed that Laura "is an unexpected detective because, in a way, she is seeking her own killer" ("Caspary's Females" 46), supporting McPherson in his official capacity as investigator. But in my view, the more salient form of reconnaissance here is the reflective process through which Laura comes to apprehend and eventually emancipate herself from the ill treatment of men, of which the homicidal attack—by spurned lover

Lydecker, as it turns out—is the most egregious instance. In sorting through the acquisitive motives of the men who surround her, Laura comes to recognize and repudiate their masculine prerogatives; Caspary uses Laura's new cognizance as a means to disparage the bourgeois romanticism to which she has formerly given credence. Freeing herself from the constraints of an ideology that requires the shackling of women to enable the empowerment of men, at novel's end, Laura can claim that "I belonged to myself" (*Laura* 174).

The reader is able to validate this claim, in part because, from the beginning, Laura is positioned in the novel as the controlling agent of her own discourse and destiny, whose force of character deflects the men's efforts to skew her persona into mere otherness. While, as I hope to show, the film dematerializes Laura, robs her of personhood and turns her into an emblem of the eternal feminine in order to advance its misogynist agenda, the novel presents readers with a flesh and blood woman whose complexities establish her humanity and disallow sexual reductivism. The fictional Laura has a specific history, palpable likes and dislikes, hobbies, habits, tastes, and predilections; she has a dwelling place and a workplace, and has stamped both with the impress of her personality. Eugene McNamara has catalogued the idiosyncrasies that make Caspary's Laura sufficiently substantial to stave off the erotic mystification that the film imposes:

> Through her narration the reader learns that she came to New York from Colorado Springs, Colorado, that she is hovering on the age of thirty, likes the music of Jerome Kern and is a baseball fan. A ball autographed by Cookie Lavagetto is in a prominent place on her desk. She reads Jonathan Swift. She has good taste in Scotch and has a quick temper. She conked Diane Redfern on the head with a trayful of *hors d'oeuvres* at a party. (*Laura as Novel* 30)

The details of her life and habitation that precede her entrance into the story—"She worked like a dog"; "she had more friends than money"; she cheerfully shelled out dollar bills to street musicians; she lived in a "comfortable" flat with faded chintz curtains and daisies planted in the window-boxes (*Laura* 33, 38, 41)—expressly debar exotic fantasies, fixing Laura in the reader's (and McPherson's) imagination as a vibrant but down-to-earth person who lived her life deliberately and characteristically.

To propel forward Laura's quest for ownership of herself, Caspary structures the novel's narrative to authorize Laura as verbal arbiter of the discourse. The story is advanced by a "prismatic narrational scheme" (McNamara, _Laura as Novel_ 31), meshing together several points of view that in combination yield the full story. Laura's own account is one of the assemblage, which also includes an opening segment from Lydecker, portions told by McPherson, and a transcript of an interview of Shelby Carpenter. As feminist theorists have argued, women's discourse functions as a counter to the male morphology of classical story-telling, with its relentless drive toward closure, univocal speaker, and linear momentum. Female narrative tends to destabilize this paradigm by delaying denouement through obfuscation, affording multiple speakers and dialogic conversation, and undermining progression through interruptive exposition and jagged chronology—all tactics to topple male dominion over the signifying system.

Caspary's novel reflects this subversive design, giving voice to Laura's perspective and effectively disenfranchising the males for whom she would otherwise be, in Lacanian terms, the other of a discourse grounded in her exclusion. Each subsequent retelling of the events serves to discredit the various male speakers while it enhances Laura's authority over her own story. The opening section is narrated by Waldo Lydecker: his agenda is to represent Laura as an ingrate whose emotional betrayal made her perversely responsible for her own death. Lydecker's script is then undermined by McPherson's revisionist account which recasts Laura as tragic martyr to male predation. A subsequent interview with Shelby Carpenter foils McPherson's interpretation, painting Laura as a rejected lover whose possessiveness has turned her murderous. When Laura steps in to reclaim her life and seize her own story, the self-serving masculine posturing of the others is set in relief against her own knowing and candid appraisal. Bolstering the potency of Laura's voice as the instrument of her subjectivity, Caspary uses an irregular narrative momentum and fragmented time structure to derail the engine of male desire which has so disserved her.

Interestingly, in this vein, the novel does not end with Laura's self-vindicating narrative; it is actually McPherson who speaks the final segment in which Lydecker is unmasked as the killer. But the pattern of structural destabilization persists, since McPherson's voice in this concluding segment is tentative rather than authoritative, and the romantic pairing of Laura and McPherson is deferred indefinitely by the story's vague termination. If we understand closure in narratives of bourgeois romance to entail female sexual capitulation culminating in marriage, such completion is arrested in the novel, leaving readers with the sense that the fixed social and linguistic codes upon which patriarchy rests have been disrupted. This is not to suggest that Laura will not ultimately unite with McPherson, but their potential matrimony is clearly to be subject to her desire and will, and its delay confounds the teleological drive of the narrative, calling attention to its deviation from standard patriarchal romance.

In light of the novel's incipient feminist argument, its cinematic transformation into a fetishistic fantasy is more than disturbing. Indeed, Preminger's *Laura* might be called a textbook example of the kind of classical Hollywood film built around and reliant upon psychical mechanisms rooted in male spectatorship and driven by male desire, wherein, as Mary Ann Doane has put it, "the camera almost literally enacts the repression of the feminine—the woman's relegation to the status of a signifier within the male discourse," and the film itself may be understood as a "compensatory [structure] designed to defend the male psyche against the image of the woman" ("*Caught*" 196).

In this sense, the film is committed to deepening the reassuring divide of sexual difference upon which Western patriarchy rests. Jettisoning the novel's affirmation of Laura as female subject, the film relocates interest in the mission of the male principles to verify their masculinity by bridling and ultimately obliterating the woman. For this to happen, Laura must be turned into an avatar of essential femininity and then censured and quashed as such, while the power and potency of conventional manliness must be upheld. Hence, Laura is conveniently circumscribed for most of the film in the frame of a portrait of her that the men safely adore as a *memento mori*; when she disturbs the sexual equilibrium by resurfacing as a living woman, she is conceptualized as a temptress whose erotic menace warrants her suppression. Between them, the men enact a series of tactics to nullify Laura: making her into a gratifying fantasy, probing her private heart, silencing her voice, shooting, and finally domesticating her. That McPherson (played by a very hard-boiled Dana Andrews) emerges the victor depends in part upon his superior strategies for containing Laura: his brand of maleness is championed, while Lydecker (memorably acted by Clifton Webb) and Carpenter (Vincent Price) are denigrated for theirs. To achieve the emphatic gender polarization upon which the film depends, values and behaviors associated with "the feminine" must be seen as adulterated, and the women's discourse that propels the novel is choked off, leaving the patriarchy intact at film's end.

To justify the suppression of the feminine that the film sets out to achieve, the character of Laura must be recast as blameworthy and threatening to masculine composure. Hence, the Laura that viewers see is hardly the likable but vulnerable person of the novel. Indeed, Caspary professed to have been stupefied by the dangerous woman of the world that Preminger made out of what she saw as a "kind," "bright-eyed," "warm," "independent girl who earned her living and pampered her lovers," and offended by the director's insinuation that Laura's sexuality made her tainted ("My 'Laura'" 36-37).

That Preminger conceived of Laura as a vitiated woman has been corroborated in the remembrances of those who worked with him on the film's production. David Raskind, composer of the movie score (which, as I will subsequently argue, contributed substantially to the filmic project of dematerializing Laura from person to fantasy-object), reports that in his initial consultation with Preminger, the two discussed using Duke Ellington's *Sophisticated Lady* for the theme music. Raskind dissented, but "Preminger defended his choice, saying, 'This is a very sophisticated girl.' When I pretended not to understand how he meant that, he said, 'My dear boy, this girl is a whore!'" (Prendergast 67). Producer Darryl Zanuck reiterated the perception that Laura was a sexually compromised woman. He expressed dissatisfaction, for example, with Jay Dratler's script, objecting that Shelby Carpenter, whom he described as a "pimp," was insufficiently "charming and debonair" to be paired with someone as worldly as Laura. Later, giving instructions to Preminger as he staged the scene in which McPherson inspects Laura's personal belongings, Zanuck insisted that among other things, the detective "look at her lingerie" at which point "she begins to get under his skin" (Behlmer 182-83), again affirming the sexualized construction of Laura that dominated the intentions of the male auteurs.

The whole film follows this reading of Laura. Its assignment is to depict her as corruptive so that vindictive reprisal is merited; hence the novel's diegesis must be reconstituted to accuse Laura, and the film becomes a kind of catalogue of her implied sexual treacheries. That this résumé of her character was the one successfully conveyed to spectators is evident from the consensus among contemporary reviewers that Laura was a loose woman. Bosley Crowther, writing for the *New York Times*, thought Gene Tierney too naive and wholesome for a role that called for sophisticated vice (24). Manny Farrel, writing for *The New Republic*, typified critics' reactions when, following the film's

October 1944 screen debut, he described Laura as a woman "bound to become the mistress of anybody in pants, who can lie and be as tricky as the next society type," noting with righteous disapproval that "during the picture she falls in love with four men and out of love with three" (568). The fact that Farrel's assessment is technically inaccurate is less important than what it reveals about the film's effectiveness in rendering Laura as a seductress whose behavior incites male anxiety and defensiveness—a strategy necessary to justify her cohibitive treatment in the film. Even relatively contemporary commentators have reechoed the film's governing conception of Laura's "not so innocent life" (Peary 143) or "amoral" character (Leese 950).

From the outset, Laura's feminine sexuality is under assault. Lydecker, whose recollection opens the film, purports to eulogize the "dead" Laura (he has, of course, murdered someone he thought to be her), but his telling discloses, against his conscious intention, the simmering hatred he bears for the woman he views as a "betrayer." The narrative and camera act as co-conspirators in the series of scenes flashing back Waldo's memories of Laura, scenes structured to make her seem an alluring prevaricator. First, she invades his private lunch table against his wishes and then uses her charm to make a sales pitch, prompting Lydecker's defensive response ("You think the mere fact of being a woman exempts you from the rules of civilized conduct") and inviting the spectator to read her behavior as coy manipulation.

Soon after, Laura is seen taking advantage of Lydecker's social and professional contacts and then rewarding his generosity with coquettish glances and intimate encounters, vignettes which suggest that she has in some sense prostituted herself for success. When she cancels a dinner date with Lydecker with no explanation and then is seen entertaining a male visitor late that night, she is wanton and duplicitous; later, when Lydecker demeans one of her beaux in a snide newspaper column, Laura is shown tittering over his derisive remarks, thus setting her up as a faithless user of men—the very antithesis of her character in the novel. Laura's popularity among rival suitors is presented as a teasing ploy on her part: when she arrives at a party on Lydecker's arm, she resists one man's invitation by saying, "I'm not alone," only to abandon Lydecker and conduct a tryst with the man, thus appearing to confirm Lydecker's treacherous image of her.

The film's spectatorial and structural mechanisms collude to endorse Waldo's paranoid reading of Laura as desirable object and perfidious woman. Visually, from her first appearance on screen, Laura is made the embodiment of sultry sexual promise, the invitation to danger and the activator of the cinematic gaze. In the flashback scenes, she is regularly positioned in a succession of familiar groupings with men, looking up into their faces, laughing secretively with them, beautifying herself in a mirror before admiring onlookers, lighting a cigarette and blowing smoke in tandem, dallying with a shadowy figure behind an opaque window shade—all coded gestures suggesting sex.

Laura's screen persona is set up as an artifact of male desire. Actress Tierney claimed to have coveted the part because "it was an escape from . . . all the half-caste girls I had played . . . a Polynesian, a Eurasian, an Arab, and a Chinese" (quoted in Behlmer 187). Ironically, however, she was in all likelihood cast expressly to evoke those very Oriental associations which for Western patriarchy denote exotic vice, called up here to equate Laura with sexual venality. Tierney's facial properties (subtly slanted eyes, liquid black pupils, sleek, dark hair, sulky lips) are features which, beyond their Eastern connotations, had come to signify sexual availability in the covert parlance of 1940s Hollywood. Moreover, the actress's characteristic expression, a kind of faraway look that suggests unfathomability, augments the iconography of erotic power upon which the characterization of Laura as corrupt woman depends. As Richard Dyer has argued, "women in film noir are above all else, unknowable. It is . . . their unknowability . . . that makes them fatal" (92)—and in Laura's case, that prompts, as we shall see, the efforts of the threatened male characters to subdue her through carnal knowledge.

Lydecker's conception of Laura as vile deceiver is also given credibility by the voice-over technique that enables him to control the audience's view of Laura extra-diegetically. The unlocalized voice-over—an auditory privilege almost exclusively accorded male speakers in classic cinema, as Kaja Silverman demonstrates (*Acoustic Mirror* 48-52)—works to underscore Lydecker's discursive power, while his invisibility and "on-high" status as disembodied commentator exempt him from the gaze of the camera and viewer. Unlike the novel, where his narrative is undermined by conflicting versions of the story, most particularly Laura's own, the film ratifies Lydecker's account by granting it unchallenged verbal license.

McPherson's consciousness eventually replaces Lydecker's as the story progresses, but though less overtly malicious, he also construes Laura as sexually defiled. Driven by hardened preconceptions about women as "two timing dames" out to entrap men, and threatened by Laura's liberation from the secure confinement of death, McPherson makes Laura into a vessel of sexual prodigality which he can then contemplate, condemn, and control. We see this when he reconnoiters her apartment for evidences of her intimate life, scrutinizing her clothing and possessions and poring over her private letters for the data of her secret self. We see it too when he mutters innuendoes to others about cheating women, and when he bombards her with hostile questions ostensibly meant to elicit a murder confession but actually designed to ferret out and then impugn her sexual history. When Laura appears to violate a promise not to contact Carpenter after her unexpected return, McPherson muses to a fellow officer, "Dames are always pulling a switch on you," a conclusion the viewer is forced to ratify given the deceitful behavior shown us. Later, when Lydecker faints from the shock of seeing her alive, McPherson's cynical accusation ("Don't tell me you're in love with him, too") casts her as promiscuous, a judgment reinforced when even her loyal maid assumes she has been carrying on and covers up evidence of a man's presence in the apartment the night of the murder.

McPherson's sexual mistrust of Laura is corroborated by auditory and visual detail. Lydecker's lewd interjections, following upon his recriminatory voice-over, implant additional doubts (mocking her fiancé as "a very obliging fellow," berating what he deems her fixation with "lean, muscular bodies," and depicting her demeanor before McPherson as "disgustingly earthy"). Then, in the scenes following her re-entrance, Laura is repeatedly situated among a coterie of males, made to look both guilty (with darting, evasive eyes, closed-in body language, and non-communicative expressions) and seductive (flirtatious gestures, imploring glances, helpless posturing). She is caught in a series of contradictions: claiming to want freedom from overbearing men but clinging to Carpenter's custody; maintaining that she knew nothing of the murder that took place in her apartment because the radio at her country house was broken—then forced to explain why it works, which she does by revealing that she has cajoled an obliging repairman to fix it, which in turn makes her seem like a tease.

Because the filmic evidence seems to indict her, viewers are thus invited to sanction the misogynist view of Laura as sexual traitor, even while she is technically innocent of such a charge— indeed, it is a paramount irony that though the film foregrounds the putative corruption that her sexuality implies, she is enjoined from actual sex. Her libidinal life is virtually nil, and even after romance develops with McPherson, Laura is restricted to a single perfunctory kiss. She is vindicated diegetically of the imputations of infidelity when it is made clear that she has cast off Waldo and Carpenter not out of fickleness or promiscuity, but rather for their own failings of character—or, as it is more properly understood, of manliness. Her sexual guiltlessness is also affirmed when we learn that she has misled McPherson only to protect others, that she is in fact the prey rather than the assassin, and that on the night of the crime she has gone alone to her country house to ponder her future rather than keeping a lovers' liaison in her apartment. Significantly, however, though actually exonerated by the story line, Laura continues to stand accused by the extra-diegetic components of the film whose collective power to vilify her outweighs the acknowledgment of her innocence offered by the plot. And she must be vilified to justify the repression practiced upon her.

To ensure that Laura cannot contest her sullied image, her speech is muffled. Unlike the novel, where she asserts herself through narrative, here she is denied discursive authority, forbidden to advance her own viewpoint. As Silverman argues, women's voices in mainstream cinema are almost invariably "associated with unreliable, thwarted, or acquiescent speech" ("Dis-Embodying" 131). Refused a voice-over, Laura's articulations inside the frame of the story are severely restricted: she is often silent (as when she refuses to answer McPherson's direct query about her role in the killing); or her utterances are made ambiguous or inconsistent (as when she purports to have broken with Carpenter, only to be "engaged" again after spending time alone with him); or her verbal reticence is sentimentalized ("The ways she listened were more eloquent than speech," Lydecker says). Hence, Laura's impeded voice is actually used against her to disempower and censure her.

That keeping Laura mute was part of the male moviemakers' design is well documented. Preminger objected forcefully when attempts were made to adjust the script to incorporate a segment narrated by Laura (Pratley 60), and producer Zanuck similarly rejected the move, complaining that permitting her to speak for herself would skew the (masculine) psychology that shaped the story (Behlmer 183). Indeed, Laura must be barred from verbal agency because her importance to the film's system of meaning is visual: she must remain subject to the male gaze, "poised at the center of all forces, object of love and hate" (McNamara, *Laura as Novel* 67).

Laura is kept on dumb display in the portrait that dominates the film's *mise en scene*. Painted by a former lover and thus made for male gratification, the portrait functions on many levels to denote the film's anti-feminist agenda and sustain what Eugene McNamara calls the "progressive derealization" of Laura (*Laura as Novel* 44) that drives the text. Since Laura is presumed dead for nearly half the story, the painting serves as a kind of frozen surrogate for her, an icon that enables the men to covet her without actually having to confront a living woman. Held inside her frame, made eternally enticing and thus conveniently culpable for their lust while unable to counteract their objectification of her, Laura languishes in her specular prison, the very epitomization of Mulvey's notion of the enforced "to-be-looked-at-ness" (67) of the conventional film female, bearer of but banned from being maker of meaning.

While Laura's painted visage pervades the film space, it stands not for a personified agent to be reckoned with, but rather for the kind of structuring absence that, as Lacan argues, fuels (male) desire. Thus Laura "can be seen to be the subject of the film only insofar as she agrees to be its object" (Penley 4), a point borne out by the way the portrait has been conceived and situated in the film frame, and by the deportment of the male characters who view it. As Kristin Thompson has noticed, its placement in the film's scenographic space invites the audience to share the looker's perspective, thus intensifying the gaze process (94). The portrait itself is laden with exhibitionist suggestibility: Laura's body forms a serpentine twist, head tilted coyly, one hand clutching her breast, the other dropping downward in a beckoning gesture, a strapless black dress accentuating bared neck and shoulders. Apparently complicitous in the erogenous sign system that entreats onlookers to imagine ravishing her, Laura's painted face is turned frontally toward the viewer, as if she were "offering herself up for examination" (Thompson 98). It is "as if all the fetishism of the cinema were condensed onto the image of the face," as Mary Ann Doane has written. "Apprehending the image becomes the mode of possession" (*Femmes* 46, 47). Thus, the image in the picture is both eroticized and commodified, made "the site of structures both of exchange and of looking" (Borzello et al. 11), and reminding us of the connotative linkage between posing and prostitution in Western art.[1]

The portrait itself functions to augment the case against Laura as reproachable temptress. It serves as an instrument of fascination, ensnaring those unlucky enough to fall under its spell, "inciting a psychopathic possessiveness" in observers ("Laura" 3). The beautiful face that looks out from the canvas can be doubly denounced for enthralling onlookers then being inaccessible to them, "a contemporary version of the Giaconda smile . . . that remains forever out of reach" (McNamara, "Preminger's Laura" 26). Though the text is contrived to make Laura the bewitching force, conversely, it is actually she who is victimized by confinement in the claustrophobic frame of male fantasy. She is denied ownership of her own image—her face is, after all, not for herself but for her spectators, an index to her powerlessness and otherness. She cannot return the gaze or control the captivating impact of her image, nor can she protect herself from the violence of her would-be executioner whose frustrated desire spills over into a killing mania. Quarantined inside the pictorial space, Laura can be devitalized into a relic, while paradoxically kept alive as the fount of carnal imagining. By contrast, the portrait occupies an insignificant role in the novel, since there Laura is the subject of her own story rather than a lure for scopophilia.

Indeed, the entire textual system of the film, dedicated to advancing its patriarchal agenda, conspires to vaporize Laura, relegating her permanently to the dreamy, evanescent figure residual in the memories of generations of filmgoers. She is locked into an impotent visibility. Structurally, for example, she is systematically displaced from the action for much of the story. At the outset, she functions as mere memory, called up in flashbacks that, as Kristin Thompson has recognized, "bolster the idea that we will never see Laura in the 'present' tense sections" of the film (97). The skewed time sequences make her seem no more than a beguiling ghost, an impression not reversed when she appears in the flesh, since the same bloodless vagueness attends her presentation in those later scenes. She speaks rarely, occupies minimal screen time, and is situated passively in the film frame sandwiched between men who initiate the action.

Moreover, the film's indefinite milieu, restricted almost exclusively to interiors and disconnected from any real markers of temporality or locale, amplifies the sense of witnessing events "free-floating" in fictional space. The sets are self-consciously artificial and the urban landmarks generic studio contrivances; the spurious decor of Laura's apartment belies her occupancy. The indeterminacy of the setting tends to diminish her reality as metropolitan resident, weekend commuter, and uptown employee, tangible facets of her life in the novel which are effectively rubbed out of her celluloid representation, making her seem a disembodied feminine essence rather than a person. An added factor is the age transformation from the novel's thirtyish sophisticate to the film's twenty-two year old ingenue, a process which robs Laura of substance and self-possession, and underscores her revised characterization as a compliant pin-up.

In addition, the film's monothematic score is critical to the process of making Laura appear immaterial. Perennially described by hearers as a "haunting" tune evocative of an elusive woman, the song was composed for the film under Preminger's express instructions to create music befitting its *femme fatale*. Raksin contends that he composed the melody having just been jilted by his wife (Behlmer 198), a detail which might explain its piquant mixture of nostalgia and sultriness. Johnny Mercer's lyrics (written after the film) emphasize Laura's exotic mystery. She is "the face in the misty light," the one whose "footsteps . . . you hear down the hall," suggesting a kind of dream lover or succubus: "You know the feeling/Of something half remembered/Of something that never happened/Yet you recall it well." The language here underlines not only Laura's insubstantial being, but the film's insistent construction of a male spectatorship; Laura is a vision manufactured to unnerve then gratify a masculine sensibility.

Inside the filmic apparatus, the music works to "render the viewer an untroublesome viewing subject . . . [increasing] the spectator's susceptibility to suggestion" and "removing defenses against unconscious fantasies," as Claudia Gorbman has argued about cinematic music in general (5). In *Laura*, then, the "haunting" score makes possible the (male) viewer's ownership of the fantasy of the tantalizing female, immersing him in a "melodic bath" of primal pleasure which reinforces Laura's status as signifier of the erotic imagination. Laura is explicitly identified with the song: first heard in the opening credits with her portrait in the foreground, it is replayed constantly in the early phases of the story when she is presumed dead, always when her portrait occupies the screen, and whenever the other characters call her to mind.

When Laura comes back to life, however, she threatens to capsize the system that oppresses her, breaking out of her frame to challenge the process by which she has been depersonified. Not surprisingly, her reappearance induces retaliatory action from the males in whose interest it is to preserve her extinction, and sets in motion a series of tactics meant to stymie her self-assertion. Lydecker, who had slain her when she resisted his control and transgressed his cerebral fantasy, needs her dead, and McPherson has become infatuated with a phantom who obliges his lust while remaining safely inert. As Eugene Archer argues, he "hates her, and cannot forgive her for coming back to life" (13). Both men, along with Carpenter whose status as charming reprobate is threatened by Laura's presence, want to squelch the resurrected woman whose volition calls into question their potency, since, as Janey Place explains it, "in film noir, it is clear that men need to control women's sexuality in order not to be destroyed by it" (36).

Lydecker tries to regain psychological mastery of Laura through deft verbal assaults aimed at shaking her self-confidence and personal esteem. Eventually, he is driven to reprise the murder, intending to immortalize his chaste goddess in quaint prose for his own perpetual indulgence. (Importantly, the novel has Lydecker plan his own suicide to coincide with Laura's murder; the film, however, reconceptualizes the homicide to make clear the necessity of Laura's death as appeasement for Lydecker's masculine ego.) McPherson alternately cajoles and bullies Laura, using romantic overtures to soften her self-protective shell, then invading her fragile female psyche. The movie's Laura, unlike her fictional source, is no match for this assault upon her feminine self. Whatever power she may have once commanded—social, professional, sexual—is effectively eradicated by the frenzy of endangered manhood, and she capitulates before the onslaught. McPherson saves her from Lydecker's homicidal rage only to ready her for the domestic incarceration that their implied marriage will ensure.

Ultimately, the film's project is to buttress the traditional gender roles that have tottered following the social changes of the period. This means reviling and suppressing the feminine, as we have seen, but it also requires that conventional notions of masculinity be vindicated, and in this objective, *Laura* has much in common with other *noir* films of its time wherein "the phallic regime of masculine identity . . . has to be consolidated and perpetually protected against various forms of deviance and disruption," as Frank Krutnik has argued (85). This becomes McPherson's task as he takes on the status of the story's sanctioned male exemplar. As I have shown, suppressing Laura, the female other, is one means of fortifying his manhood; he must also define his heterosexual identity against what Krutnik calls "alternative figurations of masculinity" (243), and thus distinguish himself from the more feminized models represented by Lydecker and, to a lesser extent, Carpenter.

Caspary saw Lydecker as a failed suitor whose sexual impotence doomed his romantic pursuit of Laura ("My 'Laura'" 37). Thwarted libido explained his viperish temperament, turning his pen into a prosthetic phallus and provoking murderous anger. In the film, however, Lydecker must be made effeminate, differentiated sharply from McPherson's tough guy manliness, in order that McPherson's position as protagonist be solidified. Thus through coded cinematic cues, a process which discredits Lydecker's claim to masculine authority and leaves McPherson as the triumphant personfication of patriarchy, the film reconceptualizes Lydecker from a dysfunctional lover into a homosexual aberrant.

In shaping Lydecker's screen identity, Preminger clearly capitalized upon actor Clifton Webb's fastidious theatrical persona and prissy public image. In spite of the casting director's objection that Webb was too "effeminate," Preminger pushed ahead with the assignment (Pratley 56), since Webb's demeanor exactly suited the director's intention to build his film around competing prescriptions of masculinity. From the outset, viewers read Lydecker as latently gay, responding to a series of visual and verbal indices. In the opening scene, for example, he is seen lounging in a bathtub; the room's fussy decor and Lydecker's elaborate soaking and preening ritual along with his gossipy dialogue immediately mark him as "feminine" while, by contrast, McPherson's stilted posture and taciturn manner brand him as "manly." The insinuations progress as Lydecker stands up to get dressed. His upper torso is thin and flaccid; though viewers cannot see below the waist, McPherson's apparent smirk when he casts an embarrassed eye in Lydecker's direction suggests that the man's maleness is somehow suspect. It is hardly a stretch here to recognize the degree to which the film plays up the latent castration anxieties of its male audience. Later, Lydecker dresses (in McPherson's presence) in a dandyish suit with a silky handkerchief folded into the pocket and jaunty carnation poked through the lapel; set against these "vestimentary codes" implying homosexuality,[2] McPherson's broad-shouldered jacket, low-slung fedora, dangling cigarette, and erect stance signal "straight male" to the spectator.

The implicit sexual polarity between the two men persists throughout the film. Lydecker is constructed as epicene, assigned mannerisms identified as womanish (he passes out when in shock, primps before mirrors, has a "perfumed style of talking [that] expresses a lot of auntyish effeminacy" [Farrel 568], and even refers to himself as "Old Mother Hubbard"). He scorns the conventionally male activities like baseball that appeal to McPherson. The accoutrements in his apartment suggest a lady's domain (cluttered Victorian knickknacks, sumptuous furniture, ornate fixtures, fancy glassware and cutlery) and are reduplicated in the dwelling places of the two prominent women in the film (Anne Treadwell and Laura) to underline their feminine associations. Indeed, one strategy used here to vitiate female sexuality is to align it with acquisitiveness and precious excess, what McNamara deftly labels "a kind of pornography of antique decor" ("Preminger's *Laura*" 29).

Not surprisingly, McPherson's virile cop is given gender prerogative over Lydecker's decadent queen. In spite of his oppressive treatment of Laura, or rather because of it—since to estrange himself from and put down the female other is to confirm his own masculine ego—McPherson surfaces as the vanquisher. Dana Andrews plays McPherson as ultra-hard-boiled dick, reflecting the filmmakers' antipathy to Caspary's conception of the character as "tough-minded but warm-hearted" ("McPherson" 145). Andrews was coached to project a rigid, no-nonsense mien; his vestimentary and verbal codes all flash manliness: granite jaw, five o'clock shadow, scruffy apparel, laconic speech, sports metaphors, misogynist one-liners. In the end, he can handle Laura, where Lydecker (and Shelby, who is constructed as a weak dandy, attractive to women who want to mollycoddle him) cannot.

Indeed, Lydecker's incompetence is so manifold that he fails twice to kill Laura. In the elaborate final scene, he bungles the second attempt on her life, and the film comes to a close as his demasculinized voice flutters across the airwaves reciting sentimental Edwardian poetry:

> They are not long, the days of wine and roses
>> Out of a misty dream
>
> Our path emerges for a while, then closes
>> Within a dream.

Discerning viewers should not fail to notice that the thrust of these lines from Dowson, quoted by Lydecker during a taped radio address and recorded when he expected Laura to be dead, is to celebrate the kind of disembodied, desexualized romance he had tried to impose upon her. But now they sound only ironic, reminders not so much of the dematerialization done her, but of the unmanning done him by the filmmakers, whose purpose is to vindicate McPherson's authorized style of maleness.

Ultimately, *Laura* reverses the implicit feminist message of its source. Caspary's novel champions the female subject while Preminger's film targets the feminine for extinction. Caspary reaches to broaden and complicate concepts of gender, allowing her heroine latitude to find a life-route for herself that permits romance but disavows the patriarchal rules that have traditionally governed it, so that romance is no longer a decoy to inveigle women into the fetters of bourgeois marriage. Preminger means to re-excavate the gender divide, separating irrevocably the masculine from the feminine to vindicate the most traditional conception of manhood. Yet, while Caspary's novel is long out of print, the film continues to be revered by viewers, demonstrating how fully its reactionary message remains integral to gender politics in American culture and reminding us how difficult it is to tell women's stories in classical forms.

NOTES

[1]This idea has been advanced by many feminist art historians, but its primary articulation is in Berger, 45-81.

[2]The phrase, coined by Marjorie Garber in *Vested Interests* (161), defines clothing as a system of signification.

WORKS CITED

Archer, Eugene. "Laura." *Movie* Sept. 1962: 12-13.

Bakerman, Jane. "Vera Caspary's Chicago, Symbol and Setting." *Midamerica* 11 (1984): 81-89.

____. "Vera Caspary's Fascinating Females: Laura, Evvie, and Bedelia." *Clues* 1.1 (1980): 46-52.

Behlmer, Rudy. *America's Favorite Movies: Behind the Scenes.* New York: Ungar, 1982.

Berger, John. *Ways of Seeing.* London: British Broadcasting Corporation; Harmondsworth: Penguin, 1972.

Borzello, Frances, Annette Kuhn, Jill Pack, and Cassandra Wedd. "Living Dolls and 'Real Women.'" *The Power of the Image: Essays on Representation and Sexuality.* Ed. Annette Kuhn. London: Routledge, 1985. 9-18.

Caspary, Vera. *Laura.* 1943. New York: Avon Books, 1970.

____. "Mark McPherson." *The Great Detectives.* Ed. Otto Penzler. Boston: Little, Brown, 1978. 143-46.

____. "My Laura and Otto's." *Saturday Review* 26 June 1971: 36-37.

Crowther, Bosley. "*Laura.*" *New York Times* 12 Oct. 1944: 24.

Doane, Mary Ann. "*Caught* and *Rebecca*: The Inscription of Femininity as Absence." Penley 196-215.

____. *Femmes Fatales: Feminism, Film Theory, Psychoanalysis.* New York: Routledge, 1991.

Dyer, Richard. "Resistance through Charisma: Rita Hayworth and *Gilda.*" Kaplan 91-99.

Farrel, Manny. "Murdered Movie." *The New Republic* 30 Oct. 1944: 568.

Garber, Marjorie. *Vested Interests: Cross Dressing and Cultural Anxiety.* New York: Routledge, 1992.

Gorbman, Claudia. *Unheard Melodies: Narrative Film Music.* Bloomington: Indiana UP, 1987.

Kaplan, E. Ann, ed. *Women in Film Noir.* London: British Film Institute, 1980.

Krutnik, Frank. *In a Lonely Street: Film Noir, Genre, Masculinity.* New York: Routledge, 1991.

"Laura." *Daily Variety* 11 Oct. 1944: 3.

Laura. Prod. and dir. Otto Preminger. With Gene Tierney, Dana Andrews, Clifton Webb, Vincent Price, and Judith Anderson. 20th Century-Fox, 1944.

Leese, Elizabeth. "Laura." *Magill's Survey of Cinema: English Language Films, First Series.* Ed. Frank N. Magill. 4 vols. Englewood Cliffs, NJ: Salem P, 1980. 2: 948-51.

McNamara, Eugene. *Laura as Novel, Film, and Myth.* Lewiston, NY: Edwin Mellen, 1992.

____. "Preminger's *Laura* and the Fatal Woman Tradition." *Clues* 3.2 (1982): 24-29.

Mulvey, Laura. "Visual Pleasure and Narrative Cinema." Penley 57-68.

Peary, Danny. *Cult Movies 2.* New York: Dell, 1985.

Penley, Constance, ed. *Feminism and Film Theory.* New York: Routledge, 1988.

____. "Introduction." Penley 1-24.

Place, Janey. "Women in Film Noir." Kaplan, 35-67.

Pratley, Gerald. *The Cinema of Otto Preminger.* New York: Castle Books, 1971.

Prendergast, Roy M. *A Neglected Art: A Critical Study of Music in Films.* New York: New York UP, 1977.

Silverman, Kaja. *The Acoustic Mirror: The Female Voice in Psychoanalysis and Cinema.* Bloomington: Indiana UP, 1988.

____. "Dis-Embodying the Female Voice." *Re-Vision: Essays in Feminist Film Criticism.* Eds. Mary Ann Doane et al. Los Angeles: American Film Institute, 1984. 131-49.

Thompson, Kristin. "Closure within a Dream: Point-of-View in *Laura*." *Film Reader* 3 (1978): 90-105.

A Train Running on Two Sets of Tracks: Highsmith's and Hitchcock's *Strangers on a Train*

MaryKay Mahoney

Highsmith's Strangers on a Train *provides a psychological analysis of Guy Haines and Charles Anthony Bruno and their intertwined relationship. Hitchcock transforms the material into a thriller, focusing on action, suspense, and surprise. In the novel, the personalities of the characters, Highsmith's stylistic techniques, and the plot structure emphasize the similarities between Haines and Bruno; in the film, however, the visual links between the two are confused by the transformation of Haines into an innocent hero.*

It begins with a casual conversation between two men on a train. When one of them shifts the topic to a "trade" of murders—"I kill your wife and you kill my father" (Highsmith, *Strangers* 30)—the first strands are spun of a web of violence that will entangle both men. Readers of suspense fiction and fans of Alfred Hitchcock films will immediately identify this plot: Patricia Highsmith's novel *Strangers on a Train* (1950) and Alfred Hitchcock's 1951 film adaptation of the same name.

Highsmith describes the starting point for her novel: "the germ of the plot for *Strangers on a Train* was: 'Two people agree to murder each other's enemy, thus permitting a perfect alibi to be established'" (*Plotting* 4). Highsmith's own novel deals somewhat ironically with that plot germ, since Guy Haines does not, on the train, "agree" verbally to the trade of murders suggested by his fellow "stranger" Charles Anthony Bruno. In Guy's revelations about his wife, Miriam, to Bruno, and in his silence after Miriam's murder, however, there is an implicit consent, and Guy eventually becomes a full accomplice in the exchange of murders, killing Bruno's father as his part of the trade. In Hitchcock's film, on the other hand, the exchange of murders is far more one-sided, with Bruno killing Miriam but Guy, in return, attempting instead to warn Bruno's father, the intended second victim.

103

As suggested by the dramatic plot change in the film, the two works are substantially different in focus and direction. Highsmith focuses on the psychological analysis of the two men and their intertwined relationship, whereas Hitchcock's transformation of the material into the genre of the thriller means a corresponding focus on action and the characteristic Hitchcock elements of suspense and surprise. According to John Russell Taylor, "In *Strangers on a Train* Hitch had managed, by instinct rather than conscious thought, to find a deeply disturbing subject—that of an exchange of guilt—which could be satisfactorily externalized in thriller form" (218). Hitchcock himself commented, "*Strangers on a Train* wasn't an assignment, but a novel that I selected myself. I felt this was the right kind of material for me to work with" (qtd. in Truffaut 193).

As various film critics have pointed out, Hitchcock's opening shots for the film capture a sense of the film as a whole:

> Extremely low camera placements in the opening sequence prepare us for a film that will take place largely in a subterranean world of anxiety and nightmare. The credits run over a scene looking back from the inside of a cavernous train station to the brightness of the world outside. As they end, a cab turns into the entrance. It disgorges Bruno, or more accurately, Bruno's garish shoes and trouser legs. A second cab pulls up at the dark curb and unloads Guy's legs, feet, and tennis racquets. The film begins with a movement into darkness from which it will return only at the very end. . . .
>
> As the action of guilt and entrapment commences, images of descent and imprisonment proliferate. The camera stays at knee level for a minute and a half after the credits, until Bruno's foot and Guy's bump under a table in the lounge car. This opening sequence includes an expressive shot of the shadow of the train proceeding along the intersecting and diverging tracks of the railyard. . . . The image of the converging rails at the beginning of *Strangers on a Train* serves as an emblem of the plot, in which characters in a chaos of unconnected human lives coincidentally converge and collide, turn apart, and pursue crucial actions in parallel. (Brill 76-77)

Those opening shots of the two pairs of feet moving towards each other and of the converging railroad tracks emphasize the connection between the two men, the deliberate image of them as doubles. Robin Wood points out that, in the process, our sense of the opposition between the two pairs of shoes seen in the opening sequence—Guy's modest dark shoes and Bruno's flashier two-toned spats—becomes a parallel "imposed by the editing on what would otherwise be pure contrast" (Wood 170). This sense of Bruno and Guy as doubles is reinforced both visually and linguistically throughout the scenes that follow by such elements as Guy's lighter with its engraving of crossed tennis racquets, the link between the "doubles" of tennis player Guy and the scotch doubles ordered for them both by Bruno, and Bruno's thoughtful murmurs of "Crisscross" as he lies back in his private compartment, holding the lighter Guy has left behind and contemplating the trade in murders he has just suggested to Guy.

Yet despite the film's technical brilliance in suggesting the idea of doubles,[1] the viewer's sense of Bruno as the representative of Guy's unexamined and repressed desires is shortcircuited by the plot level of the film, resulting in a significant departure from the dynamics of the Highsmith novel. In plot terms, Guy is an innocent man, guilty on a conscious level of neither Miriam's death nor Bruno's plans to have his father killed. Hitchcock's editing techniques visually link Guy and Bruno; for example, when Hitchcock cuts from a scene in a telephone booth where Guy, drowned out at first by a train, shouts about Miriam, "I said I could strangle her!" to a shot of Bruno's curved, upheld hands, the sequence directly links Guy's desire for Miriam's death to the means by which Bruno will accomplish that death. Yet the essence of the film's plot is that Guy, the innocent hero, will eventually emerge uncorrupted from the world of darkness into which Bruno has temporarily plunged him.

When Hitchcock's Guy, having entered Bruno's father's bedroom at night in accordance with Bruno's murderous plan, attempts to warn the father (only to find a suspicious Bruno there in his place), the opposition, rather than the likeness, between the two men becomes marked. Even though Guy carries a gun with him on his nocturnal expedition, the speed with which he pockets the gun outside the bedroom and calls out the name of Bruno's father makes it nearly impossible to believe that Guy is seriously tempted to carry out the killing to protect himself from Bruno's blackmailing threats. As a result, the scene's suspense derives from Hitchcock's deliberately misleading the viewer, rather than from any sense of Guy as a potentially complex and unpredictable character torn between two possible choices. When Guy is confronted on the staircase by an apparently vicious guard-dog and the viewer is swept into fear for Guy's safety, that very anxiety (considering that Guy *may* be about to kill a defenseless old man in cold blood) is

designed to force viewers to deal with the moral ambiguity of their
own reactions. Yet the viewers' moral dilemma is patently
manufactured if there is no real chance of Guy's killing Bruno's
father, and this converts the whole sequence to the level of a clever
trick. (Interestingly, Wood, in revising his essay on the film, shifts
from seeing this problem as simply a "misjudgment" to commenting
that "'Major lapse in artistic integrity' is perhaps not too strong a
description" [179].)

This confrontation between Bruno and Guy reveals to Bruno as
well as to viewers that Guy will not succumb to Bruno's dark
desires. In retaliation, Bruno threatens to find an appropriate
revenge for the "betrayal": he will falsify evidence of the innocent
Guy's guilt. After Bruno's decision, the film moves quickly to two
dramatically crosscut races against time: Bruno's attempting to
rescue Guy's lighter from a sewer so he can use it to incriminate
Guy, and Guy's attempting to win his tennis match at Forest Hills as
quickly as possible so he can thwart Bruno's plans. This crosscutting
emphasizes the differences between the two men by means of a
striking visual contrast: the darkness of the sewer scenes and the
open, sunlit scenes of the tennis match represent each character's
moral condition.

As the film progresses, viewers clearly discern the men's
dramatic opposition despite the chaos of events and the confusion
of the police. In the film's climactic scene Guy follows Bruno to the
carnival grounds where Bruno killed Guy's wife, Miriam. There the
police are misled by the ambiguity of a carnival worker's cry;
looking towards the two men, he exclaims: "He's the one. He's the
one who killed her." As the accidental shooting of the carousel
operator sends the carousel hurtling at top speed, Guy is swept
dramatically from the ordered safe world he craves into the
instability and disorder linked with Bruno.[2] Nevertheless, the
opposition between the two men remains paramount, captured in
miniature by a vignette where a young boy attempting to help Guy
is pushed viciously by Bruno and nearly falls from the wildly
spinning carousel; Guy risks himself to save the child, with the
result that he himself is nearly killed by Bruno.

As soon as the carousel's crash and the discovery of Guy's
lighter in the dead Bruno's hand have revealed Guy's innocence to
the police, Guy is able to return to a harmony with the ordered
world beyond the carnival gates. The film ends, however, not with
the death of Bruno, but with a humorous parallel that indicates the
degree to which Guy is free of Bruno and the threat to Guy's world

and his sense of self that Bruno represented. A minister on the same train as Guy and Anne (the woman Guy loves and intends to marry) inadvertently repeats Bruno's opening question, "Aren't you Guy Haines?"; Guy and Anne look at each other and exit the car, leaving behind the bemused minister. The repetition of Bruno's comments by this clearly harmless "stranger" underlines Guy's return to a world of order and normalcy.[3]

Earlier in the film, the use of other minor "strangers" on trains also de-emphasizes the idea that the link between Guy and Bruno is predestined, necessitated by something within Guy himself rather than by random chance. Just as the minister's question is a harmless repetition of Bruno's, so another passenger has earlier nudged the foot of another man accidentally, just as Guy had nudged Bruno's. And Guy's supposed acquiescence to Bruno's murder plot—"Now, you think my theory's okay, Guy? You like it?" "Sure, Bruno, sure. They're all okay"—is humorously repeated, on the same night that Bruno kills Miriam, when Guy casually assures the drunken Professor Collins, in response to a confused question about differential calculus, "Yes, I understand."

The clear separation between Guy and Bruno during the later part of the film is responsible for an element of moral ambiguity in the film as a whole: Guy's pleasant future of marriage to Anne and a political career has been provided for him courtesy of Bruno, who has removed Miriam, the only obstacle to Guy's happiness. Guy's ability both to separate himself from that murderous desire and to profit from its results has been described variously: Spoto calls it "one of Hitchcock's darkest ironies" (218), whereas Wood notes that "the effect seems at times two-dimensional, or like watching the working out of a theorem rather than a human drama" (181).

In contrast to the portrayal in Hitchcock's film, Highsmith's novel makes the link between Guy and Bruno a major component of the book's overall direction. Highsmith's use of both Guy's and Bruno's narrative points of view acts structurally as Hitchcock's crosscutting does in his adaptation: forcing us to picture the two men as inextricably linked doubles, rather than as separate individuals. But whereas in the Hitchcock film this visual fusing runs counter to the development of the plot itself, in Highsmith's novel the personalities of the characters, the stylistic techniques, and the structure of the plot all emphasize the doubling.

The fusing of the two main characters in Highsmith's novel begins, as does Hitchcock's visual linking, with the train journey. The encounter between Highsmith's Guy and Bruno is accidental only in the most superficial way; though the encounter is not planned, the sense of shared identity arises immediately and is reinforced by Guy's denial of its existence: "All he despised, Guy thought, Bruno represented. All the things he would not want to be, Bruno was, or would become" (30). Despite these protests, Highsmith's Guy is quickly drawn to something in his companion, unlike Hitchcock's Guy, who is presented as alternately amused, annoyed, or irritated by Bruno and his notions. When Bruno propounds his theory that "a person ought to do everything it's possible to do before he dies, and maybe die trying to do something that's really impossible," Guy's reaction reveals a likeness to Bruno: "Something in Guy responded with a leap, then cautiously drew back. He asked softly, 'Like what?'" (19).

Highsmith continues to stress the psychological links between the two men through her portrayal of Guy's passive vulnerability when he is confronted with Bruno's aggressive curiosity. Hitchcock's adaptation de-emphasizes this sense of passivity, instead presenting Guy as a successful professional tennis player—a career choice which helps emphasize his physical presence and suggests that he is a man of action. In the film, Miriam's threat to Guy is minimal, existing only because it is impossible for Guy to refute her false charge that the child she is carrying is his and she an abandoned wife. This strong, active, tennis-playing Guy effectively resists Bruno's murder scheme by attempting instead to warn the intended murder victim. In contrast, Highsmith's Guy is not a tennis player but a successful architect with a tendency to live in his mind, to see the world in ideals and abstractions while refusing to recognize or fully acknowledge his own suppressed emotions and needs.[4] Until he meets Bruno, his companion on the train is a volume of Plato, an old high school text that he accidentally leaves in Bruno's compartment and that later becomes a clue to be used against him. He has brought the book as "an indulgence to compensate him, perhaps, for having to make the trip to Miriam" (9). But while the words he reads make sense to him, an inner voice questions, "But what good will Plato do you with Miriam" (9).

Guy's inability to face his tangled feelings about Miriam makes him an easy prey for Bruno, with his cool, unshockable curiosity. Finding in Bruno the stranger to whom he can admit Miriam's unfaithfulness, Guy realizes that "he had never told anyone so much about Miriam" (22). Bruno evokes in Guy the feelings he has tried both to conceal and ignore; when Bruno asks how many lovers Miriam had, Guy, in answering, finds himself caught in a surge of emotion: "'Quite a few. Before I found out.' And just as he assured himself it made no difference at all now to admit it, a sensation as of a tiny whirlpool inside him began to confuse him. Tiny, but realer than the memories somehow, because he had uttered it" (25).

Despite, or perhaps because of, this whirlpool of emotion, Highsmith's Guy remains vulnerable and passive, enabling Miriam to control him through his inability to confront difficult situations. He is willing to give up the chance to bring into actuality the Palmyra, a building he has designed, rather than face the emotional chaos and failure of his relationship with her. Miriam recognizes Guy's weakness and taunts him about his decision to give up the Palmyra to keep her from coming with him: "Running away? . . . Cheapest way out" (37). Guy later tells Anne that, because of Miriam, he had decided the Palmyra simply wasn't part of his "destiny" (51).

While Hitchcock's stronger, more active Guy Haines successfully resists Bruno's attempts to draw him into crime, Highsmith's confused, passive architect fails to resist Bruno because Bruno represents a part of Guy himself. In fact, in the novel the interaction between Guy and Bruno immediately takes on an overtone of mutual sexual attraction downplayed in the film's presentation of their first encounter. In the film, Bruno has no sooner met Guy than he launches into innuendoes about Guy's publicly known relationship with Anne, a senator's daughter, and his desire to get a divorce so that he and Anne can marry. In the novel, Bruno's conversation focuses on Miriam, the hated and destructive other. He knows nothing about Anne, and later feels cheated when he learns about Guy's relationship with her. However, the novel's Anne is significant in her absence, since Guy is thinking about Anne when he initiates the meeting with Bruno: "Suddenly he [Guy] felt helpless without her. He shifted his position, accidentally touched the outstretched foot of the young man asleep, and watched fascinatedly as the lashes twitched and came open" (9-10). Thus begins the complex triangle as Guy's allegiance shifts between her and Bruno.

Later in the novel, Guy's relationship with Anne and Bruno becomes an almost mystical *ménage à trois*. During his wedding, Guy discovers Bruno in the church: "He [Guy] was standing beside Anne, and Bruno was here with them, not an event, not a moment, but a condition, something that had always been and always would be. Bruno, himself, Anne. And the moving on the tracks. And the lifetime of moving on the tracks until death do us part . . ." (175). Soon, however, three becomes a crowd. Guy and Anne's home is invaded by an uninvited Bruno, who is as immediately comfortable as if he were one of the inhabitants. Before long, Bruno comes to view Anne as the invasive presence and begins to think and act destructively toward her. Anne's prized sailboat is damaged on a surreptitious sail that Guy and Bruno take together; and Bruno finally considers eliminating Anne as the only obstacle left between himself and Guy: *"Anne is like light to me,* Bruno remembered Guy once saying. If he could strangle Anne, too, then Guy and he could really be together" (228).

Guy's suspension between Anne and Bruno represents the struggle between the creative and destructive elements within himself, a struggle which Hitchcock's secure playboy is never forced to endure. For Guy, his architectural designs represent in concrete form the grace, beauty, and order that he discovers in the act of creation; as Kathleen Klein describes it, "His work is, for him, a spiritual act, defined by unity and wholeness; it rejects disorder, fragmentation and shallowness" (176). His ultimate dream as an architect has always been to build that visible symbol of unity and balance, a bridge—he imagines designing "a white bridge with a span like an angel's wing" (192). Guy's vision of Anne as an ideal— the light opposed to the darkness represented by Bruno—links her directly with the creations of his mind; and at Guy's wedding, Bob Treacher, who later offers Guy a chance to realize his dream, notes that Anne is "as beautiful as a white bridge" (174).

Similarly, Guy recognizes a starker, destructive side of himself mirrored in Bruno. As Guy journeys to Great Neck to kill Bruno's father, he defines the relationship between them quite differently than at their first meeting: "He was like Bruno. Hadn't he sensed it time and time again, and like a coward never admitted it? Hadn't he known Bruno was like himself? Or why had he liked Bruno? He loved Bruno" (134). After the murder, that sense of shared identity tightens; as Guy considers how good and evil, hate and love exist simultaneously in the human heart, he thinks, "Bruno, he and Bruno. Each was what the other had not chosen to be, the cast-off self, what he thought he hated but perhaps in reality loved" (163). This insight is confirmed by a dream later that night, in which Guy imagines himself waking to find Bruno springing into his room. To Guy's question, "Who are you?" Bruno finally answers, "You" (164).

While he and Bruno are on the train early in the novel, Guy sees how the intelligence and clarity of his creative professional life run counter to the confused emotion and blindness of his personal life; once he has murdered, Guy understands a starker contrast:

> He felt rather like two people, one of whom could create and feel in harmony with God when he created, and the other who could murder. "Any kind of person can murder," Bruno had said on the train. The man who had explained the cantilever principle to Bobbie Cartwright two years ago in Metcalf? No, nor the man who had designed the hospital, or even the department store, or debated half an hour with himself over the colour he would paint a metal chair on the back lawn last week, but the man who had glanced into the mirror just last night and had seen for one instant the murderer, like a secret brother. (185)

Guy is at peace in his work on the Palmyra project because of his belief that it will reach perfection: "And the more he immersed himself in the new effort, the more he felt recreated also in a different and more perfect form" (90). The house that Guy designs for himself and Anne is likewise beautiful in both design and final form. But the idea of that house, like the finished and inhabited house itself, becomes infected and changed by becoming linked with the thought of Bruno. On the night Guy learns that Miriam is dead, he has been visualizing the house he will build, seeing it in his hotel room as "shining white and sharp against the brown bureau across the room" (78). After the phone call reporting Miriam's murder, he looks again at the bureau: "Now, where he had seen the vision of the white house, a laughing face appeared, first the crescent mouth, then the face—Bruno's face" (81).

Symbolically, the design of the house, planned by Guy before his encounter with Bruno on the train, reflects Guy's position as the focal point of a triangle. The house is conceived of as "Y"-shaped; and while Guy has considered dispensing with one of the arms of the "Y" in the interests of economizing, "the idea sang in Guy's head only with both arms" (78). The house is designed to project from a white rock, and to look "as if alchemy had created it from the rock itself, like a crystal" (78); Guy, in fact, considers naming the house "The Crystal." As Guy imagines the house, it is a work of proportion and balance, in harmony with both itself and the environment from which it has sprung.

The idea of the house as a crystal echoes and contrasts with Guy's earlier mental description of himself when he thinks about ways in which he has sabotaged himself and chosen to fail: "There was inside him, like a flaw in a jewel, not visible on the surface, a fear and anticipation of failure that he had never been able to mend" (37). The jewel image is repeated when Guy drops overboard the gun he has used to kill Bruno's father. Bruno has sent Guy a Luger for the murder; Guy rejects the gun for its ugliness and ungainliness, and uses instead a gun he had bought as a teenager, an object purchased solely for its cleanness of design and aesthetic appeal. Guy's use of his own gun indicates the degree to which he is fusing what he considers the best of himself, his sense of beauty and design, with this act of destruction; it also emphasizes that he is acting of his own volition, rather than being compelled by Bruno. After the murder, despite the fact that the gun is the one concrete piece of evidence linking him to a crime, Guy is reluctant to eliminate its loveliness: "How intelligent a jewel, he thought, and how innocent it looked now. Himself—" (200). Highsmith's Guy, unlike his creations or the beautifully designed gun, is "flawed," and he is unable to achieve within himself the harmony and balance he values. This inability renders him vulnerable to Bruno's suggestions and makes him utterly unlike the Guy Haines created in Hitchcock's film.

In the opening minutes of the Hitchcock adaptation, the shot of railway tracks coming together, and then diverging, sets the tone for the film: Guy's and Bruno's lives will converge, and then separate. In Highsmith's novel, however, the image of train tracks is used throughout to emphasize Guy's sense of imposed direction, a cessation of choices: "the lifetime of moving on the tracks" (175).

In the film, the encounter with a stranger asking "Aren't you Guy Haines?" can be answered differently (and in a sense replayed) and so escaped. But for Highsmith's Guy, a meeting with another "stranger," Miriam's lover Owen, to whom he goes to confess his guilt, brings a fear of being further swept into a cycle rather than a sense of escaping one; as he describes the murder scheme and hears himself voicing Bruno's ideas, he has "a horrible, an utterly horrible thought all at once, that he might ensnare Owen in the same trap that Bruno had used for him, that Owen in turn would capture another stranger who would capture another, and so on in infinite progression of the trapped and the hunted" (246). Guy can be renewed and escape from the cycle only by capture, confession, and punishment. True to his nature, the novel's Guy achieves a new ending for his script by passivity and acceptance rather than by action. He attempts to purge himself by going to Owen, telling him of the two murders, and waiting for him to make the appropriate decision. When Owen refuses to act—and indeed shows little interest in the whole situation—Guy is rescued from his passivity by the actions of the detective Gerard, who has listened to the confession by means of a telephone connection.

Despite the status of the Hitchcock film as an adaptation of Highsmith's novel, the differences in focus and plot ultimately make the two very different and individual works of art. And in spite of the drastic shift in overall effect caused by Hitchcock's plot changes, Highsmith considers *Strangers on a Train* one of the best of the films made from her novels (*Plotting* 106). Perhaps the key to her ability to accept Hitchcock's vision of her novel as well as her own can be found in a comment Highsmith made on the artistic process:

> Every human being is different from the next, as handwriting and fingerprints prove. Every painter or writer or composer has consequently something different to say from the next (or should have). A Rembrandt or a Van Gogh is identifiable from a distance and at once. I believe in individuality, in being oneself, in using the maximum of one's talent. . . . That is what the public finally loves— something special and individual. (*Plotting* xiv)

NOTES

[1]Raymond Durgnat's discussion of the film lists other doubles of various types and purposes (217-31).

[2]The nightmarishly vivid scenes of the out-of-control carousel have been interpreted in a variety of ways. Wood describes Guy as having to "reenter the chaos-world in order to retrieve it [the lighter], thereby risking final submersion" (180). Sabrina Barton analyzes the scene in terms of its image of intercourse and "the fusing of images of 'disordering' homosexuality with disordered cinematic representation" (92).

[3]Darker interpretations of this final scene are also possible. Donald Spoto, for example, sees the movement away from the minister as an indication of a problematic outcome for Guy and Anne's planned marriage (216, 218). And Bill Desowitz has pointed out that copies of the film currently shown on television may omit this final scene altogether, using a version Hitchcock designed for release in the United Kingdom, in which the minister scene was removed as potentially offensive (4-5).

[4]In fact, the tennis racquets and other sports equipment that show up during Guy and Bruno's meeting on the train all belong to Bruno, who travels with them to please his mother—and because they're "good to hock" (12).

WORKS CITED

Barton, Sabrina. "'Crisscross': Paranoia and Projection in *Strangers on a Train.*" *camera obscura* Jan.-May 1991: 75-100.

Brill, Lesley. *The Hitchcock Romance: Love and Irony in Hitchcock's Films*. Princeton: Princeton UP, 1988.

Desowitz, Bill. "Life With Video: Strangers on Which Train?" *Film Comment* May-June 1992: 4-5.

Durgnat, Raymond. *The Strange Case of Alfred Hitchcock, Or The Plain Man's Hitchcock*. Cambridge, MA: MIT, 1974.

Highsmith, Patricia. *Plotting and Writing Suspense Fiction*. New York: St. Martin's, 1983.

____. *Strangers on a Train*. Baltimore: Penguin, 1950.

Hitchcock, Alfred, dir. *Strangers on a Train*. Warner Brothers, 1951.

Klein, Kathleen Gregory. "Patricia Highsmith." *And Then There Were Nine . . . More Women of Mystery*. Ed. Jane S. Bakerman. Bowling Green, OH: Bowling Green State University Popular Press, 1985: 170-97.

Spoto, Donald. *The Art of Alfred Hitchcock*. New York: Hopkinson & Blake, 1976.

Taylor, John Russell. *Hitch: The Life and Work of Alfred Hitchcock*. London: Faber & Faber, 1978.

Truffaut, Francois. *Hitchcock*. Rev. ed. New York: Simon & Schuster, 1983.

Wood, Robin. "*Strangers on a Train*." *A Hitchcock Reader*. Ed. Marshall Deutelbaum and Leland Poague. Ames, IA: Iowa State UP, 1986: 170-81.

The Perils of Adaptation:
John D. MacDonald's Travis McGee Novels on Film

Lewis D. Moore

Robert Clouse's film Darker than Amber *furnishes a seemingly plausible version of John D. Macdonald's novel of the same name but removes the book's moral force without replacing it with a believable alternative. Andrew V. McLaglen's television film version of* The Empty Copper Sea *faithfully follows the novel's plot but fails to provide the sense of danger and excitement needed to drive the action forward.*

Bringing a novel to the screen presents the adapter with difficult choices. First, one can merge or fuse the film's vision with the novel's sense of direction, making any necessary changes but keeping the novel intact in the process. If this is done, the basic plot conflict and character roles remain the same while the setting faithfully reflects the novelist's descriptions and sense of atmosphere. As director and screenwriter Edward Dmytryk observes, "In adaptations, it is mandatory to clearly define the *theme*, the *characters*, and the *action* to be retained, and to determine what can be eliminated without damage to these three elements of the over-all story or of any particular part of it" (48-49). For William Miller, it is important that "the adaptation retain the key elements from the original and catch its flavor—the 'personality' or feeling-tone of the original" (210). And in a letter to Dan Rowan after reading the script for *Darker than Amber*, John D. MacDonald states that for new Travis McGee projects, "I will do . . . a simplified treatment which will retain character, retain the essence of the plot and the good visuals, but delete the things that I can get away with in a book which, by reason of their complexity, will just not come off on the screen" (*A Friendship* 61).

If skillfully done, the adaptation can employ some of the novel's dialogue, and if a character serves as a narrator, he or she can sometimes do much the same in a film, thus preserving the tone of the original work. In contrast, an adapter can start with a novel and change it to reflect a new vision of the original's dynamics. At

115

one extreme, little but the title remains, and sometimes not even that. New characters, new plot elements, new settings fill the shell and create a work that rarely engages the novel. Finally, a more ambiguous revision occurs when major plot and character shifts embed themselves in the general plot structure while the setting and many of the relationships stay essentially the same.

The films based on MacDonald's Travis McGee series demonstrate two of these possibilities. The first method generally applies in Andrew V. McLaglen's television film version of *The Empty Copper Sea* (*Travis McGee: The Empty Copper Sea* [1983; novel, 1978]). The third describes Robert Clouse's *Darker than Amber* (1970; novel, 1966), which furnishes a seemingly plausible version of MacDonald's work of the same name, but robs the novel of its moral force without replacing it with a believable alternative. In contrast to the problematic changes in *Amber*, the adaptation of *Copper* reveals the pitfalls of producing a film faithful to a novel's events but not asserting a dominant vision that brings the film to life. Thus, neither McGee film creates a visual and dramatic equivalence of the novels, a disappointing outcome given MacDonald's impressive body of mystery/detective fiction.

The place to start in analyzing the adaptation of *Darker than Amber* is to discover through a scene-by-scene analysis of both the novel and the film what has been added or changed and what remains the same. For present purposes, I will define a new scene as any major shift of setting that reflects more than a few characters going from one location to another. In these terms, the novel has 57 scenes and the film 61. However, many scenes in the novel do not appear in the film, and the latter alters certain important actions in the novel and adds several new ones. In general, screenwriter Ed Waters, who also wrote the screenplay for *Man Trap* (1961), based on MacDonald's *Soft Touch* (1958) (Shine 143), follows the novel's plot and incorporates some of MacDonald's dialogue. Although McGee's ruminations at times shift the pace of the novel's action, slowing it while adding depth to his character, MacDonald has a strong sense of visual imagery and a gift for dialogue honed in his many works of fiction. The novel's use of the first person allows the reader to enter McGee's life in ways that admittedly are difficult to duplicate on the screen. But while the film does not attempt to duplicate the first-person point of view, it suffers little from the change; McGee's remains the most important perspective if not the only one.

Most of the film's 61 scenes figure McGee prominently, but at least four scenes or groups of scenes focus wholly or in part on Terry

Bartell (Ans Terry in the novel) played by William Smith. Smith is a convincing villain whom Howard Thompson describes as "a truly horrendous giant of a psycho" and about whom MacDonald himself remarks, "The gem part of the picture is a performance by a young heavy name of Bill Smith. He can really scare you. He is like an elemental force" (*A Friendship* 144). Although Bartell's personality is the same as Terry's, he remains the chief antagonist after the death of Griff (Robert Phillips). There is a directness about this, but Bartell's character must carry more than the novel has indicated. And by focusing so much on Bartell, the film flattens out the forces with which McGee and Meyer (Rod Taylor and Theodore Bikel) struggle, thereby simplifying the moral issues the two must face.

In the four episodes when Bartell does not interact with McGee, Waters and Clouse change him from the novel's weakly corrupt, muscle-bound goon into a controlling, manipulative figure who never loses his taste for violence. The film's first and third scenes which feature Terry Bartell show Griff, Terry, and Vangie (Suzy Kendall) at night in a convertible parked short of a bridge south of Miami. Terry sits in the back with Vangie while Griff drives. They are waiting for a break in the traffic to throw the weighted Vangie off the isolated bridge. Terry is a remorseless figure who enjoys his work. Second, Terry interrogates and beats to death for little apparent reason Burk (James Booth) who operates Burk's Landing where McGee and Meyer rent their fishing boat the night of Vangie's attempted murder. Third, Terry, who previously has identified McGee, tracks him to his cabin on the cruise ship *Sunward* (*Monica D.* in the novel) and—having already killed Del Whitney (Ahna Capri), his lover, who has abandoned him after McGee reveals Terry's part in her friend Vangie's death—fights with McGee. Finally, Merrimay Malloy (also played by Suzy Kendall and named Merrimay Lane in the novel), posing as Vangie, induces a violent reaction in Terry, preceded by flashbacks of his having thrown Vangie from the bridge and later to her death in front of a car. The latter scene shifts Bartell closer to the Terry of the novel, moving him from the controlling, calculating figure to a more susceptible one whose senses were earlier propelled on the road to derangement by finding in his stateroom's tub and wrapped in vines the leg weights previously attached to Vangie.

The roles of two other characters in the film, Del Whitney and Noreen Walker (Janet MacLachlan), change largely for the same purpose which motivated the transformation of Ans Terry into Terry

Bartell: to simplify and make more direct their parts in the plot. In both cases, these changes reveal one paradox of adapting a novel to film since their impact is both intensified and flattened. In the novel, Del is little more than a name before McGee confronts her in Nassau with Vangie's death and convinces her that the murder ring plans the same for her. After this revelation, McGee uses deception to trap Del, Ans Terry, and ultimately the murder ring. This reasonably nonviolent solution matches McGee's usual desire to use indirect means to accomplish his ends; as Walter and Jean Shine note, he "depend[s] a bit more on his wits than on his physical prowess and reflexes to keep him out of the hospital or morgue" (148). Convincing Del that the best way to ensure that the police believe she committed suicide is to write a confession detailing what she knows about the ring's activities is an example of this method. After Terry's capture at the dock, McGee has Merrimay anonymously report Del to the police who have previously received her confession.

Apparently not wishing to lose this flavor of deception, the film begins McGee's actions in Nassau in a similar way. He contacts Del in a store, takes her for a drink, and convinces her that she will be killed as Vangie was. Del agrees to abandon Terry, but little else remains of the novel's complex deception besides having Merrimay pose as Vangie on the Miami dock and leaving the weights (in the novel, a doll resembling Vangie) under water in Terry's stateroom on the *Sunward*. The decision to remove Del thus focuses largely on her murder and the violent fight between McGee and Terry and sharply limits and removes the nuances of McGee's personality.[1]

In the novel, Noreen Walker provides information about Vangie and, inadvertently, about where she hides her money, along with comments on race relations in the United States. Occasional social commentary is both the joy and bane of readers of the Travis McGee series, but MacDonald generally integrates it into his plots in such a way that it develops the action and the characters, giving both additional depth. While the novel convincingly depicts Noreen as a maid during the day and a college-educated CORE activist at night (90), the film does only a little of this but adds a stereotypical racial confrontation between McGee, Walker, and a white man in a local cafe. This scene has two limitations. First, it minimizes Noreen's ability to control her environment as she does in the novel. There, she speaks with McGee privately at a friend's house, not letting his problems interact with her civil rights work (90). Second, it again portrays McGee as someone who either initiates or cannot avoid violent confrontations. While MacDonald's descriptions of violent scenes in the series are memorable, McGee seldom "stumbles" into them as he does in the cafe scene.

It is arguable that both Travis McGee as a character and the series of novels featuring him motivated those who created the film. *Darker than Amber* is the seventh novel featuring McGee. As in many series of novels, characters change and develop, building up a complex fictive life. Presumably this character "history" played an important role in attracting Clouse's and Waters' attention. McGee's lifestyle, his work and its peculiar rules, his character and life history, his friends—all of these are part of him and define him in the series. The film's makers could have ordered an original screenplay on any subject and shot that, but they did not; something about the character and his attributes generated their interest. Such interest would seem to preclude any drastic change of an important element of the fictive history which would weaken the connection between film and source. However, such a change— one that violates the essential nature of a character in the novel— does appear, with no discernible motivation, in the film. This change is McGee's deep emotional response to Vangie, one that blurs any moral stand he takes in the story. Possibly this kind of thing is what inspired MacDonald's characterization of the script as "cheap, ordinary, vulgar and impossible," a "perversion of my book" and replete with "illogic and trite characterization" (*A Friendship* 61).

In the novel, McGee's reactions to and evaluations of Vangie are varied, but do not approach love. He admires her "toughness of spirit" (40) when she does not cry as Terry throws her from the bridge (33, 40) or later when he and Meyer remove a fishing hook from her thigh (16-17, 40). In addition, he credits her with "remarkable buoyancy" (40) that allows her to shake off her near death. McGee also admires Vangie's physicality, her well-kept body— especially her legs—as they take out the hook without anesthetic, giving her only brandy. However, McGee also has another, more cautious sense of Vangie's physicality. When Meyer asks, "[W]hat's your reaction to her?" McGee responds, "Wariness, I guess. Like they say about stalking a panther, you're never sure of who's after who" (24). Later, after McGee hesitates over whether or not to help Vangie recover the money in her apartment, particularly if it belongs to somebody else, he witnesses Vangie explode: "'Somebody else!' She pulled the dark glasses off and looked directly into my eyes. That dark amber was as merciless as the eyes of the big predator

120 It's a Print!

cats, and as empty, and as hungry" (53). This view presents her as an amoral force, lacking a human conscience, which would devour him if hungry. As McGee earlier described her to Meyer, "She's a hard one" with "gambler's nerves" (24).

Vangie elicits some sympathy from McGee when she tells him and Meyer about her past: institution for delinquent children at 10, loss of mother at 12, affair with resident director of the same institution at 13, and prostitute for vice ring at 14 (38-39). Nonetheless, McGee has no false optimism regarding Vangie, "Her twelve years on the track had coarsened her beyond any hope of salvage" (40). Although he does not see her as a "total waste" (413) as Carol Cleveland does, he has a feeling of moral revulsion, mingled with other emotions, toward her: "I realized I felt proud of her. This reaction was so irrational it startled me. . . . It was the inevitable sense of ownership" (40). His involvement is in the life of someone whose "dark eyes were like twin entrances to two deep caves. Nothing lived in those caves" (17). He also refers to an "utter emptiness behind those dark eyes" (20) and to Vangie as a "dead-eyed cookie" (27). These observations and references to her as a "whore" (40), "hooker" (41), "bitch" (59), and "slut" (66); his sense that "I'd felt no slightest itch of desire for her" (50) and that once a woman "reaches her own number" (50) of too many sexual encounters, "she suffers a sea change" (51); and, among other negative images, McGee's description of her mouth as "a windy cave from whence, with each moisturous gasping, comes a tiny stink of death" (51)—these lead to his complex feeling that "I could not want her on any terms. But I could like her. And wish her well" (51). Meyer, who suggests to McGee that "You like women as people" (60) and who acknowledges Vangie's sense of "revulsion" toward her "murder for profit" activities (59), likewise knows that Vangie "is case-hardened beyond redemption" (60). Ultimately, McGee, who might avenge her death because her feelings of revulsion "partially redeemed" her (Geherin 81), remembers "the girl-hands on my wrist" (67) as he dived to a depth of 20 feet and released her from the cement block wired to her ankles and feels "annoyed" (67) that someone has killed what he struggled to save.

Given this extensive and complex relationship, what transpires between Vangie and McGee in the film significantly alters McGee's motivation for breaking the murder ring. After McGee rescues Vangie, Meyer revives her; the two men bring her back to the *Flush* where they remove the fishing hook from her thigh. Vangie then settles into a companionable few days with both men and quickly develops a sexual relationship of some emotional intensity with McGee. Before this occurs, however, three incidents foreshadow their move from rescued and rescuer to lovers. First, even before Vangie wakes up the morning after her experience, Meyer speculates on McGee's apparent inclination to become involved in her troubles. McGee's reply about someone's using an "eighty-five pound weight for a 110 pound girl" sets the tone for his subsequent decision to take the side of the attractive and threatened woman. Second, during a conversation between McGee and Vangie on the *Flush*'s bridge after she asks him, "What's your way to go McGee?" and after she reveals her name, McGee explains his salvage business and ultimately his code that sex is nothing without emotion. Third, Meyer remarks later to McGee, with no negative overtones, that Vangie has gotten to him.

This extraordinary switch from novel to film occurs because the film obscures Vangie's real past. Before Meyer's statement that she has gotten to him, Vangie has a flashback to the only murder, apparently, with which she involved herself. But Vangie conveys this neither to McGee nor Meyer, and after she approaches the sleeping McGee in the night in order to make love and he responds as if attacked, she speaks ambiguously about her past and suggests that it would have been better if they had not been under the bridge to rescue her. Later that same night, McGee goes to her stateroom and they make love. Of course, this storyline erases the complex relationship McGee has with Vangie in the novel and renders him morally neutral with regard to her. Vangie reveals little, McGee and Meyer ask less, and both men seem the victims of a pretty face and body.

In the film, the motivation for McGee's pursuit of the murder ring after Vangie's death is as shallow as his reaction to her while alive. After McGee discovers where Vangie lives, he speaks to her maid, Noreen Walker, an educated black woman with another, though unnamed, job. At one point Noreen states that Vangie was a hustler. McGee's briefest of nods speaks volumes about the moral vacuity with which Clouse and Waters have endowed his character. When Del later says on the *Sunward* that Vangie went on only one trip, McGee has no reaction to this. Did he know and not care that the trip involved the murder of an innocent man, or not know and not ask when questions about her predicament were in order? The film is silent. At the end of the film, McGee tells Merrimay that it will take time to get over Vangie and that he is not ready for another relationship, quite in contrast to his happy response in the novel to her call for a "CARE package" (189) when her acting tryout falls through and she seeks comfort from him. To seal the mawkish, almost infantile, and surely fatuous change, a song to Vangie accompanies the final credits.

The contrast to McGee's far more realistic motivation in the novel is stark. In addition to many surmises by McGee and Meyer, hints by Vangie, and outright statements by her and McGee about her murderous past (*Amber* 42, 49, 50, 53, 54), Meyer's two-page summary of her remarks (54-56) leaves little doubt that treachery and murder were part of her recent life even if she had begun to feel guilty about her activities (59). After Meyer's statement regarding the moral responsibility he and McGee share because of their knowledge of the murder ring, McGee decides to think about breaking it up (58). In addition, McGee believes they might be able to help Vangie with the law if she returns for their aid. Failing that, he decides, they will make an attempt to "bust the operation wide open and let the law pick up the stragglers. . . . And if we come out of it with a little meat, we share" (61). In addition to making a final reference to $32,000 as a motivation (67), McGee feels a sense of resentment (66) and annoyance (67) after he recognizes her body at the City memorial morgue in Broward Beach (64).

In marked contrast, McLaglen's faithful if somewhat dull television film of MacDonald's *The Empty Copper Sea*—described by Tom Shales as "drowsily static and talky" and by Lissa August as a "humdrum murder mystery" (9)—surprises with its failure to generate more tension than it does. The problem could, of course, be MacDonald's novel, not one of the most gripping in the series. As David Geherin remarks, "*Copper* is weakened by its awkward denouement and its relative paucity of action. Because there is so little for McGee to do, he spends an inordinate amount of time questioning local townspeople, most of whom repeat the same information" (142).[2] MacDonald confronts McGee and Meyer with a single question: What has happened to Hubbard Lawless, Kristin Petersen, and the missing money? Their search for an answer leads to an explanation rather than a confrontation with Lawless, and the novel thus spends more time telling than showing. Aside from McGee's fights with Nicky Noyes, a former Lawless employee and present drug dealer, and the confrontation with Tuckerman on the beach at the end as the latter digs out the jeep containing Lawless's and Petersen's bodies, the novel supplies little tension for Stirling Silliphant and McLaglen to adapt to the film.

Teleplay writer Silliphant follows MacDonald's plot structure, and he and McLaglen use the California, rather than Florida, scene effectively, if not spectacularly. However, they do not infuse the film with a sense of danger and excitement to drive the action forward. With *The Slender Thread* (1965), *In the Heat of the Night* (1967), *The Towering Inferno* (1974), and *The Enforcer* (with Dean Reisner, 1976) (Clark 294), Silliphant has demonstrated his ability to write tense mystery/suspense screenplays. Yet, even though Richard Meyers believes that "only the script could have been termed anything approaching satisfactory," he also observes that it "was rudimentary and unnatural" (428).

A novelist could hardly wish for a teleplay that follows his work more closely than Silliphant's does MacDonald's. While a scene-by-scene analysis of the novel and the film reveals 66 scenes in the former and 40 in the latter, Silliphant generally retains the novel's order and adds relatively little new material. Two minor characters, Felicia Ambar and DeeGee Walloway, appear in the novel but not in the film. Felicia is one of the two young women who accompanied Lawless and John Tuckerman on the *Julie* the night Captain Van Harder supposedly got drunk, Tuckerman "accidentally" ran the boat onto a sandbar, and Lawless fell overboard and possibly drowned, all of which led to Harder's losing his license. Walloway was the former mate on the *Julie* and knows Harder. McGee questions him in the novel about Harder's protestations that he had only one drink and does not know why he became unconscious. Walloway says, "I think they decided there was no way they could buy Van off. He's straight. So they give him a mickey" (151). In the film, Silliphant uses Mishy Burns, the other young woman on that night's cruise, to supply information about what she and Felicia saw. Tuckerman admits both in the film and in the novel that Lawless drugged Harder (123).

A number of other changes do surprise the viewer who knows the McGee series well. Some are minor: The scene switches from Florida to California, a state that MacDonald uses only for parts of three other McGee novels (*The Quick Red Fox* [1964], *A Deadly Shade of Gold* [1965], and *The Green Ripper* [1979]) and one novel in which important actions occur without McGee's presence (*Free Fall in Crimson* [1981]); McGee's boat changes from motor to sail; and actor Sam Elliott is shorter than McGee's 6'4".[3]

More fundamentally, Elliott does not adequately project the potential for violence that MacDonald gives McGee. While MacDonald's McGee is generally more reactive than aggressive, he carries with him the aura of past conflicts. But even though the film depends on him, Elliott does not create enough suspense to make up for what the plot lacks and deserves John J. O'Connor's comment that he portrays McGee "in a style so laid back as to be almost comatose."[4] A clue to the sense of lethargy which leads Alvin H. Marrill to call McGee "John D. MacDonald's world-weary private eye" (427) might lie in McGee's confession both in the novel and in the film that he has not felt any clear purpose in his life lately, that he has experienced a sense of drifting, "[a] bleakness" (254). In fact, in the film, McGee communicates this loss of direction to Meyer from the very beginning; but even so, nothing adequately replaces it.

An additional weakness in the novel comes from the character of Van Harder, the man who hires McGee to recover his reputation for $10,000, half of the value that he puts on it (11). However, McGee has little contact with Harder after the beginning of the novel and shows only a small degree of personal interest in him. McGee thus searches for an idea and not a person or thing. MacDonald demonstrates in *The Deep Blue Good-by* (1964), the first novel in the series, that looking for something, in this case the gems brought back from World War II by Sgt. Dave Berry and stolen by Junior Allen, adds an edge to the action. Of course, looking for something frequently means looking for someone, and Allen's violent character gives *Blue* a strong flavor of excitement. But the only character in *Copper* similar to Allen is the much weaker figure of Noyes, a minor character not involved in Lawless's disappearance, who dies relatively early in the book and film.

Pursuit, another staple of mystery and suspense fiction, works well in many McGee novels. Combined with the first person narrative, the hunt for an absent antagonist is a device that often leads to a satisfying climax as the reader experiences the difficulties and dangers the narrator undergoes to find and confront his prey. Cody T.W. Pittler in *Cinnamon Skin* (1982) clearly establishes this possibility. Pittler appears indirectly at the beginning and directly at the end, and the hoped for clash with him builds the tension that culminates in his death in the Mexican jungle. The contrast with *Copper* is marked. The northwestern Florida town of Timber Bay is sorely hit by Lawless's business failures. Before that, he added an element of hope and possibility to the whole town, and his disappearance leaves many deflated, especially his good friend Tuckerman. However, the search for Lawless leaves only the tale of his death and his and Petersen's macabre burial on the Gulf shore near Tuckerman's home. Earlier, Julia Lawless's statements that

Hubbard is dead (90, 219 and film) override the contrary positions that the emotionally disturbed Tuckerman and Noyes maintain (41, 124, 135, and film). Since the film uses the same plot as the novel, it also winds down before McGee's brief but anti-climactic fight with Tuckerman at the end.

The Empty Copper Sea provided Silliphant and McLaglen difficult structural problems. If they followed MacDonald's plot, they trapped themselves in a story with insufficient conflict. However, to create conflict they would have had to make major changes. One possibility would have been to make Lawless the character with whom McGee and Meyer struggle. Of course, making this and other changes would have required a major rethinking of the novel, an effort which they apparently were not prepared to undertake for a pilot for a new television series (Parish and Pitts 549). But without this alteration, McGee and Meyer have no worthy antagonist, no one who sufficiently calls forth their abilities to think and act.

In addition, neither MacDonald nor Silliphant injects a sense of evil into their works. The image of the physically powerful and elusive Paul Dissat in A Tan and Sandy Silence (1971) clarifies what is missing from Copper. Dissat is an amoral killer who discovers a pleasure in torturing his victims (190). In Copper, Lawless is dead before the novel and film begin. A loud, ambitious man whom Tom Shales styles "a profligate entrepreneur," he tried to run when he saw his businesses failing but demonstrated no more evil than Noyes who shoots at McGee when he is high on drugs, seeing McGee's questions about Lawless as a symbol of everything that has gone wrong with his own life. Kristin Petersen, Lawless's lover with whom he planned to run away, is ambitious and greedy; but nothing more is hinted about her, and Tuckerman kills her after Lawless's deception and death leave him emotionally unstable (Copper 250 and film). Thus, McGee and Meyer overmatch their few adversaries. Following MacDonald's lead, Silliphant and McLaglen raise expectations of serious conflicts, especially with regard to Lawless, that they do not fulfill.

It might be argued that MacDonald's novel and McLaglen's film are more works of social and psychological realism than detective fiction. Peggy Moran observes that "The Empty Copper Sea seems to me MacDonald's most serious—and, in some ways, most hopeful—study of the male-female relationship" (87). And, Larry Grimes speculates that at the end of Copper McGee will "affirm life by actively participating in it for its own sake" (107). MacDonald's response to Grimes is that McGee will do that and return "to the vocational formula as of old" ("Introduction" 70). This acknowledges his awareness of the formula and his desire "to move my suspense novels as close as I can get to the 'legitimate' novels of manners and morals, despair and failure, love and joy" ("Introduction" 73). However, John G. Cawelti observes that "This is a very delicate matter, for if a character becomes too complexly human he may cast a shattering and disruptive light on the other elements of the formula" (12). If MacDonald overbalances toward the more traditional novel and away from the detective fiction formula, an overbalancing duplicated by McLaglen, this changes the critical perspective and requires that greater emphasis be placed on the themes of recovery and discovery, shifting both the readers' and viewers' assumptions of what it is they experience.

MacDonald was unfortunate in the efforts to film the Travis McGee series. For all the potential, no one has stepped forward who could successfully transform these novels to film. It surely is not an impossible task, but the novels need someone who understands them thoroughly and can then determine ways to bring that understanding to a different medium. Recent television productions of P.D. James's Adam Dalgliesh and Agatha Christie's Jane Marple and Hercule Poirot show the possibilities. However, neither Clouse's *Darker than Amber* nor McLaglen's *Travis McGee: The Empty Copper Sea* achieves the level of quality found in those adaptations and which the Travis McGee series continues to hold for some future adapter.

NOTES

[1]Del Whitney's death, along with McGee's fierce battles with Griff and Terry, is another reason for the *Variety* reviewer's statement that "The very liberal doses of brutality and violence are obvious exploitation devices" (Murf). Commenting more generally on MacDonald's fiction, Peter Wolfe believes that MacDonald's "relish for violence" is part of his "dark side" (427).

[2]Richard Meyers agrees that *The Empty Copper Sea* "was not the best McGee to adapt. It was a middle-era McGee, nestled uncomfortably between the crackling early efforts and the more challenging recent works. The plot is both far-fetched and labored . . . a *bad* combination" (428).

[3]Rod Taylor, described by James Robert Parish and Michael R. Pitts as "stocky" (154), has the same problem in *Darker*.

ˈBok comments that Elliott "played at such a laid-back pace that the pace of the show remained low-key and subdued." While more complimentary about Elliott's performance, Judith Crist's review largely focuses on the same low-level style: "Sam Elliott is just fine as the moody, macho, introspective yachtsman-detective looking into the death of a real-estate developer" (A56).

WORKS CITED

August, Lissa. "Picks & Pans." *People Weekly* 23 May 1983: 9-23.

Bok. "*Travis McGee.*" *Variety Television Reviews*. Ed. Howard H. Prouty. 15 vols. to date. New York: Garland, 1989- . 13: n.p.

Cawelti, John G. *Adventure, Mystery, and Romance: Formula Stories as Art and Popular Culture*. Chicago: U of Chicago P, 1976.

Clark, Randall. "Stirling Silliphant." *American Screenwriters*. Ed. Robert E. Morseberger, Stephen O. Lesser, and Randall Clark. Detroit: Bruccoli Clark-Gale, 1984. 294-99.

Cleveland, Carol. "Travis McGee: The Feminists' Friend." *The Armchair Detective* 16 (1983): 407-13.

Clouse, Robert, dir. *Darker than Amber*. Writ. Ed Waters. Rod Taylor, Suzy Kendall, and Theodore Bikel. National General, 1970.

Crist, Judith. "This Week's Movies." *TV Guide* 14 May 1983: A5, A56.

Dmytryk, Edward. *On Screen Writing*. Boston: Focal-Butterworth, 1985.

Geherin, David. *John D. MacDonald*. New York: Ungar, 1982.

Grimes, Larry E. "The Reluctant Hero: Reflections on Vocation and Heroism in the Travis McGee Novels of John D. MacDonald." *Clues: A Journal of Detection* 1.1 (1980): 103-08.

MacDonald, John D. *Cinnamon Skin: The Twentieth Adventure of Travis McGee*. 1982. New York: Fawcett, 1983.

———. *Darker than Amber*. 1966. New York: Fawcett, 1982.

———. *The Deep Blue Good-by*. 1964. New York: Fawcett, 1982.

———. *The Empty Copper Sea*. New York: Fawcett, 1978.

———. "Introduction and Comment." *Clues: A Journal of Detection* 1.1 (1980): 63-74.

———. *A Tan and Sandy Silence*. New York: Fawcett, 1971.

Marrill, Alvin H. *Movies Made for Television: The Telefeature and the Mini-Series: 1984-1986*. New York: Zoetrope-Baseline, 1987.

McLaglen, Andrew V., dir. *Travis McGee: The Empty Copper Sea*. Writ. Stirling Silliphant. Sam Elliott, Gene Evans, and Katharine Ross. Warner Bros., 1983.

Meyers, Richard. "*TAD* on TV." *The Armchair Detective* 16 (1983): 428-30.

Miller, William. *Screenwriting for Narrative Film and Television*. New York: Communication Arts-Hastings House, 1980.

Moran, Peggy. "McGee's Girls." *Clues: A Journal of Detection* 1.1 (1980): 82-88.

O'Connor, John J. "TV: Three-Part Series on Blacks in the Military." *New York Times* 18 May 1983: C27.

Parish, James Robert, and Michael R. Pitts. *The Great Detective Pictures*. Metuchen, NJ: Scarecrow, 1990.

Rowan, Dan, and John D. MacDonald. *A Friendship: The Letters of Dan Rowan and John D. MacDonald: 1967-1974*. New York: Knopf, 1986.

Shales, Tom. "ABC's Tired 'Travis McGee.'" *Washington Post* 18 May 1983: B13.

Shine, Walter, and Jean Shine, comps. and eds. *A Bibliography of the Published Works of John D. MacDonald with Selected Biographical Materials and Critical Essays*. Gainesville: Patrons of the Libraries, U of Florida, 1980.

Thompson, Howard. "Screen: 'Darker than Amber' Opens." *New York Times* 15 Aug. 1970: 16.

Wolfe, Peter. "The Critics Did It: An Essay Review." *Modern Fiction Studies* 29 (1983): 389-433.

Creation, Adaptation, and Re-Creation: The Lives of Colin Dexter's Characters

Joanne Edmonds

The transformation of Dexter's novels into television films poses special problems. Not only are different screenwriters involved, but in addition to films based on novels, one encounters adaptations of ideas and an original storyline by Dexter plus several films based on his characters. Dexter's novel The Jewel that was Ours *furnishes a final complication since it is based in part on the storyline Dexter wrote for television's* The Wolvercote Tongue, *which furnishes a different solution than the novel.*

Several years ago, the guides who escort groups of tourists around the university city of Oxford, England, began incorporating some new bits and pieces of information into their canned lectures. Today, as visitors walk north on St. Giles's Street, they may be informed that notable alumni of St. John's, the college on their right, include not only A.E. Housman, Philip Larkin, and Kingsley Amis, but also Colin Dexter's Chief Inspector Morse. As they pass the Eagle and Child, the well-known pub where C.S. Lewis and J.R.R. Tolkien used to drink and chat, they may be reminded that Morse also has been known to frequent the Bird and Baby, as he likes to call it. And if they take the right fork of St. Giles's and head north on the Banbury Road, they will catch a glimpse of the Thames Valley Police Headquarters in Kidlington, base of operations for Morse and Lewis, his sergeant.

Undoubtedly, Morse found a place in these Oxford tours partly because of the immense popularity of the television programs which have presented adaptations of most of Dexter's novels[1] as well as some more unusual kinds of adaptation which will be discussed below. Thanks also to the television series, the earlier novels have been reissued in the U.S. in Bantam paperback editions picturing actor John Thaw, the television Morse, against a background of "dreaming spires."

These programs, filmed as they are on location in Oxford, clearly acknowledge the importance of maintaining, or at least seeming to maintain, the atmosphere of Dexter's novels. The episodes give us panoramic vistas of towers and spires as well as looks at streets in the city centre crowded with double-decker buses, shoppers, and tourists—vistas and streets well known to Chief Inspector Morse and Sergeant Lewis. We need to ask ourselves, however, whether Morse and Lewis as we see them in the television adaptations actually inhabit the world, manifest the characteristics, and move through the plots which we associate with their counterparts in the novels.

One might think these questions easy to answer: almost every episode of the Inspector Morse series has been filmed on location in Oxford, and every episode stars actors John Thaw and Kevin Whately as Chief Inspector Morse and Detective Sergeant Lewis. In other words, a quick glance at these programs shows all of them looking and sounding much alike. One might, therefore, think it a small matter to do a standard comparison/contrast of novels versus television programs in order to discover what changes have occurred and what these do to the spirit of Dexter's work.

Complications arise, however, when we realize the implications of dealing with several *types* of adaptation. To begin with, we are examining the work of a number of different screenwriters, some more faithful than others to Dexter's novels. In addition, an "original storyline" by Dexter was adapted for television as *The Wolvercote Tongue* before Dexter published a revised version as a novel (*The Jewel that was Ours*). Moreover, ideas by Dexter have become programs (*The Ghost in the Machine* and *Deceived by Flight*, for example), and a number of other films (among them *The Infernal Serpent, Masonic Mysteries, Promised Land,* and *Fat Chance*) are "based on the characters created by Colin Dexter."[2]

I should say here that I am writing from a position of tolerance vis-à-vis "tampering" with texts, not insisting on literal and all-inclusive re-creation of Dexter's work. I am interested in determining the extent of fidelity to the spirit of Dexter's work—both from respect for what he does well in the novels and from curiosity regarding what happens during the adaptation process. Therefore, I want first to describe the principal characteristics of the novels themselves in order to clarify the source of their life. While doing so, I will look at the most important changes that occurred in these areas when the novels were adapted for television. After examining these relatively conventional examples of adaptation, I will turn to the more unusual adaptations—of characters, of ideas, of a storyline.

What, then, accounts for the life of the novels, and has this life survived the change in medium? As I have already suggested, much of Dexter's appeal comes from his skillful and very specific use of the Oxford setting. Although a number of writers of English mysteries have occasionally used the Oxford setting, Dexter has used it ten times and is, in fact, the only mystery writer I am aware of who has been so faithful to this particular city. On that evidence alone, we might conclude that the Oxford setting is central to Dexter's purposes.

On one level, Dexter uses the setting simply to appeal to what he thinks his audience wants. It is, he says, "a very big plus to live amid the Oxford setting, because so many people have either been to Oxford or would like to visit it in their imaginations" (qtd. in Herbert 31). For these lovers of this particular place, Dexter gives detailed and precise information. When Morse walks from where he has parked his car "beneath the towering Italianate campanile of St. Barnabas' church" (*The Dead of Jericho* 22) to number 9 Canal Reach in the district of Jericho,[3] readers can follow his progress exactly by examining the map in the front of the book—an accurate city map to which Dexter has added the cul-de-sac on which the first murder victim lives. Repeatedly in the novels, Dexter not only tells us where Morse is going but which streets he travels to get there; the result for readers is a strong sense of walking or driving with Morse through a city they know.

It would seem that the television adaptations of the novels also use the Oxford setting to provide the kind of basic appeal of the city which Dexter capitalizes on in the novels. Pubs and parks, college quadrangles and towers provide an attractive backdrop for the action. Indeed, as Mark Sanderson notes, the backdrop in the films is probably more visually attractive than in the novels, for the "seedier locales of Oxford" have been "generally eschewed to widen the appeal of the programme" (20). Despite the visual appeal, however, the television films may in one respect provide less satisfaction than the novels for those who know the city well. Whereas the novels accurately map Morse's and Lewis's movements through the city, the television adaptations offer location shots these viewers will realize do not always make sense. A typical instance occurs in the adaptation of *The Dead of Jericho* when Morse offers to escort Anne Stavely (called Anne Scott in the novel) to her home in the Jericho district. They leave the pub where they have been drinking (The White Horse, in the Broad Street), cross the street, and stroll between the Clarendon Building and the Sheldonian Theatre, entering Catte Street directly across from the Bridge of Sighs. Traveling a short distance down this street, they cross Radcliffe Square towards Brasenose Lane. Alastair Reid, the director of this episode, has here used lovely shots of some of Oxford's best-known sights—and because they are well known, many viewers will realize that Morse and his companion have begun walking away from, not towards, Jericho, circling well out of their way before heading back in the general direction of their supposed destination.

These inaccuracies may not matter except to die-hard Oxford enthusiasts. In many respects, the visual composition of the films is so carefully evocative that some literal errors may be winked at. In *The Dead of Jericho* for example, a "pervasive sense of melancholy" is created by "the haze in the chapel; the sun streaming into the gloomy court-house; the dazzling, antiseptic, white light that silhouettes the blind boy in hospital" (Sanderson 35). Scenes like these make forgivable, perhaps, a wrong turn by Morse and Anne Stavely. Nevertheless, this is an error the novels would not contain.

In the novels, the Oxford setting also helps Dexter characterize his protagonist: Chief Inspector Morse, Homicide Division. A working police investigator, Morse also attended an Oxford college, though he left without taking a degree. In his present life, he fills a role more clearly town than gown, yet his university background also marks him. Consequently, he is neither the one thing nor the other. Morse—who attends meetings of the Oxford Book Association and listens to Dame Helen Gardner on T.S. Eliot, who scolds his sergeant because of his poor spelling, who is appalled by the pedestrian prose of the *Oxford Mail* (the local paper), who listens to Wagner, Mozart, and Bach—is a man with some academic and cultural standards. Morse is also, however, sometimes cynical about public school/varsity elitism. Whether talking about the frowned-upon "three Bs—bullying, beating, and buggery" (*Service of All the Dead* 110)—or delightedly uncovering corruption in the entrance examination system (*The Silent World of Nicholas Quinn*), Morse the townsman is only too happy to embarrass any of what he considers the wrong kind of gownsman. For readers, then, he becomes an embodiment of unresolved tensions between town and gown, tensions woven into the texture of the novels.

In the adaptations of the novels, however, Morse's dual identity as townsman/gownsman is not consistently maintained. At times, adaptors ignore Morse's background as a university man. The adaptation of *The Dead of Jericho* makes nothing of Morse's history as a student or of his continuing interest in literature, although the novel has him receiving a luncheon invitation from a head of college (96) and resolving to renew acquaintance with Eliot's *Four Quartets*, which he studied while an undergraduate (26). The adaptation of *The Silent World of Nicholas Quinn* omits the scene in which Morse, observing a trio of "long-haired, bearded undergraduates" who are "T-shirted and bejeaned," remembers his own college days: "He had worn a scarf and tie himself—and sometimes a blazer. But that seemed a long time ago" (112).

The films' near obsession with Morse's love for classical music also helps shape a Morse far less complex than the novels. Though the novels do make much of Morse's love of music, particularly Mozart and Wagner, they also abound in references to Morse's knowledge of literature. For instance, in *Service of All the Dead* Dexter writes that "Morse was a believer neither in the existence of God nor in the fixity of the Fates. About such things he never quite knew what he should think; and, like Hardy's, his philosophy of life amounted to little more than a heap of confused impressions, akin to those of a bewildered young boy at a conjuring show" (42). As he solves crimes, he ponders quotations from Gibbon (*Service* 250), analyzes the plot of *Oedipus Rex* (*Jericho* 180-87), and is well able to cope with such suspects as Bernard Crowther, an English don whose specialty is Milton (*Last Bus to Woodstock* 89-101). Such literary references are minimized in the films; instead, adaptors most often represent Morse's educated and sensitive side by frequent references to his musical activities, even at the cost of significant departures from the novels. For instance, the adaptation of *The Dead of Jericho* invents a choral group for Morse to belong to, eliminates his attendance at meetings of the Oxford Book Association, and drops all the references to the publishing industry which are a part of the texture of the novel.

Not only is the television Morse less "fleshed out" ("Criminal Dexterity" 36) than the original, but the Jericho setting loses "character" as well. In *The Dead of Jericho*, Dexter uses the connection between that district and the Oxford University Press to establish contrasts and contradictions in both his protagonist and the scene of the various crimes committed. Omitted altogether from the adaptation is exploration of the relationship between the venerable

Press and inhabitants of the formerly working-class and now somewhat gentrified district.

Not surprisingly, the same films which dilute the richness of the Oxford setting and the personality of Morse also thin out the plots. To turn the novels into two-hour episodes, writers of the screenplays have dropped secondary characters or stripped them of some of their background. For example, we learn less from television than from the novel about Morse's attraction to murder suspect Ruth Rawlinson (*Service*). Mrs. Murdoch and sons Michael and Edward get replaced by one character—Ned (*Jericho*). And Joyce and Frank Greenaway, who name their infant son Nicholas, after the man who died on the day the new infant was born, do not exist in the television adaptation of *The Silent World of Nicholas Quinn*. These more sparsely developed and populated plots are perhaps an inevitable result of the change of medium, but they do diminish the "felt life" of the pieces.

Retained, however, is the crossword puzzle aspect of plotting so prized by Dexter himself. A creator of crosswords as well as of novels, Dexter enjoys "putting before his sleuth a puzzle or a test of wits that requires not only a certain amount of procedure but a 'sort of moment of epiphany' in which Morse at last makes sense of the clues that have been carefully placed before the sleuth and reader until that moment" (Herbert 31). Dexter emphasizes that his books are "whodunits," not the "whydunits" popular with some writers today: "The emphasis for me, if someone were to read the book, is always to say, I would never have thought it would turn out like this" ("Criminal Dexterity" 36). Although thinning out the plot in ways indicated above, the television adaptations do allow Morse his "moment of epiphany" in which all the clues suddenly suggest the answer, an answer which will perhaps surprise even more than in the novels; because the suspects are less fully developed than in the novels, we may theorize that viewers will be less likely than readers to come up with the solution ahead of time. For viewers who want to be surprised, this is perhaps an advantage of the change of medium. For those who delight in reaching the solution along with the detective, it is a disadvantage.

This kind of detecting may in any event be less important for television viewers than for readers. Certainly a major draw of the adaptations is the portrayal of Morse by John Thaw, an actor whom Marilyn Stasio calls so "damnably distracting" that "one's mind keeps straying off the plot" (17). Stasio's comment echoes Melanie McFadyean, who calls Thaw's Morse "the thinking man's cop and the thinking woman's crumpet" (24). Dexter himself has praised Thaw and Kevin Whately for their interpretations of Morse and Lewis ("Criminal Dexterity" 37), and Thaw is now so closely identified with Morse that critics such as Cathleen Schine tend to consider Thaw's Morse as interchangeable with the Morse of the novels—even when they discuss his role in a program adapted not from Dexter's text but from his characters or ideas.

It seems clear that the continued success of the television programs owes much to Thaw and to Whately, who provide a consistency of characterization despite the fact that writers, directors, and producers vary from adaptation to adaptation. Although Thaw is white-haired and stocky rather than "dark-haired" and "lightly built" (*Last Bus* 10), and although Whately is considerably younger than the Lewis of the novels, who becomes a grandfather in *The Dead of Jericho* (224), they enact their roles convincingly, providing a continuity which allows viewers to believe in them even when they are placed in plots which Colin Dexter didn't create. Even Dexter is convinced. He admits, in fact, that his "view of Lewis" has changed because of Whately and that recently, when he has written about Lewis, he has "solved the problem by ignoring it and not giving him too much physical description" (qtd. in Sanderson 20).

Generally speaking, the television adaptations most removed from the world of Dexter's novels are those based on his characters but not on his ideas or his writing. As with the adaptations mentioned earlier, thinner plots and less complex characters allow smaller scope for the kind of crossword puzzle putting together of clues valued by Dexter in his novels. *The Infernal Serpent* and *Masonic Mysteries* represent the worst and the best of the adaptations based on Dexter's characters, with the latter winning high marks for entertainment value despite its departure from what we expect to find in Dexter. It is almost as if the screenwriters of these adaptations have sometimes forgotten about Dexter entirely. In *The Infernal Serpent*, written by Alma Cullen, Morse has great trouble getting the information he needs to solve the case because he is treated like a non-university man by the Master and his wife, who consistently patronize him. When Lewis complains at one point that because he isn't an alumnus he doesn't "have the rank" to pursue his inquiries within the college, Morse responds wearily, "I don't have the rank either." Although John Thaw does his best to portray the Morse we have known all along, there is no escaping the fact that in this one episode Morse is not portrayed as an Oxford alumnus who is a policeman, but as an ordinary copper who doesn't have the credentials to extract information from the Oxford establishment.

Dexter's characters lead somewhat more convincing lives in *Masonic Mysteries*, written by Julian Mitchell. Here, the educated, music-loving Morse is back with us, this time involved as chorus member in a local production of *The Magic Flute*. We might quibble that the Morse of the novels listens to music rather than makes it, but at least the music is Mozart, a composer we know Morse admires. The plot is an engrossing one, well paced and suspenseful; however, it smacks more of Arthur Conan Doyle than of Colin Dexter. Morse is framed by Hugo de Vries, a Moriarity-like adversary so cunning that he has convinced Morse he is dead, created a new and sordid past for Morse and planted this record in the computer files of the Thames Valley Police, and cold-bloodedly killed a woman with whom Morse is involved, arranging for this to happen backstage at a dress rehearsal of *The Magic Flute* and for Morse to be apprehended with the murder weapon in his hand.

John Thaw and Ian McDiarmid enact the struggle between Morse and de Vries with wit and intensity, while Kevin Whately does a creditable job of portraying a loyal but extremely worried Lewis. But in this episode they inhabit a world different from the one Dexter gives them. Dexter's villains are not evil geniuses but ordinary sinners leading, for the most part, lives of quiet desperation. Even when clever Oxford dons get involved in wrongdoing, Dexter has them do so out of mundane greed or lust or professional jealousy. Mitchell's screenplay for *Masonic Mysteries* pits Morse and Lewis against a more dramatic and less realistic kind of opponent. They acquit themselves well in this new world, but after the episode has ended, we realize that it is not the world they normally occupy.

More crucially, the episodes based solely on Dexter's characters are at times jarringly at odds with the basic ethical pattern of Dexter's novels. Mystery editor Irma Heldman believes that good mysteries today do two things: present a "plausible puzzle" and show "concern with a particular contemporary social problem—these days, rape, sexual abuse, runaway children—that will interest and inform the reader" (qtd. in Anthony 24). Dexter's plots certainly puzzle, but although his novels do contain elements of some contemporary problems—drugs (*Jericho*), a runaway (*Last Seen Wearing*), rape (*Last Bus*)—they are not given a particularly trendy or contemporary slant. Characters in *The Silent World of*

Nicholas Quinn flock to see *The Nympho-maniac* at a local Oxford cinema because of their "baser instincts" (225) and the seedy Soho establishments in *The Riddle of the Third Mile* exist because of flawed human nature, not because Dexter wants to express concern about the rise in pornography, giving Morse himself, according to Cathleen Schine, "an ironic sense of his own destiny: he knows he'll solve the crime, but not the sin behind it" (174).

The adaptations based solely on Dexter's characters, however, bring to the foreground the kind of up-to-date subject matter Heldman refers to. In *The Infernal Serpent*, the motive for the attack on Julian Dear, senior fellow and revered, almost saintly environmentalist, seems to be an effort to cover up the involvement of his college with an environmentally unsound corporation. The motive for murder, however, turns out to be not this contemporary problem but another—child abuse. Furthermore, one of the suspects in the case is a young environmental activist being blackmailed because he once posed for homosexual pornographic photos, yet a third contemporary topic.

In another recent film based on Dexter's characters, trendy topics once again dominate. *Fat Chance* brings together two unlikely "bedfellows"—controversy within the Anglican church over the ordination of women priests and suspicious goings on at a weight-loss center. Despite the beauties of New College chapel, where the visually striking opening scene was filmed, despite admirable performances by Maurice Denham and Zoe Wanamaker in supporting roles, the parts of the film fail to add up to a coherent whole. As in *The Infernal Serpent*, screenwriter Alma Cullen seems more interested in exploiting current topics than in exploring common human failings. Moved to the background is the Morse of the novels, a man who wrestles with human duplicity knowing he'll never really win.

The Ghost in the Machine is another kind of adaptation, one based on an idea by Colin Dexter. The screenplay by Julian Mitchell presents a Morse and Lewis whom we recognize, the relationship between the two of them complementary as always, with Morse listening to Maria Callas—while Lewis asks if the music is from *Cats*—and criticizing Lewis's grammar: "You'll never get on if you can't master your subjunctive." The Oxford part of the story takes place in a college called Courtenay, with a number of location shots of this invented community filmed in or near Oriel College. Most of the action, however, takes place at Hanbury House, located near but not in Oxford, and involves an aristocratic family. Consequently, both setting and characters seem foreign. Except for the occasional jaunt to a country pub or journey into London, the novels are firmly placed in a very specific Oxford setting, a setting peopled by dons, by policemen, and by ordinary middle-class and working-class people—but not by the likes of the Hanburys. Actress Patricia Hodge does a fine job as the appalling Lady Hanbury, but she and her historic gardens and her stately dwelling provide a foreign background for Morse and Lewis. Screenwriter Julian Mitchell is clearly fond of plots and settings different from Dexter's; here, he puts Morse and Lewis in the stereotypical world of the country-house murder—not a world they usually visit.

Furthermore, the plot is much more a "Howdunit" than a "Whodunit": few viewers can have been surprised by the identity of the guilty parties; for most of the two-hour program, the only real puzzle is how they did their deeds. Because Dexter has not published the idea upon which the program is based, we cannot know what Julian Mitchell has done to it; what we can say, however, is that both setting and plot differ from what both novels and adaptations of the novels have led us to expect. If Mitchell's adaptation *is* faithful to Dexter's idea, then Dexter has strayed from what he claims is most important for him: a "puzzle" of a plot which will surprise his audience.

Deceived by Flight, written by Anthony Minghella, is also based on an idea by Dexter. In her final comments, host Diana Rigg explains that the idea for the story came from a conversation between Dexter and Kevin Whately, who told Dexter he'd longed as a boy to grow up to be an England test batsman. In the program, Whately as Lewis gets to play cricket, although as a bowler, in an attempt to discover a murderer among members of a cricket team of old boys who are also chums from Morse's own Oxford days. This program gives us the Morse of the novels—the uneasy townsman who has also been a gownsman. Most of his old college chums can't understand why he has become a policeman, although the most sympathetically drawn of the group (Anthony Donn, well played by Daniel Massey) respects him and is interested in learning about his life. This is one of the programs featuring Amanda Hillwood as coroner Dr. Russell, an "invention" who does not appear in the novels. Her character (a feisty woman in what has been a male profession) and also some secondary incidents (the bombing of a local shop which sells what Lewis describes as "left wing books" and other "way-out stuff," including explicit homosexual literature) gives a note of contemporary realism which works better here than in *The Infernal Serpent* and *Fat Chance*. On all levels—within the police force, within fringe groups of political extremists, within the privileged world of Oxford alumni—changes are afoot. The causes of crime, however, remain the same. Except for Diana Rigg's description, we do not have a "text" for Dexter's idea, but Minghella's screenplay is more respectful of Dexter's world than some of the scripts discussed earlier.

The final and most complicated kind of adaptation involves *The Wolvercote Tongue*, with a screenplay written by Julian Mitchell from a storyline by Colin Dexter. Here we cannot compare Mitchell's adaptation with the unpublished story; we can, however, compare *The Wolvercote Tongue* with the novel *The Jewel that was Ours*, a novel published *after* the program aired, a novel with a different title but the same characters (some with different names), a novel with the same victims but different murderers. Readers of the novel who have also seen the television program consequently find themselves in the interesting position of being teased not only by the conventional red herrings of detective fiction but also by characters whom they have encountered before and discovered to be guilty or not guilty of murder, but whom they now find to be both the same and quite different—at least in terms of innocence and guilt.

Certain things remain the same: in both works, a Celtic jewel, the so-called Wolvercote Tongue, disappears from the hotel bedroom of a wealthy American tourist who had been intending to donate it to the Ashmolean Museum to reunite it with a buckle, already in the museum's collection. In both works, this tourist dies at about the same time the jewel disappears, causing Morse to wonder whether her heart gave out as a result of discovering someone in the process of filching the jewel. In both works, the death of a second victim, Dr. Theodore Kemp of the Ashmolean, suggests a connection between the two deaths. However, the deaths are in fact connected in only one of the works; the murderer in the first is a suspect who turns out to be innocent in the second, and the clues which help Morse solve the mystery in the first work mislead him in the second—although he eventually has the requisite moment of epiphany when all things are revealed.

Here, in other words, Dexter himself is the adaptor. In the Acknowledgements section of his novel, he writes that *The Jewel that was Ours* "is based in part on an original storyline written by Colin Dexter for Central Television's *Inspector Morse* series." Although we cannot be sure whether Dexter is also adapting from the television show which adapted his storyline, or whether he is adapting "back to" his original storyline, which had been changed by the television program, we certainly have a situation in which the novelist knows that many of his readers will have seen on television a plot somewhat different from the one he is constructing in his novel. Changing the identity of the "who" in the "whodunit," he tantalizes his readers with situations which looked the same in the television program but which have quite different meanings now. This reversal of what usually happens, with the book coming after instead of before the film, allows for especially complex plotting. By the nature of their medium, novels allow for more detailed plots than do films. In addition, the plot of this novel is complicated further, for those who have seen the film, by Dexter's well-thought-out changes. In this kind of adaptation, plot does not suffer; it is enriched.

To this improved plot, Dexter also adds the texture and complexity more easily obtained in the novel than on television. Characterization is more "fleshed-out": especially interesting here is the presentation of the group of American tourists who are staying at the Randolph, Oxford's premier hotel, when one of their number dies. In the television film, most are portrayed quite stereotypically as brash Americans abroad. Loud and complaining, they are treated with contempt by Sheila Williams, their English tour organizer, and little happens to suggest that her contempt is unjustified. In the novel, however, Dexter plays with the stereotype but eventually undercuts it. Although American accents get mocked ("Arksford" for Oxford, "Bairth" for Bath), and some Americans are represented as classic know-it-alls and others as know-nothings, Dexter corrects this image a number of times in the novel, as when Cedric Downes, a don responsible for leading the group on a tour of historic Oxford, thinks to himself that he "sometimes felt a bit dubious about 'Americans'; yet like almost all his colleagues in Oxford, he often found himself enjoying actual Americans, without those quotation marks. That morning he knew that as always some of their questions would be disturbingly naive, some penetrating, all of them *honest*" (76).

This re-creation by an author of a screen adaptation of his own original story has worked well in this instance. Producers should consider cajoling Dexter to write new storylines which his editors could encourage him to adapt into novels after the programs have aired. These kinds of novels, written in part for readers who have already seen a related television program, might come to constitute a new sub-genre of detective fiction, one in which the novelist's puzzles, red herrings, and clues lie both within and outside his written work. Here both characters and readers would inhabit a perplexing parallel world in which solutions, when they finally occur, bring particular satisfaction.[5]

NOTES

[1]Dexter's ten novels, with dates of publication, are: *Last Bus to Woodstock*, 1975; *Last Seen Wearing*, 1976; *The Silent World of Nicholas Quinn*, 1977; *Service of All the Dead*, 1979; *The Dead of Jericho*, 1981; *The Riddle of the Third Mile*, 1983; *The Secret of Annexe 3*, 1986; *The Wench is Dead*, 1989; *The Jewel that was Ours*, 1991; *The Way Through the Woods*, 1992.

[2]In citing the television programs based on Dexter's work, I use "adapt." before the name of the writer of the screenplay when he is working from text written by Dexter. I use "writ." before the name of the writer of the screenplay when he or she is working from ideas or characters, but not from written text.

In this paper, I discuss many but not all of the adaptations seen on PBS as of spring, 1993. In all, six "series" have been shown in this country, beginning in 1988. These include adaptations of five of Colin Dexter's novels: *The Dead of Jericho, The Silent World of Nicholas Quinn, Service of all the Dead, Last Seen Wearing, Last Bus to Woodstock*; adaptations of Dexter's characters: *The Settling of the Sun, The Infernal Serpent, Masonic Mysteries, Driven to Distraction, Sins of the Fathers, Second Time Around, Fat Chance, Promised Land*; adaptations of Dexter's ideas: *Ghost in the Machine, Deceived by Flight, The Secret of Bay 5B*; and adaptations of stories by Dexter: *The Wolvercote Tongue, The Last Enemy*.

The Last Enemy (which first aired in the U.S. on 31 May 1990) contains many of the same elements of plot as *Riddle of the Third Mile* (1983) and could almost be considered a "loose" adaptation of that novel. The opening credits, however, insist that it is "based on a story by Colin Dexter." In any event, as the television program comes after the novel (and story), it is a less complex kind of adaptation than that discussed in connection with *The Jewel that was Ours*.

[3]Interestingly, P.D. James also has used St. Barnabas's "soaring campanile," as she calls it, as part of the setting for her mystery *A Taste for Death*. However, she moves the church to the banks of the Grand Union Canal, London.

⁴Worth noting about this novel are the similarities between Quinn, the first murder victim, and Dexter himself. Both attended Cambridge, taught grammar school briefly, and then moved to Oxford where Quinn took a position with the Foreign Examinations Syndicate, and Dexter with the Oxford Delegacy of Local Examinations. Both are deaf, and Dexter has noted that his own tendency to "mishear so much" helped him to write the novel (Sanderson 15). In the television adaptation, Dexter, who makes fleeting appearances in most of the films, crosses paths at a social gathering with the unfortunate, soon-to-be deceased Nicholas Quinn.

⁵I would like to thank Nathan Hasson of WGBH, Boston, for information about the six seasons of Inspector Morse films which have been shown in the U.S. Special thanks to Janet and Philip Budd for "local" information about the effect on the city of Oxford of the filming of the series.

WORKS CITED

Anthony, Carolyn. "Crime Marches On." *Publishers Weekly* 13 Apr. 1990: 24-25.

The Dead of Jericho. Adapt. Anthony Minghella. Dir. Alastair Reid. Prod. Kenny McBain. *MYSTERY!* PBS. WGBH, Boston. 4, 11 Feb. 1988.

Deceived by Flight. Writ. Anthony Minghella. Dir. Anthony Simmons. Prod. Chris Burt. *MYSTERY!* PBS. WGBH, Boston. 30 May and 6 June 1991.

Dexter, Colin. "Criminal Dexterity: An Interview with Colin Dexter." With Markman Ellis. *Waterstone's News Books*. London: Blackmore, 1991.

____. *The Dead of Jericho*. 1981. London: Pan, 1983.

____. *The Jewel that was Ours*. London: Macmillan, 1991.

____. *Last Bus to Woodstock*. 1975. New York: Bantam, 1989.

____. *The Riddle of the Third Mile*. 1983. New York: Bantam, 1988.

____. *Service of All the Dead*. 1979. London: Pan, 1980.

____. *The Silent World of Nicholas Quinn*. 1977. New York: Bantam, 1988.

Driven to Distraction. Writ. Anthony Minghella. Dir. Sandy Johnson. Prod. David Lascelles. *MYSTERY!* PBS. WGBH, Boston. 23, 30 Apr. 1992.

Fat Chance. Writ. Alma Cullen. Dir. Roy Battersby. Prod. David Lascelles. *MYSTERY!* PBS WGBH, Boston. 8, 15 Apr. 1993.

The Ghost in the Machine. Writ. Julian Mitchell. Dir. Herbert Wise. Prod. Chris Burt. *MYSTERY!* PBS. WGBH, Boston. 17, 24 May 1990.

Herbert, Rosemary. "Aiming Higher." *Publishers Weekly* 13 Apr. 1990: 30-32.

The Infernal Serpent. Writ. Alma Cullen. Dir. John Madden. Prod. David Lascelles. *MYSTERY!* PBS. WGBH, Boston. 16, 23 May 1991.

James, P. D. *A Taste for Death*. London: Faber, 1986.

The Last Enemy. Adapt. Peter Buckman. Dir. James Scott. Prod. Chris Burt. *MYSTERY!* PBS. WGBH, Boston. 31 May and 7 June 1990.

Masonic Mysteries. Writ. Julian Mitchell. Dir. Danny Boyle. Prod. David Lascelles. *MYSTERY!* PBS. WGBH, Boston. 9, 16 Apr. 1992.

McFadyean, Melanie. "The Man for the Job." *The Guardian* 19 Sept. 1991: 24.

Promised Land. Writ. Julian Mitchell. Dir. John Madden. Prod. David Lascelles. *MYSTERY!* PBS. WGBH, Boston. 22, 29 Apr. 1993.

Sanderson, Mark. *The Making of Inspector Morse*. London: Macmillan, 1991.

Schine, Cathleen. "Inspector Morse." *Vogue* May 1990: 174.

Second Time Around. Writ. Daniel Boyle. Dir. Adrian Shergold. Prod. David Lascelles. *MYSTERY!* PBS. WGBH, Boston. 25 Mar. and 1 Apr. 1993.

The Secret of Bay 5B. Writ. Alma Cullen. Dir. Jim Goddard. Prod. Chris Burt. *MYSTERY!* PBS. WGBH, Boston. 13, 20 June 1991.

The Settling of the Sun. Writ. Charles Wood. Dir. Peter Hammond. Prod. Kenny McBain. *MYSTERY!* PBS. WGBH, Boston. 3, 10 May 1990.

The Silent World of Nicholas Quinn. Adapt. Julian Mitchell. Dir. Brian Parker. Prod. Kenny McBain. *MYSTERY!* PBS. WGBH, Boston. 18, 25 Feb. 1988.

Sins of the Fathers. Writ. Jeremy Burnham. Dir. Peter Hammond. Prod. David Lascelles. *MYSTERY!* PBS. WGBH, Boston. 7, 14 May 1992.

Stasio, Marilyn. "Crime." *The New York Times Book Review* 19 Apr. 1992: 17.

The Wolvercote Tongue. Adapt. Julian Mitchell. Dir. Alastair Reid. Prod. Kenny McBain. *MYSTERY!* PBS. WGBH, Boston. 15, 22 Dec. 1988.

Watching Warshawski

Kathleen Gregory Klein

Hollywood Pictures' V.I. Warshawski (1991) transforms plots in which Sarah Paretsky carefully weaves professional and personal stories, and where detection is a metaphor for living life, into a simplistic—and essentially unresolved—linear narrative. In the process, Paretsky's detective, V.I. Warshawski, is objectivized and fetishized from an independent, complex woman into a passive object of male desire.

Hollywood Pictures' release of *V.I. Warshawski* starring Kathleen Turner did not prove to be one of the hot-weather blockbusters of the summer of 1991. In my neighborhood it barely lasted a week. Overall, the movie grossed only $11 million (Krupp 131); neither Turner nor anyone else associated with the film was even nominated for an Academy Award.[1] In short, it was not a commercial success. Nonetheless, I want to argue that the movie was made with exactly that kind of success in mind and that such intentions made impossible the faithful transfer of Sara Paretsky's character and plots from fiction to film.

Seen in the novels from the inside out, a first-person feminist narrator of her life, her profession, and her ideology, V.I. Warshawski is seen on film through the camera eye, an ostensibly objective, omniscient narrator. Objectivized and fetishized by the "male gaze" of technological apparatus—the camera eye—the previously independent and self-defined V.I. becomes "other," a manifestation of the gaze, and a product of patriarchal capitalism. The plots in which Paretsky so carefully weaves professional and personal stories, where individuals become victims of institutions, and where detection is a metaphor for living life become, instead, a simplistic—and essentially unresolved—linear narrative.

The V.I. Warshawski of Sara Paretsky's novels is a complex woman far from the standard definitions of the hard-boiled detective as a man isolated—by choice or necessity—from his community. V.I.'s fictional history identifies her, rather, as a woman of her communities. She is tied into the city of Chicago through her childhood, extended family, police (and criminal) contacts, and her

145

earlier work as a public defender. She is connected with the feminist community through activism in a student underground abortion referral network and through her continuing rejection of gender role stereotypes. Disappointed by most of her relatives, after the deaths of her parents she builds an extended family bound by ties of affection and shared values.

Using V.I.'s attachment to these communities, Sara Paretsky creates plots in which the personal and the professional—the communities and the criminal—intersect to draw Vic deeply into her role as detective. Only the first of her cases begins in the conventional style with a paying client hiring her for a job; and even this case in *Indemnity Only* turns out to have family connections. The other novels all focus first on the "family" and are then enlarged to encompass the crime and the institutional world which it threatens. In a striking departure from typical detective novels, Paretsky's conclusions seldom resolve the crime or the underlying institutional arrogance; there is no return to order at the end of these novels because, as the readers clearly understand, there was no edenic status quo before the crime. Dr. Lottie Herschel, V.I.'s closest friend, lives a perfect metaphor for the society in which the novels are set: a Holocaust survivor whose family died in the concentration camps, she operates a clinic for Chicago's poor. Power and powerlessness, the haves and the have-nots: no one, certainly not the lone doctor or the lone detective who mediates between the two extremes, can eliminate either.

The interplay of these communities creates the structure for both narrative and plot in the seven Warshawski novels: Paretsky consciously chooses to make personal and professional stories intersect.[2] The novel which most closely resembles the film is *Deadlock*, the second in the series. In it, V.I. chooses to investigate the apparently accidental death of her cousin, the former hockey player Boom Boom Warshawski. She follows his trail through the Eudora Grain Company where he had been hired after an ankle-shattering accident left him unable to skate. There he was alternately labeled an accident, a suicide, or a troublemaker. Vic's motive for "hiring" herself to check out his death begins in guilt for not having responded quickly to his last telephone message. What she finds, not surprisingly, is murder, betrayal, explosions, capitalism gone amuck, and a hint of insanity.

As the novel develops two story lines—the criminal and the personal—the narrative also carries two plots—the original criminal activity and V.I.'s detection of the crime. The former is fairly straightforward: V.I. determines that Boom Boom was murdered by Clayton Phillips, a vice-president of Eudora Grain, to hide evidence of invoice tampering which would prove fraud and theft. The detection plot is considerably more complicated. V.I. begins to chase the paper trail of evidence from Eudora Grain to Grafalk Steamship and its owner, Niels Grafalk. Her investigation leads Warshawski to "stow away" on a grain freighter on the Great Lakes as she tries to interview sailors who had worked with her cousin. During V.I.'s process of discovery, nine additional people are killed: a security guard at Boom Boom's apartment building, the driver of car hit by Vic when her brakes fail, four crew members on an exploded ship, the debt-ridden hockey player who planted the explosives, and the two villains, Clayton Phillips and Niels Grafalk. Vic's own life is clearly in jeopardy on three specific occasions: her car brake lines are cut; she is on the exploded ship; and she is discovered on his sailboat by Niels Grafalk. Along the way she tackles Phillips's grasping wife, Jeannine, and Grafalk's mistress, Paige Carrington, who had agreed to become Boom Boom's lover in order to keep tabs on him. When Vic puts together all the pieces of the case, she shares the complete story with Claire Grafalk, Niels's wife. This pattern of information sharing, begun in *Indemnity Only* with Anita McGraw, represents a deliberate expanding of the knowledge base and an extension of her range of "communities."

Warshawski's decision to share information typically reserved to the detective and client marks one aspect of the feminist changes in the formula which Paretsky's seven novels reflect. Other changes revolve around both the protagonist and the plots. Even though she sees herself as a "Doña Quixote," attempting to right wrongs against enormous odds, V.I. does not ordinarily impose her own code of morality; rather than create a heroic individualistic detective, Paretsky has imagined her protagonist expanding the collective base of power through her inclusive style. With the novels' villains so firmly entrenched within the power system (corporate business, unions, the Chicago political system, the Catholic church, the medical community, and the police), no lone avenger—no naive Don Quixote—could hope to have any marked impact. Against criminals entrenched within and protected by the system, she concentrates on helping ordinary people.

And then there is the film. Despite having access to a complex character and range of plot and narrative lines developed through seven novels, producer Jeffrey Lurie and director Jeff Kanew chose to flatten V.I. Warshawski into a one-dimensional mold and park her in the middle of a no-dimensional plot. Disney Studios and Hollywood Pictures bought the rights to one of the most provocative feminist private eyes in contemporary detective fiction and threw away everything about her which mattered. They turned a hot property into cold cuts. What happened to *V.I. Warshawski* can be answered, albeit in a roundabout way, by looking at the film through a feminist lens.

Because an already well-developed theory and methodology of film criticism was in place, feminist film theory developed early, shortly after feminist theory and criticism of literature and history. According to Annette Kuhn, "1972 in fact seems to be a watershed year for feminist film theory" (75). Both New York and Toronto held Women's Film Festivals in the early 1970s; three books and two journals of feminist film criticism as well as some of the most important articles in the field were published during the first half of the decade.[3] Three central concerns of feminist film theory—from its beginnings to the present—illuminate the filmic impulses behind the production of *V.I. Warshawski*: representation, absence, and the "gaze."

The typical form of mainstream "Hollywood" cinema is what Annette Kuhn calls classic realism (28) which articulates its characters as narrative function (31). Such a model leans heavily on the persuasive implication of normative behavior or so-called natural order. Such films, like novels whose narrative trajectory they borrow, rely on the audience's acceptance of most of their elements as previously encoded knowledge; thus the audience is freed to address only the unique elements the directors and producers wish to foreground. But such expectations of and by audiences discount the presence and impact of ideology. If, as feminists, cultural critics, and theorists have insisted, dominant cinema is part of the ideological process of making meaning—or the process of making ideological meaning—then audiences must denaturalize the filmic text. Feminist film and cultural critics have been most insistent about this necessity because of the oppressive nature of the culturally dominant representation of women.

The continuing representation of Woman to meet patriarchal ideology rather than the authentic presentation of women— unpacked by numerous film and fictional critics in their readings of "images of women"—raises questions about whose natural order is being served. We see that transgressive women are punished either by being killed or driven insane in nineteenth-century fiction (Gilbert and Gubar), or limited to basic biological functions in the modern day Gilead of *The Handmaid's Tale*, or fly off into the sunset and certain death like Thelma and Louise; if not punished, they are recuperated to traditional family roles, like Mildred Pierce (Kuhn 35). But what's the difference?

In short, as E. Ann Kaplan puts it: "Women in film, thus, do not function as signifiers for a signified (a real woman) as sociological critics have assumed, but signifier and signified have been elided into a sign that represents something in the male unconscious" (310). In classic cinema, the absence of real women as objects of the male unconscious is frequently carried to extremes where even the representation of Woman is absent or excluded. The complete erasure of women from realistic cinema occurs in war movies, prison stories, and male buddy or bonding films. The virtual absence of women can be found in westerns with their token schoolmarm or saloon girl, in adventure films where secretaries and short-term sex objects appear briefly, or in gangster and other corporate-male movies where wives and mistresses are merely window dressing. The absent-while-present equivalent is at work when women or sex are occasions of male actions, catalysts to be used and forgotten: victims and even murderers in crime stories and revenge films or films where women in traditional male positions are brought down by culturally dominant mores. As Budd Boetticher, a cult director of Hollywood B Westerns, states: "What counts is what the heroine provokes, or rather what she represents. She is the one, or rather the love or fears she inspires in the hero, or else the concern he feels for her, who makes him act the way he does. In herself the woman has not the slightest importance" (qtd. in Mulvey 62). Psychological theories of representation would argue that all women are absent; only eroticized fetishes for male satisfaction remain in the two-dimensional images on screen.

The theory of the gaze, first enunciated by Laura Mulvey in 1975, is psychoanalytic in its base; it draws on Freud's analysis of both voyeurism and scopophilia (defined by E. Ann Kaplan as "male pleasure in his own sexual organ transferred to pleasure in watching other people have sex" [310]) leading to fetishism. Writing of voyeurism, Kaplan continues:

> The original eye of the camera, controlling and limiting what can be
> seen, is reproduced by the projector aperture that lights up one frame
> at a time; and both processes (camera and projector) duplicate the
> eye at the keyhole, whose gaze is confined by the keyhole "frame."
> The spectator is obviously in the voyeur position when there are sex

scenes on the screen, but screen images of women are sexualized no matter what the women are doing literally, or what kind of plot may be involved. (311)

This inevitable eroticization of women comes, according to Mulvey, from the three forms of the male gaze: as the camera, as the characters within the film, and as the spectator who mimics those first two gazes. Let me further summarize Mulvey's reading of the visual pleasure worked out in "illusionistic narrative film" (67): first, the voyeuristic fantasies of the audience are heightened by the film's self-contained existence and the traditionally darkened theatre which promote the necessary sense of separation and secrecy. Second, the traditional role of women as representations *to-be-looked-at* meshes neatly with the dichotomy of male/active and female/passive. The spectator's necessarily active "look" is identified with the filmic "look" of the strong male character(s), "so that the power of the male protagonist as he controls events coincides with the active power of the erotic look, both giving a satisfying sense of omnipotence" (Mulvey 63). But—and here's the serious downside for the otherwise satisfied male spectator—in psychological terms the female always represents an absence: the lack of a penis; to represent sexual difference, she must also evoke castration anxiety. The male unconscious chooses one of two escape routes: voyeurism, by reenacting the original trauma; or fetishization which turns the represented figure into a manageable object. The latter route, Mulvey's fetishistic scopophilia, attempts to disavow the possibilities of castration altogether through gaining power over the representation of the absence of a penis. Mulvey concludes:

It is the place of the look that defines cinema, the possibility of varying it and exposing it. . . . Going far beyond highlighting a woman's to-be-looked-at-ness, cinema builds the way she is to be looked at into the spectacle itself. Playing on the tension between film as controlling the dimension of time (editing, narrative) and film as controlling the dimension of space (changes in distance, editing), cinematic codes create a gaze, a world, and an object, thereby producing an illusion cut to the measure of desire. (67)

And, as Teresa de Lauretis writes, in classic Hollywood cinema, "the male is the measure of desire" (67).

No doubt the male measure of desire goes a long way to explain the choice of Kathleen Turner as protagonist-hero-private-eye V.I. Warshawski. No interview or story about Turner misses the opportunity to refer to her sultry, sexy role in *Body Heat* even though subsequent roles have offered her a much wider range of opportunities; it is as though she is defined by that image. The commercial appeal of a star-name on the product and the publicity which could be garnered by pairing "body heat" and "private eye" was thoroughly exploited by Hollywood Pictures. After all, the original (working) title for the film was *Fully Loaded* (Benenson 20). No feminist—film theorist or not—should have been surprised by the result. From the moment the newspaper advertising began, the only misleading information was the credit phrase "Based upon the V.I. Warshawski novels by Sara Paretsky."

The full-page newspaper ads, also reproduced on movie-theatre billboards, trumpet the star's name across the top in large, bold, upper case lettering. Similar type at the bottom announces the film's title, *V.I. Warshawski*; the bracketing placement of the two, similar type and bold print, imply the pairing statement used in other publicity contexts: "KATHLEEN TURNER is V.I. WARSHAWSKI." Between these two names stands a full-body shot of Turner/Warshawski against a background of the letter "W" as if it were cutting through to the gray, gritty background of a large city; on the billboards and video cover, the W is scarlet. Turner/Warshawski stands, in a dark, short-skirted suit and very high heels facing forward; her legs are spread apart to match the lower edges of the "W" and she holds a large gun pointing upward, level with her eyes, off to her left side. She stares directly out of the picture. The pose is explicit: the viewer focuses immediately on the white space between her legs which is also the space between the two lower points of the "W". Both the "W" and her legs are cut off before the crotch by the slim, thigh-length skirt she wears; but the viewer's eye completes the image. The two incomplete triangles rest on each other, simultaneous and contiguous, ending at the acute angle at her crotch where the triangle (point down, of course) often employed to symbolize women's sexuality begins.

Were Turner/Warshawski holding the gun in front of her body, braced with both hands in the now familiar stance of cops and private eyes from every television show and movie, the message of her open position might be misread; but here there can be no doubt that this visual emphasis on the space between her legs is meant to titillate. The upraised gun is placed graphically in one of the open "V's" forming the top of the "W," coming up directly from the point of the triangle into the open space. One hand is gripped around the gun and on this wrist Turner/Warshawski appears to be wearing a bracelet or watch; the other hand is held down by her side, fingers spread in a more conventionally feminine gesture. Finally, the triangles of the "W" and her legs are matched by the V-necked blouse and suit jacket Turner/Warshawski wears.

Should the newspaper reader be unable to deconstruct the visual meaning, the ad makes explicit its message. Immediately under the figure and above the name V.I. WARSHAWSKI in dark, easily visible type are the phrases "Killer eyes. Killer legs. Killer instincts." Below the movie's title one reads, "A private detective with a name as tough as she is." Having seen the eyes on a level with the phallic gun and observed the widely spread legs, the reader is reminded again of them with the slang adjective "killer." Matched with "instincts," a tough name and a tough person, the message is twofold: most obviously, V.I. is defined as someone to be wary of. More subtly, she is posed as a challenge; how tough is she? In this representation of the detective as "killer" and "Woman," the two contradictions are resolved in the quasi-shooter, completely sexual stance: spike heels on widely spread-open legs. The woman/private eye is an oxymoron graphically and verbally exposed. This is an ad for a movie made to sell; and its audience is only too clearly encoded from the outset.

The film's absences are, as might be expected, far less obvious than the blatantly sexual come-on of its advertising. What's missing is, by definition, hard to see. And by the definitions of the feminist film critics cited earlier, *V.I. Warshawski* might seem to be among the least guilty of new releases: after all, it features a woman as the hero-protagonist; and, unconventionally, it does not seem to show her as male-defined. Professionally, Warshawski usurps the traditional male role, in fact, all the male roles: protagonist, hero, detective, private eye, crime fighter, shooter, and sexual actor. But there are absences; in this film they are two-fold. One is marked by an erasure, a disappearance; the other by a presence. For the V.I. Warshawski of Paretsky's novels has a well-defined ethnic background which plays an important part in defining her character and personality; and she is child-free, no less significant a factor in explaining her subjectivity.

Film adaptations of novels have to consider the extent to which readers of the original works carry impressions of the text—plot, setting, characters—with them into the movie theatre. Sara Paretsky comments on the transformation of her character: "V.I. is about 5 foot 8, with short dark hair, gray eyes and Italian-Polish features . . .

Kathleen Turner doesn't look a bit like her. Serious fans of the book are upset that Turner is in the role, but I think when they see the final result they'll be happy. At least I hope so" (quoted in Benenson 20). The negation of Warshawski's ethnicity by the producers' decision (initially at Tri-Star Productions and later with Disney Studios) to cast the blonde, "all-American" Turner has two significant effects. The first is more global; the American look is defined as blonde, blue-eyed, and not recognizably ethnic. Vic is the embodiment of the cheerleader Peggy Sue fantasizing an exciting grown-up life. The rest of the casting also denies American multi-ethnic/cultural diversity to stay firmly white except in throwaway roles. The second effect of Turner/Warshawski's lack of ethnicity is to make her average; the contributions of her Jewish-Italian mother and Polish father—both major influences on her upbringing in the novels—are erased. This erasure is not neutral; it does not leave a space where the audience might interpolate its own background information but marks an absence of ethnicity which in contemporary America is a defining characteristic of its own.

The absence of natural maternity for V.I. is similarly marked. In *Of Woman Born*, her study of motherhood as both social institution and personal experience, Adrienne Rich concludes that the single most important cultural element defining women is the capacity to bear children; and, she continues, the fact that all women are potential mothers is more important than the reality that some women never have children. Because of the oxymoron implicit in the premise of *V.I. Warshawski*—a woman private eye—the producers solved the dilemma of how to keep Turner/Warshawski's femininity sufficiently foregrounded to compete with her gun by giving her a child, in fact, a thirteen-year-old daughter, Boom Boom's daughter Kat.[4] V.I.'s encounter with the soon-to-be-killed Boom Boom moves her quickly from bar pick-up, to involuntary babysitter, to employee of her young charge, to mother substitute; the girl's natural mother is so self-centered that audiences are doubly impressed by V.I.'s caring attention and shared wisdom: "Never underestimate a man's ability to underestimate a woman's." The script, as a consequence, erases the child-free woman;[5] it concludes that inasmuch as V.I. has unaccountably neglected to fulfill this vital aspect of her potential, even a temporary child is better than none. The film's final scene in which V.I. and her too-visible lover Murray decide to shield the girl from her mother's treachery is a clear-cut triumph of the on-going sentimentality about parents and children, with Vic and Murray as mom and dad; by contrast, throughout the novels, Warshawski consistently shares information, especially the painful kind, with those who have a right to know. From start to finish, the kid is a studio cop-out in the face of a potentially strong woman in an unconventional role.[6]

The gaze of the spectator which turns the female character into the representation of male desire—a sex object—is immediately apparent in this film. In the dark, the viewer watches as a camera/projector frames scenes designed to evoke pleasure. What that viewer sees almost immediately is a female body offered up to the male gazes within the film as a signal of how to watch the film. Following quickly on the establishing shots of Chicago, the camera tracks V.I. getting out of bed to go jogging. Thus far, the camera and the viewer are the carriers of the "gaze"; since a woman getting out of bed is an already established social sign, the first scene is anything but neutral. The next two scenes complete the clear-cut articulation of Turner/Warshawski as a fetishized object. While jogging outdoors, V.I. encounters a group of male joggers, apparently college students/athletes going in the opposite direction; they stare to the point of turning around and jogging backwards to continue looking at her. To emphasize their objectification of her—and their general crassness—they make hooting animal sounds at her. With their disappearance, the camera takes over their role, focusing on her bare, running legs. When her legs and running shoes are replaced by stockings and spike heels, the camera pans up.

If the first look duplicates the college students' gaze, the second is explicitly linked to the look of a prospective client with whom V.I. is seen subsequently. That he too is explicitly vulgar—she's perfect for the case because, according to him, she's a "female dick"—ties the two episodes together verbally as the camera unifies them visually.[7] Immediately and economically, the audience is instructed how to view the film: the spectator's gaze fetishizes Turner/ Warshawski; she becomes an object "to-be-looked-at." She is merely a body whose representation valorizes male desire and negates authentic female experience; in the way the gaze is psychoanalytically encoded, the actress and the role are essentially irrelevant, becoming only vehicles to carry the gaze.

Two subsequent episodes within the film's first 15 minutes carry the message of Warshawski/Turner's "to-be-looked-at-ness." When she returns to her apartment (coincidentally finding Murray ensconced without her permission thanks to a stolen key), V.I. takes a bath in an old-fashioned tub. Her first viewer is the film audience, followed in quick succession by Murray, Kat, and Boom Boom himself. The girl's question, "Are you fucking my dad?" reinforces the sexually objectified role Warshawski/Turner has been seen in up to that point, and the parade of gazers through her bathroom intensifies the apparent protagonist's function as a visual fetish.[8] Moments later—after the departure of Murray and Boom Boom followed by a little smart-mouthed kid talk—Kat leaves to find and help her father. Apparently taking her role as detective-baby-sitter-mother seriously, V.I. chases after her—in her underwear and bathrobe. While in a cab, she slips out of the robe and into a dinner dress. (How the dress comes to be in the cab is too silly to explain.) The shot-reverse-shot makes clear the function of this episode: the cabdriver's eyes are seen in the rearview mirror; then, V.I. is seen undressing, in her bra, and slipping on the dress in the back seat; the cabdriver's eyes in the rearview mirror return. When V.I. wisecracks that he's getting a look instead of a tip, the clear implication is that they've made a fair exchange: the body/money economy is satisfied. These four episodes in the early portion of the film establish rapidly and effectively the real function of the hero(ine). While she may call herself a detective, she is there "to-be-looked-at"; anything else is both incidental and coincidental. Because every significant male figure in the film—Murray, her father's old friend Lt. Mallory, Boom Boom's murdering brother, Boom Boom himself, and smalltime crime boss Earl Smeeson—reinforces her status as the representation of a gender role, whether fetish, sex object, or wife/mother, the audience is never allowed to forget the lesson of the introductory scenes. V.I. Warshawski need not act to fulfill her function in this film; she is there to be viewed. She need only appear; it does not matter whether she is seen as V.I. Warshawski, Kathleen Turner, a detective, or a woman, so long as she is "seen."

The point of all this? In Raymond Bellour's analysis of the first scenes of Alfred Hitchcock's *Marnie* and *Psycho*, he draws some conclusions about American films generally: "a number of precise analyses (of Hawkes' films, of Minelli, of Lang, of westerns, of musical comedies, of horror films, films of the fantastic, etc.) show clearly that the central place assigned to the woman is a place where she is figured, represented, inscribed in the fiction through the logical necessity of a general representation of the subject of desire in the film, who is always, first and last, a masculine subject" (Bergstrom 192-93). The desiring subject in *V.I. Warshawski* is no single male protagonist but rather the entire male cast of the film; in this role, they stand in for the entire audience, male in its desire and in its gaze. Neither Sara Paretsky's independent character nor Kathleen Turner's star status nor V.I. Warshawski's lead role can rescue *V.I. Warshawski* from its commercial parameters and its consequent failure.

NOTES

[1]*Glamour* magazine implies that Turner/Warshawski's sartorial shortcomings ("Guns and long-sleeved blouses don't work together" [Krupp]) might have been responsible for the low returns. Their suggestion: "hire Linda Hamilton's trainer."

[2]Paretsky's seventh novel, *Guardian Angel*, was published in January 1992 and undoubtedly available in manuscript during the filming of *V.I. Warshawski*. Its style and content follow the previous novels, signaling no change in Paretsky's focus.

[3]*Popcorn Venus* by Marjorie Rosen (1973), Joan Mellen's *Women and Their Sexuality in the New Film* (1974), and Molly Haskell's *From Reverence to Rape* (1975). Among journals, *Women and Film* was published from 1972 to 1975 and was followed in 1976 by *Camera Obscura*. Among the most influential theoretical articles, Laura Mulvey's "Visual Pleasure and Narrative Cinema," appeared in *Screen* in 1975.

[4]I suspect that this is hardly what Nancy Chodorow had in mind when she emphasizes the "reproduction of mothering" experienced by women.

[5]There is no successful terminology for the woman who has no children; whether stated in the positive or the negative—child-free or child-less—the implication remains that the connection between woman and child is irreducible.

[6]Kat is loosely based on Jill Thayer, a teenage girl who hires V.I. in *Indemnity Only*; Jill, however, plays a minor role in the novel and no role in the investigation. Although Vic is concerned for the girl, she does not take on a maternal role.

[7]The persistent references in hard-boiled novels to women detectives as "female dicks" carry an interesting overtone of castration anxiety when transferred to the fetishized female detective of film.

[8]The emphasis by the camera, the film, and Warshawski on shoes—a conventional fetish object—cannot be overlooked; the red spike heels she slips on in the bar and pushes out into the aisle to trip Boom Boom are a sexually explicit invitation requiring no translation.

WORKS CITED

Benenson, Laurie Halpern. "Kathleen Turner: Going Public as a Private Eye." *New York Times* 14 Apr. 1991: 20.

Bergstrom, Janet. "Alternation, Segmentation, Hypnosis: Interview with Raymond Bellour—An Excerpt." Penley 186-95.

Chodorow, Nancy. *The Reproduction of Mothering: Psychoanalysis and the Sociology of Gender.* Berkeley: U of California P, 1978.

De Lauretis, Teresa. *Alice Doesn't.* Bloomington: Indiana UP, 1984.

Gilbert, Sandra M. and Susan Gubar. *The Madwoman in the Attic: The Woman Writer and the Nineteenth-Century Literary Imagination.* New Haven: Yale UP, 1979.

Haskell, Molly. *From Reverence to Rape: The Treatment of Women in the Movies.* New York: Penguin, 1973.

Kaplan, E. Ann. *Women and Film: Both Sides of the Camera.* London: Methuen, 1983.

Krupp, Charla. "Word On . . . " *Glamour* Dec. 1991: 131.

Kuhn, Annette. *Women's Pictures: Feminism and Cinema.* London: Routledge & Kegan Paul, 1982.

Mellen, Joan. *Women and Their Sexuality in the New Film.* New York: Dell, 1973.

Mulvey, Laura. "Visual Pleasure and Narrative Cinema." Penley 57-68.

Paretsky, Sara. *Deadlock.* New York: Dial, 1984.

____. *Guardian Angel.* New York: Delacorte, 1992.

____. *Indemnity Only.* New York: Dial, 1982.

Penley, Constance, ed. *Feminism and Film Theory.* New York: Routledge, 1988.

Rich, Adrienne. *Of Woman Born: Motherhood as Experience and Institution.* New York: Bantam, 1977.

Rosen, Marjorie. *Popcorn Venus: Women, Movies and the American Dream.* New York: McCann & Geoghegan, 1973.

V.I. Warshawski. Dir. Jeff Kanew. Prod. Jeffrey Lurie. Hollywood Pictures, 1991.

Williams, Linda. "Feminist Film Theory: *Mildred Pierce* and the Second World War." *Female Spectators: Looking at Film and Television.* Ed. E. Deidre Pribram. London: Verso, 1988. 12-30.

Mystery and Horror and the Problems of Adaptation in *Angel Heart* and *Falling Angel*

Sharon A. Russell

William Hjortsberg's Falling Angel *and its film adaptation* Angel Heart *draw from both the* film noir *and fantastic/horror traditions to pose subversive questions about the laws governing the real world. The more modern use of images and their thematic complexity gives the film a depth and unity absent from the novel, but both novel and film remain within the limits of their genres, providing closure rather than fragmentation.*

While the problems associated with adaptation from one media to another have long interested scholars, the theoretical complexities of such translations become more entangled when each version of the work transgresses genre boundaries. In 1987 William Hjortsberg's *Falling Angel* was adapted to film as *Angel Heart*, directed by Alan Parker (who also wrote the screenplay) and produced by Alan Marshall and Elliot Kasner. In an unusual example of the increasing influence of one popular form on another, both novel and film combine cinematic and literary traditions in their exploration of the relationship between horror and mystery.

It is often easy to approach analysis of an adaptation as either the destruction of great literature by a bastard medium (pick any major novel which has been adapted), or the elevation of popular potboiler into cinematic masterpiece (*The Godfather*, for example). But too often such criticism ignores the complex socio-economic factors of the film business at the same time as it misunderstands or misrepresents the inherent strengths and weaknesses of the two art forms. In addition, such criticism also fails to take note of the "high-brow/low-brow" confrontation which the public often perceives as the major problem with any adaptation; that is, people who have read the book see the film as a "classic comic book" for those who won't read. While neither *Falling Angel* nor *Angel Heart* can be characterized as a masterpiece, both have artistic pretensions which mandate that they be considered "serious" explorations of popular tradition.

159

In addition to the direct trajectory of adaptation, *Falling Angel* and *Angel Heart* are also united in their backward look at *film noir*. *Angel Heart* is actually somewhat prescient in its anticipation of the revival of this genre in the later 1980s and 1990s. But while both novel and film begin with the *"noir"* of mystery, both end with the black of magic and Satanism, the black of horror. A comparison of this movement from genre to genre in both the novel and the film focuses the relationship between the two works and the mediums they represent. Both film and novel deliberately create ties to earlier genres in order to play with their conventions in ways which connect them to the modern or even the post-modern traditions.

Given the small number of films which can be categorized as part of it, *film noir* has engendered a great deal of criticism and analysis. While some critics and historians suggest links between the genre and a specific historical period—the United States of the 1940s and 1950s—others like Frank Krutnik identify it through the application of visual or thematic criteria. According to Krutnik, early *noir* films were adaptations of "hard-boiled" novels by such authors as Dashiell Hammett, Raymond Chandler, and James M. Cain; the name itself comes from the "série *noir*" translations of such novels as *The Maltese Falcon*; *Murder, My Sweet*; and *Double Indemnity* published by Marcel Duhamel in France (15). Krutnik also points out that the 1947 film *Out of the Past* already "relies upon a knowledge of the 'hard-boiled' private-detective thriller precisely as a conventionalized Hollywood cycle . . ." (27). As *noir* films became more available to post-war audiences, the hard-boiled form became still more familiar; and gradually the narrative style of the novel became influenced by that of the film.

The hard-boiled mystery began, of course, as a reaction to the carefully plotted classical mystery novel produced by such writers as Agatha Christie and S.S. Van Dine. But Krutnik shows that stylistic shifts in this genre are also linked to Hollywood's narrative tradition. Like *noir* films, hard-boiled novels demonstrate a "narrative drive which propels the reader/spectator through a series of connected episodes" (40) and, in addition, can be seen as "reactions against the contemplative mode of the 'literary'" (40). "The question of the 'hard-boiled' influence upon *film noir* should not, then, be conceived solely in terms of what the films drew from the books. Rather it seems that 'hard-boiled' fiction was in itself a particular response to the influence of the cinema as the most innovative mode of storytelling in the modern age" (41). In addition to dealing with techniques such as the cinematic flashback which also exist in the hard-boiled novel (42), Krutnik shows that similar thematic parallels also exist, emphasizing concern with the hero's identity as a unified masculine subject as a feature shared by both film and novel (42).

The structural and thematic interdependence of the hard-boiled novel and the *noir* film has not deteriorated over time, and even in their most recent manifestations there is little of the self-referential parody found in other genres sharing common origins. The latest versions of the *noir*/hard-boiled form still take the basic concerns of the genre seriously. The absence of parody is both an indication of the continued viability of the genre and a validation of the importance of its themes for successive generations of readers and viewers.

But while the hard-boiled novel has continued to demonstrate vitality throughout its unbroken history, the *noir* film reemerged relatively recently and still makes only sporadic appearances. The novel's continued growth is evidenced by the predominance of contemporary locations and characters; on the other hand, many films of the 1970s and 1980s recreate or remake the past in tone and image. Recent films and novels retain certain basic themes, but few recent *noir* films contain the unusual generic combinations found at the height of the form's development. As Krutnik points out, the early *noir* films presented greater potential for the expansion of the genre because such expansion was indicative of both the fashionable "high brow" influence of German Expressionism and the artistic aspirations of directors who wanted to cross over into more profitable major productions with important studios (21).

More specifically, Krutnik indicates that unions of *noir* horror and fantasy were popular in the 1940s (26). Such combinations might, in fact, be one of the sources for the hard-boiled/horror combination in *Falling Angel*, since such generic transgressions are not a strong part of the tradition of the hard-boiled novel. However, now that the influence of German Expressionism has disappeared, generic transformations are not a part of the *noir* revival, and the mixture of genres may actually be one of the reasons for *Angel Heart*'s lack of commercial success. Viewers expect a return to the past to be a recreation of a collective memory of what was rather than an accurate recreation of the contradictions of a vital form. The only successful recent revival of visual elements of German Expressionism occurs in the recent work of Tim Burton who unites horror, fantasy, and adventure in his Batman films. Of course, once

Angel Heart appeared, *Falling Angel* (more of a *succès d'estime* than a popular hit when it was first published) came to be thought of as a great masterpiece destroyed through adaptation. Actually both works have problems—some shared, some unique to each medium.

The principal components of both works are, of course, the interdependent thematic elements of *film noir* and hard-boiled fiction. Central among these themes in both *Falling Angel* and *Angel Heart* is the role of the hero. Krutnik identifies three categories which detail the hero's relationship to his mission and its consequences for "the legally defined framework of law and to the law of the patriarchy which specifies the culturally acceptable positions (and the delimitation of) masculine identity and desire" (86). These are

> (i) *the investigative thriller*, where the hero . . . seeks to restore order—and to validate his own identity—by exposing and countermanding a criminal conspiracy.
>
> (ii) *the male suspense thriller*, which is the inverse of the above, in that the hero is in a position of marked inferiority, in regard both to the criminal conspirators and to the police, and seeks to restore himself to a position of security by eradicating the enigma.
>
> (iii) *the criminal adventure thriller*, where the hero . . . has to face the consequences of stepping out of line. (86)

Krutnik is referring specifically to the films of the 1940s in these categories. The first category is the one most applicable to the hard-boiled detective novel and one of its prototypes, *The Maltese Falcon*. *Falling Angel* and *Angel Heart* clearly fall into the second; examples of the third are *The Postman Always Rings Twice* (novel and film) and *The Lady from Shanghai*. He later writes of "tough" thrillers which while "seeking ostensibly to dramatise a positive trajectory—the affirmation of masculine identity and the right of 'male law' . . . tend to subject this to a series of inversions, delays, and schisms" (88-89).

In works of the second type, Krutnik suggests, the failure of the hero is the "source of fascination" (128). These films exhibit the desire to fail and a loss of confidence in masculine authority. "This 'problematising' of the hero as a viable position of narrative authority mirrors and distorts a series of cultural schisms in the relations between men and women, between men themselves, between men and their social world, and within the male psyche"

(129). In these films the hero is either falsely accused of a murder or suffers from amnesia and cannot remember whether or not he is involved (132). The world of this type of film is the world of the fractured hero, a hero trying to solve the riddle of his identity at the same time that he must attempt to unite the fragments of his own personality. These films, like the novels from which they are adapted, are not parts of series. Their central characters are too damaged to provide sequels.

In addition to the image of the fractured masculine hero of the *film noir* tradition, *Falling Angel* and *Angel Heart* also contain elements of the fantastic. In *Fantasy: The Literature of Subversion*, Rosemary Jackson argues: "Any social structure tends to exclude as 'evil' anything radically different from itself. . . . Strangeness precedes the naming of it as evil: the other is defined as evil precisely because of his/her difference and a possible power to disturb the familiar and the known" (52-53). Jackson also suggests that modern fantasy has shifted its view of the demonic from external to internal sources: "The demonic is not supernatural, but is an aspect of personal and interpersonal life, a manifestation of unconscious desire" (55). This internalization of evil breaks down the clear barriers between good and evil. "In the modern fantastic, this desire [a negative version of the desire for the infinite] expresses itself as a violent transgression of all human limitations and social taboos prohibiting the realization of desire" (57). Jackson sees modern fantasy as a force for liberation because of its ability to demonstrate the limits of the real. "Structurally and semantically, the fantastic aims at dissolution of an order experienced as oppressive and insufficient" (180).

In *Angel Heart* and *Falling Angel*, both *noir* and fantasy elements operate in the plot but are concentrated in the figure of the central character. While there are significant stylistic differences between novel and film, the basic plot and narrative structure remain the same. Harry Angel is hired by the enigmatic Louis Cyphre to trace a missing person, Johnny Favorite, a popular singer of the 1940s. Drafted and injured during the war, Johnny was brought home a vegetable. Now, 16 years later, he is supposed to be in a private hospital, and Louis Cyphre wants Harry to find him. Accounts of the meeting between Cyphre and Harry differ slightly between novel and film. In the novel Harry meets Cyphre for lunch at 666 Fifth Avenue. In the film the meeting takes place in a church in Harlem. Harry's search for the missing Johnny seems to follow the traditional structure of the genre. He goes to the hospital where

Johnny was placed after being diagnosed as suffering from shell shock. While novel and film differ in detail, Harry finds out that Johnny has been transferred, and he contacts the doctor who signed the transfer order. Harry tries to interview the doctor (a drug addict), leaves him locked in a bedroom to go cold turkey, and returns to the locked room and finds him murdered. Only the film deals with how Harry passes his time during the interval between the two visits to the doctor's house. The sequence starts with the shadow of a fan on the doctor's bed and continues with the sound of heartbeats and Harry's whispered name on the soundtrack. Harry opens the door to a church and sees two African-American nuns, but when he looks again they are gone. The scene shifts abruptly to a closeup of a hand and a key and cuts to an establishing shot of Harry in a diner. Both film and novel end this section with Harry's discovery of the dead body and then go on to trace the rest of Harry's investigation.

All the important sources Harry locates and interviews are murdered. The interval between the questioning of a subject and Harry's discovery of the person's body is left vague in the novel and indicated in the film through recurrent series of religious images, flashes from the past, heartbeats, and whispers. Harry discovers information about two women who were important to Johnny: Evangeline Proudfoot, his secret love and mother of his daughter (Epiphany), and Margaret Krusemark, his fiancée. Evangeline, who died before Harry's investigation, was an herbalist deeply involved in voodoo, and Margaret is experienced in satanic ritual. In the novel, Margaret's father is also involved in the worship of Satan. Harry learns that Johnny, with the help of Margaret, made a pact with the devil, offering his soul in exchange for success. Later, Margaret and Johnny tried to cheat the devil by switching Johnny's soul with that of another person, a soldier of the same age and sign, in a complex ritual. During the ritual Johnny ate the soldier's heart. The plan was for Johnny to disappear and then reappear as the soldier with access to the singer's money, hidden all over the world. But before Johnny could carry out this part of the plan, he was shipped out and came back unable to remember how to complete the ritual. A year after his return, Margaret and her father bribed a doctor, and took Johnny from the hospital to Times Square on New Year's Eve, the time and place of the initial encounter with the soldier. They left Johnny and somehow the ritual was completed. The big surprise is that Harry was the soldier who became Johnny. Harry is investigating himself.

In addition to having circular plots in which events fold back on themselves, both *Falling Angel* and *Angel Heart* explore a double past. On one level they describe events which occurred some time ago but are now resurfacing to affect the present—a persistent theme of both *film noir* and the hard-boiled novel. On another level, both works set their story in a period earlier than the creation of the work: the America of *film noir*.

The novel begins by making a direct reference to yet another kind of time: "It was Friday the thirteenth and yesterday's snowstorm lingered in the streets like a leftover curse" (1), establishing immediately the motifs of bad luck and coincidence which haunt it. The novel continues with a series of Times Square headlines reporting various events of the period. The first deals with Hawaii's statehood, giving the reader the year of the novel, 1959. The film indicates the time by superimposing "New York 1955" over the first image of Harry. The period is reinforced through the use of decor, clothing, and transportation. However, after the credit sequence, the film uses a different kind of cinematic time to suggest its attitude toward Harry. As Harry walks down the street, the audience hears on the sound track a phone ringing, anticipating his arrival at his office where he answers the phone and responds to the call that sets the plot in motion. From the beginning, Harry's life is predetermined by the cinematic conjunction of sight and sound. In the novel the reader may anticipate events through a personal reading; in the film the viewer's advantage over Harry is dictated by its organization. The editing controls Harry, leaving no possibility for him to control his destiny.

Both novel and film proceed as traditional searches for the missing person. Of course, no experienced viewer or reader expects merely a simple tracking of a World War II veteran. However, in these works the traditions of the genre are not confirmed even by conventional investigations of the initial problem. In both novel and film, Harry Angel's path leads him back to his own past, to the knowledge that he and Johnny Favorite are actually the same person, linked by the satanic ritual performed by Johnny to cheat the devil of his soul. But Louis Cyphre does not lose. Harry, who is also Johnny, becomes trapped in a series of murders. Every lead is destroyed after one of Harry's visits. Using a detective to discover a trail or to help a criminal cover tracks is not uncommon. But this trail leads not to the discovery of the criminal and the restoration of order but to the confusion of identities created through black magic. Ultimately the devil must be given his due, even though it is never clear if the murderer is Harry, acting as Johnny, or Cyphre.

Falling Angel suggests the presence of the supernatural by placing a page opposite the title containing strange symbols identified at the end of the novel—the signatures of the seven demons. The choice of Friday the 13th for its opening reinforces the presence of the supernatural, no matter how playful the presentation. The film opens with an anonymous murder in an alley and an exchange between a cat and dog. Both novel and film continue with Harry's phone call from Winesap, a lawyer, which sets up his first meeting with Louis Cyphre. The humorous use of names seems to be an homage to the wise-cracking style of the genre. And the initial stages of the investigation which include off-beat characters who provide a series of clues add to this tone. But dreams and visions intrude in both works, hinting at subjects outside genre traditions.

Heroes can certainly have nightmares, and Krutnik indicates that such set pieces often occur in film noir. "During the 1940's, and particularly within the generic space of the 'tough' crime thriller, such sequences represented a standardised means of simultaneously signifying and siphoning-off excess" (20). But in these later re-visions of the genre, dreams deal with more than just the day's residue. They provide obscure clues to Harry's actions and his possible involvement in the crimes he investigates. While Hjortsberg's visions always remain connected to Harry, Parker's set pieces repeat certain motifs such as sounds and images of prisons, fan blades, and elevators, reflecting on Harry's circumstances as they relate to larger images of hell.

The novel presents black magic as a series of clues which ultimately bring Harry to an understanding of his dual identity. He witnesses a voodoo ritual performed by Epiphany Proudfoot, his lover and daughter, and he photographs Ethan Krusemark's involvement in a Black Mass. In addition, Hjortsberg plays with names and numbers when Cyphre and Johnny meet—666 Fifth Avenue, for example. But in Angel Heart Parker substitutes threatening religious imagery for much of Hjortsberg's Satanism; humorous references to black magic are subordinated to a variety of traditional religious images and references to voodoo which operates as an authentic African-American religion as opposed to the kind of Reverend-Ike charlatanism Harry witnesses in the Harlem church where he meets Cyphre. Harry visits a Harlem church twice and experiences recurring images of the blood of a suicide being washed off the walls. His second visit occurs after he has agreed to continue with the case. He discovers elements of a voodoo ritual behind closed doors and is chased by members into the street just as he is about to touch a mysterious woman dressed in black seated alone in the church. As he escapes he runs into a procession and bumps into men holding a platform and chair. The minister who falls off the chair into the crowd is the same man he had seen in his first visit, the false prophet trying to get money from believers. Just before the first murder Harry sees an open church with two African-American nuns seated in the doorway. When he looks again, they are gone. Images of nuns recur as part of his visions. Late in the narrative Cyphre and Harry meet in a traditional church. Harry is the one who expresses his discomfort with the setting, just one of his phobias. The film also presents images of voodoo rituals associated with Epiphany, and, toward the end, the voodoo ritual becomes an orgy just before Harry understands his true identity.

But the true force of the fantastic in both film and novel does not reside in the ritual trappings of religion and black magic. As Tzvetan Todorov suggests, moments of hesitation between the worlds of reality and the marvelous, moments when nothing is certain for hero or audience, define the locus of the fantastic. Harry/Johnny can only resolve his dilemma through acceptance of his past and the duality of his identity. The reader or viewer's hesitation is not resolved: Who is the reliable narrator? Who really committed the murders? Did Cyphre force Harry to kill his own past? How do the murders fit into the time frame of the works? Rather than the traditional closure which explains how the crimes were committed and by whom, both the novel and its cinematic adaptation end with Cyphre's solution, his presentation of Johnny's identity shift and how it was achieved. In both works the solution provided by the police only adds an ironic note. They tell Harry he will burn for these murders. We join Harry in his knowledge of the site of that burning—hell.

The introduction of the fantastic complicates the *noir* hero's quest for identity and his attempt to restore his sense of a unified male self and the security that position entails. The traditional solution of the enigma reaffirms the patriarchal rule of the law. However, as Krutnik suggests, in the "tough" suspense thriller the search for identity and the suspense generated by delays in achieving this resolution become the focus of the work. "Indeed, it can even be claimed that these films principally manifest a fascination with the process of resisting (thereby raising the possibility of sidestepping) the conventional Oedipal closure of narrative, of suspending Oedipal law" (131). If the "tough" thriller already has problems in restoring the law of the father, a resolution which is often achieved through the hero's choice of solitude or death, the addition of elements of the fantastic problematizes the whole recuperative project.

Falling Angel and *Angel Heart* force a reconsideration of the *noir*/hard-boiled genre with their introduction of the fantastic, and the incorporation of a modern Faust story into this genre further complicates the problem of restoring order. When evil lies within the character, it cannot be eradicated without also destroying the host. Louis Cyphre may be the agent, but, in the story, Johnny Favorite ate Harry Angel's heart in a ritual designed to cheat the devil through a transfer of souls. While Cyphre is able to force a resolution of his problem, making Johnny/Harry keep his bargain, he does not provide an answer to the riddles posed by the introduction of the fantastic. Instead, Cyphre's ending only foregrounds the questions raised by the presence of the fantastic. There is no way to assign ultimate responsibility for the evil events. And without responsibility there can be no law, no resolution. Furthermore, the absence of resolution must call into question the efficacy of the patriarchal law as an agent of order. The ultimate examples of the failure of the law are the last murder committed, the murder of an innocent, and a transgression of the Oedipal order.

Epiphany Proudfoot is the product of a union between Johnny Favorite and Evangeline Proudfoot, herbalist and voodoo priestess. When she and Harry become lovers, Oedipus is recast as Electra. Epiphany, non-Christian believer in voodoo or Obeah, is the only innocent to die. She is the focus of much of the disturbance of patriarchal law in both novel and film. And her representation is also the location of the major differences between the two. Epiphany threatens the stability of the narrative on two levels: gender and race.

Epiphany's race is not a problem for the hero in either work. But she does become the occasion for racial slurs by the police in both novel and film. In *Falling Angel* she pretends to be the maid when the police come to question Harry. One of them comments, "Jungle bunnies. . . . They never should have let 'em out of the watermelon patch" (161). The comparable scene in *Angel Heart* takes place in a hotel room in New Orleans. This time the detectives see Epiphany in bed and make racist comments. The placement of both film and novel in the past permits the underscoring of racial difference at the same time that it locates the problem in an earlier time. In one sense the film further distances the problem by shifting the scene from New York to New Orleans when Harry follows Margaret's trail there. Prejudice is easily associated with southern attitudes; its presence in the north would be more disturbing to the reader of the novel in the late 1970s. However, the film's images of racism have a different impact than the verbal descriptions of the novel. In *Falling Angel*, readers find it easy to reject Johnny's racist remarks; since he is bad, racism must also be bad. But the film's visual approach allows viewers to see the effects of racism for themselves.

In *Falling Angel* the scene where Epiphany plays maid is followed by one in which she translates a Latin invitation to a Black Mass, courtesy of her education at Sacred Heart High School. In the library she also helps Harry investigate other aspects of black magic. In both novel and film she has taken over the herb store from her mother and runs it successfully. It might seem that the novel is stronger in its portrayal of the negative effects of racial conflict. But the scenes proving Epiphany is educated can be read as presenting her as the exception: Epiphany is one African-American who has made it. In the film she first appears barefoot and poor, putting an offering on her mother's grave accompanied by her child, a perfect stereotype. But by presenting this stereotype the film forces the audience to confront it. In addition, the complexity of Harry and Epiphany's relationship is conveyed in the explicit images of interracial sex which force members of the audience to confront one of their deepest fears about the consequences of integration. In both novel and film she leads a voodoo ritual with strong sexual expression. However, the film is far more explicit in all its sex scenes. Those between her and Harry actually appear in two versions, the theatrical and "uncut" video releases. The extended scene disturbs the narrative because it stands out stylistically from the rest of the film. Frank sexuality is not part of the fifties film which usually omits sex scenes or severely limits them. However, one of the marks of modern film *noir*—even a remake like *The Postman Always Rings Twice* which challenges rather than affirms the status quo—is their emphasis on explicit sex. Other than the orgy and Harry and Ephiphany's love-making there are no other sex scenes in *Angel Heart*.

The simulation of intercourse in recent *noir* films in general and *Angel Heart* in particular is especially disruptive because the threats to male identity are often located in male-female relationships. The scenes in *Angel Heart* threaten the patriarchy on two levels. First, they depict a positive interracial sexual relationship. Neither novel nor film deals directly with the negative encounter between Johnny and Evangeline which produced Epiphany. But the intercourse depicted in *Angel Heart* is a transgression against the norms of the time period and location established in the film and contains the implicit suggestion that such actions would not be condemned by the modern audience. The complexities inherent in a return to the past with modern attitudes are reinforced by the frequent use of Harlem settings in the first half of the film. Harry and Cyphre seem to be at ease in all locations. Harry fits everywhere because he fits nowhere. However, he does not like the traditional church where they meet toward the end of the film, an indication of the reintegration of Johnny into Harry's identity. Cyphre can go anywhere because he belongs to another world. The two men are beyond the societal conflicts represented by the tensions of interracial sex. But the viewer sees these actions played out in a fictional past through modern eyes. If interracial sex is no longer a transgression of societal norms, white male-African-American female sex/murder recalls an even darker historical past.

The first transgression leads directly to the second, from the social order to the disruption of natural order: a sexual relationship between parent and child. In both film and novel the Oedipal conflict is reversed. The daughter has intercourse with the father. And in both the law of the father ultimately prevails, punishing the transgression. Epiphany is killed by Harry's gun, shot in the vagina. As the policeman in the novel bluntly states, "We've got all we need, unless that's not your .38 stuck up her snatch" (242). Almost the same words appear in the film. Harry is caught not by one of the motivated murders, one of the murders which would cover his past, but by the murder of one whom he loves both as daughter and lover. It is precisely the transgressive duality of that love that destroys them both.

In *Angel Heart* the extended love scene is intercut with images of rain turning to blood in the hotel room. Harry and Epiphany's relationship, a reversal of the Oedipal pattern, reverses the usual effect of water. Before Harry meets Cyphre he sees water cleanse a wall of blood; in an early encounter with Epiphany she is washing her hair; Toots Sweet, one of the victims, sings about a rainy day. It often rains in New Orleans, but water has lost its power to clean. It turns to blood. Of course, blood is also associated with the ritual sacrifices of many religions and most specifically in these works with the black magic of Johnny's transformation and Epiphany's voodoo dance and killing a rooster.

It is also Epiphany's death that moves both novel and film into the realm of the fantastic outside the logic of the questions posed by the *noir* genre. Both novel and film contain images of Harry almost strangling Epiphany while they make love, and Epiphany's murder itself is preceded by the final revelations of Harry's conversation with Cyphre in which his true past is revealed. Harry finds his dog tags in Margaret's rooms. In the film, Cyphre's revelations lead to Harry's confrontation with his own image in the mirror in Margaret's apartment and his ultimate questioning of his identity. Cyphre says the words which are the epigram for the novel, a quotation from Sophocles's *Oedipus the King*, "Alas how terrible is wisdom when it brings no profit to the man that's wise" (vii). In both novel and film, Cyphre appears to take both the gun which will kill Epiphany and the dog tags which will be found around her neck. His final confrontation with Harry takes place in the detective's office in the novel, and he magically removes Harry's dog tags from his own pocket even though they are in Harry's pocket when he leaves the apartment. In *Angel Heart* the audience sees Harry's visualization of the other murders as he confronts the simultaneous integration and disintegration of his identity. Cyphre plays one of Johnny's records in the background and leaves with Harry's dog tags and gun. But this seeming resolution of the mysteries leads only to the final introduction of the fantastic. How can Harry kill Epiphany with a gun taken by Cyphre? How can she be wearing his dog tags? It is this "impossible" murder which finally traps him.

While the endings of both works are similar, the film's ability to show images beyond the real world of the *noir* alters its impact on the viewer. In *Falling Angel* when Cyphre confronts Harry with the final revelations about his identity, Harry tells him to "Kiss my ass!" (237); Cyphre replies, "No need for that, Johnny. . . . You've already kissed mine" (237). Harry chases after him with a hidden .45. When he arrives at the elevator Cyphre has taken, it is empty. The reader's hesitation lies in an acceptance of the reliability of Harry's perceptions. In the film, Cyphre's revelation is accompanied by the image of his supernaturally glowing eyes, an image of the fantastic. The final scene in the novel is followed closely in the film. Most of the dialogue is repeated, but the film adds several images. At the end of the scene in the hotel room, a detective is holding

Epiphany's child, and the young boy's eyes glow like those of Cyphre, underscoring the absence of any resolution of the questions posed by the fantastic. This scene is followed by a sequence intercut with the end credits. The elevator images in the film are brought to closure with a series of shots of descent, culminating in images of Harry in the elevator. At the very end of the film, the wheels stop turning, and the elevator is stationary. It has brought Harry to his final destination.

The coherence of these final images once again calls into question the visual patterns of the film. They are a final reminder of the presence of the fantastic. These images seem to make sense, but the viewer recalls the fragments present through the rest of the film and must try to decide whether they indicate the expected closure which is part of the genre. They indicate Harry's descent, but his fall is outside the logic of the *noir* film. These images generate new questions. The resolution of the murder, the restoration of order, lies outside the laws of the father, beyond the logic of the patriarchy. It is only in the realm of the fantastic that Harry's identity is revealed and is unified, a confirmation of the internal nature of modern evil. If evil is a part of Harry's "angelic" nature, evil cannot be conquered, and the order of the patriarchy is no order at all.

The absence of many of these fantastic elements from the novel allows for a stronger possibility for the restitution of order. At the end of *Falling Angel* Harry sees the policeman's smile and says, "There was only one other smile like it: the evil leer of Lucifer. I could almost hear His laughter fill the room. This time the joke was on me" (243). The novel does not abandon its re-creation of the tone of the hard-boiled model, and Harry's words can be read as the typical ironic comment of the hard-boiled hero. The police have caught him, and he must live with the consequences, with his failures.

The introduction of the fantastic into novel and film is a subversive gesture; a questioning of the real leads to a questioning of all laws governing the real world. The fantastic elements connected to the plot force confrontations with societal attitudes towards race and sex not usually presented openly in the *noir* genre. However, neither novel nor film is a traditional example of the fantastic. While fantastic fiction often returns to an earlier time, the historical gap between the time period covered by the novel and its publication date is not very great. The issues raised in *Falling Angel* are undercut by a style that verges on the pastiche or a clever trick. The film uses modern editing techniques to integrate the fantastic into the *noir*. These techniques keep the viewer off balance, heightening the impact of the fantastic. The hard-boiled tradition of the novel weakens the impact of the fantastic and lessens the importance of its exploration of the fragmentation of masculinity and the ensuing critique of society. The more modern use of images and their thematic complexity gives the film a depth and unity absent from the novel. The images of the fantastic in *Angel Heart* also give greater weight to its social critique. The viewer is drawn into an experience of the fantastic unavailable to the reader of the novel. But both novel and film remain within the limits of their genre, providing a kind of closure, and the differences are only of degree.

WORKS CITED

Hjortsberg, William. *Falling Angel*. New York: Harcourt Brace Jovanovich, 1978.

Jackson, Rosemary. *Fantasy: The Literature of Subversion*. London: Methuen, 1981.

Krutnik, Frank. *In a Lonely Street: Film Noir, Genre, Masculinity*. New York: Routledge. 1991.

Parker, Alan, dir. *Angel Heart*. Prod. Alan Marshall and Elliot Kasner. CAROLCO. 1987.

Scott Turow's *Presumed Innocent*: Novel and Film—Multifaceted Character Study versus Tailored Courtroom Drama

Andrew and Gina Macdonald

Scott Turow's Presumed Innocent *combines mystery and suspense with style and vision to produce a riveting plot and furnish penetrating analyses of the justice system, family life, and the limits of knowledge. Despite impressive vignettes, sharp characterization, and captivating suspense, the film adaptation fails to suggest psychological complications or capture the double vision and complexity which become evident at the end of the novel.*

Fictional representations of legal culture tend toward the melodramatic or, alternatively, the drily technical. Clearly, legal conflict involves both human drama and legal nicety, yet few writers are able to capture these opposite poles in readable prose. Scott Turow is an exception, particularly owing to his technical skill, which allows him to demonstrate the full range of legal perspectives in even simple questions of procedure, and his mastery of classic metaphor, a linguistic talent which permits him to explore the full interpretive range of emotions and thoughts both in the courtroom and out. While capturing the theatrical fireworks inherent in courtroom confrontation, there is no hint of the Perry Masonesque clichés which falsify so much of the rendering of legal conflict; rather, the reader gets the sense of human, rather than simply legal, maneuver, with the courtroom as just another playing field for the human need to gain advantage.

As a result of its obvious virtues, Turow's *Presumed Innocent* was an enormous success with the general reading public. It was 44 weeks on the best-seller list, sold 712,000 hard-cover copies in the U.S., and set new records for the publishing business in paper-back sales—an initial $3 million (a first-novel first) plus royalties from 18 foreign language editions. Critics also praised the book in terms usually reserved for far more esoteric and rarified works. Anne Rice says that it "transcends the murder-mystery genre . . . with an

175

elegant style and philosophical voice" and with characters "wonderfully realized." She calls it "ambitious and absorbing, the work of a profoundly gifted writer with a fine, distinctive voice." Superlatives abound in the critical reactions; for instance, Robert Donahugh praises the novel as "superbly crafted, wonderfully written"; he mentions the novel's "flesh-and-blood people and . . . thoughtful inside look at criminal and trial procedures," concluding that it is "an absolutely first-rate book . . . a great book." The adverbs and adjectives are unusual in their unqualified positive force, and these reviews are representative.

The film version stars the eminently bankable Harrison Ford, a crowd-pleasing actor perhaps best known for *Raiders of the Lost Ark* and its progeny, yet also often praised for the seriousness and intensity of his performance in films like *Witness*. Ford as Rusty Sabich is backed by a superb cast, including Bonnie Bedelia as Sabich's wife; Raul Julia as Sandy Stern, Sabich's Argentine defense counsel; Brian Dennehy as the district attorney; Paul Winfield as the judge; and Greta Scacchi as the murder victim. The director, Alan Pakula, met the challenge of adaptation with careful attention to detail, choosing a Detroit courthouse for exterior shots, Newark for early court scenes and the climactic trial, and an elaborate set which meticulously reproduced a Cleveland building. Director and star spent a week at the Detroit prosecutor's office observing a real-life murder case and studying its intricacies. The lines of the script, carefully selected for their economy, force, and character revelation, derive almost word for word from the text (the exceptions being speeches by Carolyn Polhemus's ex-husband, who replaces a son found in the novel, and the revelatory lines of Barbara Sabich in the final surprise ending). In fact, in an August 1993 *Playboy* interview, Turow describes a trailer clip from the film as "in every way the realization of what I had in my mind in terms of color, the way the characters interacted, the way Harrison Ford was behaving on the screen" ("20 Questions" 132). In other words, the film had every possible opportunity to duplicate the success of the novel on which it was based.

Yet *Presumed Innocent* on celluloid was at best a lukewarm success with audiences, and critical reviews were mixed, with even the positive reviews including a note of restraint. *Time* reviewer Richard Schickel called the movie a "slow burner" with a "portentous, not to say pretentious, air," and, though he praised some excellent acting, found its "lift . . . not enough to overcome its drag and get it airborne." John Pym of *Sight & Sound* missed the "sharpness of mind [of characters] which Turow describes," while David Denby of *New York* magazine was disturbed by the film's lack of "voice" and "personality." Such critical reservations about the film suggest that *Presumed Innocent* makes an excellent case study of the perils of moving from print to a visual medium, and the relative failures that can result. Precisely because it had everything going for it, this film raises questions as to what we value in the text as a "literary" experience, and what might make that construct of meaning and emotion satisfy in a visual medium.

Turow's *Presumed Innocent* is a complex, tightly bound psychological study that depends on point of view and characteri- zation, reinforced by metaphor, to explore the multifaceted nature of reality, to question the simplistic patterns of courtroom "justice," and to suggest the difficulty man (and more particularly his institutions) has in discovering even simple truths. The movie version, in contrast, is obviously limited to visible screen action. In effect, then, what in the novel is a careful and complex analysis of a clever, cynical man, caught up in the justice system, seemingly unburdening his soul of his fears and doubts, yet really remaining devious, a consummate politician, manipulative and never totally reliable, becomes in the movie a straightforward study of a rather naive and gullible "innocent," caught up in a plot whose origin remains hidden from viewers until the surprise revelation at the end. Setting and names of characters aside, novel and film are dramatically different stories, partly as an inevitable result of the shift in medium, but largely as a consequence of decisions made by the filmmakers, who seem unwilling or unable to reconstitute the thematic and affective intricacies of the book in their constrained, but equally powerful, medium. *Presumed Innocent* alternately demonstrates the peril of incomplete commitment to and trust in the capability of film to do what prose does, but in a different creative idiom.

Turow himself, quoting actor Brian Dennehy, sees one problem as length: "A movie of a novel is an abridgement. *Presumed Innocent* . . . [is] as good as the best *Reader's Digest* abridgement of a novel could be" ("20 Questions" 132). A scriptwriter must cut and inevitably, for a long, complex novel, those cuts involve reducing the number of characters and removing literary approaches difficult to transfer to the screen without too many awkward voice- overs or possibly confusing flashbacks: the background explana- tions, the philosophizing, the private brooding, psychological twists, and interior self-justifications. In this case, scriptwriters Frank

Pierson and Alan Pakula rightly opted to cut as a diversionary side issue Turow's concern with broad genetic patterns traceable in Sabich from his philandering immigrant father and reflected in his adored but troubled son. They capture the close professional relationship of Lipranzer and Sabich but totally cut Sabich's macho posturing and games-playing in his final man-to-man confrontation with/confession to that close friend, though in doing so they lose character complexity. The question with cuts, necessary though they are, must always be: what is lost? and what is the thin line of balance between too much cutting and too little?

However, script cuts are not the only changes in the move from novel to film. Character in a film is simply not created in the same way as is character in a novel. The film, of necessity, focuses on outward appearances, the novel on inner "reality," or at least inner phenomena. In Turow's novel, readers are so caught up in the musings of the first-person narrator that the way others see him is overwhelmed by our secret, personal knowledge of his reality; in the film, viewers react to the central character directly, from the outside, based on his overt behavior, relying in part for their judgment on the way that the other characters in the film respond to him. This "documentary realism" approach might approximately convey the issues and emotions of some novels, but not this one. In the novel, readers experience Rusty Sabich's biting internal analysis of the motives and history of those around him, the hidden motivations behind their overt acts; in the film we have only the present reality and the power of the actors or actresses to convey personality and character—what is not visible or audible remains unknown and unknowable.

Whereas the film must depend on body language—facial expressions, gestures—and verbal exchanges to give a sense of character and relationships, the novel can tailor the readers' responses and focus their observations. For example, throughout the book Turow is cynical about personal morality and legal process, and he communicates this cynicism through descriptive imagery. He describes the grand-jury room as "something like a small theater" (154), the witness stand as "a glass-and-steel cage" (194), and the internal courtroom processes as so "hedged in by the formalities of the rules of evidence," that "the truthfinding system cuts off the corners on half of what is commonly known" (292). Outside the courtroom Turow focuses on the "the churning mass" (50) of curious spectators, the "beehive of illicit dealing" (374) that constitutes police activities, and the "Medici"-like "intrigue" in which every "secret allegiance in the community comes to bear" (94) as "all the two thousand guys in blue play it for their own team" (95). Sabich calls the intricate relationships in the prosecutor's office "tangled webs" and argues that "it would require an archaeological dig to get through the sedimentary layers of resentments built up over the years" (363). Witnesses and attorneys for the prosecution are "cold as a saber's edge" (263), "Medici like" (394), "sheep" (106) with "noble poker face[s]" (56); one has "a pygmy in his soul" (16); another is "like a whipped dog" (239) with "a molten-hot personality" and "a gimlet-eyed cleverness" (317). In court, the latter "considers his armaments and reaches for the nuclear bomb" (364). And the press is "blind as ever to half tones or grays" (370). The judge in the case, Larren Lyttle, with his "princely style of oratory" (196), is "like a chieftain or a Mafia don" who owes the accused some protection while he is "in his domain" (199).

The milieu of the novel is thus rendered so complex and interrelated, so much a matter of surface and hidden substance, that our view of Rusty as a successful navigator of the human maelstrom is inevitably respectful and trusting, even when he seems less than forthcoming. Theaters, beehives, tangled webs, churning masses— at least in the imagery, the canvas is full of writhing human figures, a Diego Rivera mural of the type adorning 1930's vintage courthouses, with incidental choruses by Brueghel. Rusty Sabich's city is a tough American immigrant town, one whose rules of the game he has learned to turn to his advantage. Sabich describes himself as large and squat, with "a Neanderthal ridge over the eyes" (120), a tough Slav who has made it in his city through the school of rough experience. That Sabich has thrived in this setting makes readers expect him to control and conquer difficult events through his political savvy and his manipulation of the legal procedure and the legal personalities around him. Powerful though such images are in the book and vital though they are to characterization and interpretation, they are part of what is lost in the film—whose attitude is far more respectful and proper; in fact, the text's imagery is often in direct opposition to the seemingly sacrosanct court of the film version. In the film, the director relies only on gesture, tone, and mannerism to convey the fallibility of the characters in a setting whose venerable solidity signals its legitimacy. An exchange of glances between judge and defense lawyer or the judge's tone in questioning a move by the prosecution must speak volumes. However, in this production such substitutes for imagery never forcefully accomplish the cynical counterpoint provided in the novel.

Though film, like its distant relative theater, is often a medium for the exploration of character, its approach to human strength and weakness is through a different formula than the literary. One obvious difference is the necessity of casting. As Rusty, Harrison Ford brings with him all the baggage of his many previous roles, from *Raiders* to *Blade Runner*, and in ineffable ways this history shapes our judgment of the kind of man Rusty is supposed to be. Ford, for all his talent, is no squat Neanderthal; he is a finesse player, brutal when necessary, but ultimately civilized and ironic. He never strikes the right balance between physicality and intelligence, remaining "owlish" and "cranky" in Richard Schickel's words. Second, the mental landscape created by Rusty's internal musings is simply impossible to render visually, and fits poorly with Ford's usual understated acting style, which here is almost stolid. The film medium, even with occasional voice-over commentary, simply can't accommodate the plenitude that comes across in the novel, whose extra hours of reading time (compared to the viewer's two hours) gives it an unassailable advantage in subtlety and shading. In the book, the reader is constantly caught up in a seething volcano of passions that renders Rusty human and vulnerable, but that also reveals power and drive, hatred and cynicism, expertise and exterior control, intellectual rigor and resourcefulness. In the film we see only Harrison Ford's cool, seemingly passive, exterior, tempered by occasional submissive behavior and a slightly whining tone, that makes us interpret his character as weaker and less interesting than the character in the novel. How can such a weakling have risen to such power? True, the weaknesses Ford portrays are very much a part of Sabich's character, but in the novel Sabich's first-person narration makes these weaknesses seem minor or even perhaps an intentional strategy. The film's perspective makes it difficult to communicate this concept without significant changes in character and in plot, changes absent in Pakula's respectful approach.

The casting of the other characters also shapes our view of them. Brian Dennehy as Raymond Horgan has a physical force absent in the book, communicated quite simply by the width of his shoulders and the bulldog massiveness of his neck and head. The smooth but burned-out old politician of the book gains power from Dennehy's appearance. Instead of a man on the way down, jealous of his loyal subordinate Sabich's sexual and political success, fearful of personal exposure, and aware of the rumors that Sabich could have his job for the taking if he so chose, Dennehy by his simple presence depicts a man of power and might who can take care of himself physically and politically, and beside whom Ford looks like a dominated underling, used and manipulated.

Bonnie Bedelia's expressive face conveys more sensitivity and feeling than does the image of Barbara in the novel, where there are fewer visual pictures of her. In prose we learn of her black moods and grim, obsessive determination. Instead of the dark, brooding, problematic exterior the novel draws of a wronged woman, bitter about her wifely status and her long-thwarted career, bitter about her long-failed marriage, bitter about her rival, and contemptuous of the husband by whom she stands and whose sexual response she still needs, the film shows Bedelia's mobile features and concerned body language. Bedelia lacks Barbara's "savage deadness in her eye" (39). Inevitably, the novel's reserved woman who has married beneath her is made more sympathetic and human by the actress's performance. In the book, the wife, ignored, disappears for long passages so that even though readers have been told of her presence by Rusty's side, she drops from memory because Rusty, the narrator, ignores her; and even when she is present, Barbara is more a reflection of Rusty's love-hate response than an entity in and of herself. In the film, she is present much more often as the image of the dutiful, loyal wife. In the court scenes, she is a featured member of the tableau formed by the defense team at its table.

Other casting decisions reinforce the perspective of the novel rather than changing them. Raul Julia's Sandy Stern is slimmer in the movie than in the book and possibly smoother, more acceptable than the novel's portly Argentinean. This conventionality may be counter-weighted by another difference between novel and film: reading that someone has an accent is not the same as hearing the accent every time the person speaks, as we do with Julia (mercifully, Stephen Foster *pace*, there is no accepted and acceptable way of rendering accents in prose beyond giving subtle suggestions and reminders, as Turow does). But on balance, Julia's casting probably comes as close as possible to the spirit of the original: a cool, understated, competent cynic/idealist, quick-witted and clever, for whom knowing the truth might interfere with good courtroom practice. Since in this book we know Sandy Stern from the outside, there is no loss from the novel and much gain from Julia's impressive talent. In fact, Julia's performance is one of the high points of the film.

A number of other players work well with the sense of character given in the book. Greta Scacchi makes a fine Carolyn Polhemus, cool, blonde, and contemptuous. The distant figure of the novel comes across in much the same way in the film: a political climber, corrupt, amoral, willing to sleep her way to the top and discard past lovers when they can no longer serve her ambition. However, on film, Polhemus stands alone as her own entity; in the book, she is filtered through Rusty's imagination and memory. In the film we see her as completely scheming and seductive; in the book this is only Rusty's claim, though of course his version is reinforced by other characters' comments. There was some critical unhappiness about Scacchi's Polhemus, though the fault surely lies with the labored dialogue she was sometimes required to mouth. Her calculating look and demeanor are defining features of the film.

Despite differences in physical build, Paul Winfield's excellent portrayal of Judge Larren Lyttle probably does little to change the mental image developed by readers of the novel, but like Ford, Winfield carries baggage with him from dozens of previous roles. He is nicely street-smart, forceful, and ironic, however, and his always likable persona adds the correct note of sympathy for a judge corrupted but under forgivable circumstances.

Just as the choice of actors changes the nature of the characters in the novel, so the visual setting chosen by the director changes the character of the courtroom. What viewers see is a large, impressive, old-fashioned courtroom, all dark wood and marble; the judge's bench, elevated above the participants in this legal drama; and the jury of honest citizens, their brows furrowed, their looks intent, ready to determine right and wrong. In the novel, on the other hand, Turow's courtroom of the imagination is a place of intrigue, of political manipulation, of threat and cover-up and dubious justice, and his description is full of digressive anecdotes that bring the human element of the judicial system to life. Judge Lyttle draws on the "random and complete injustices which he witnessed on the streets" as "a kind of emotional encyclopedia" (195), to help him attack unfair prosecution. The film, in a nice throwaway line only slightly altered from the book, retains Lyttle's comment, "Now, in my neighborhood . . . he [Sabich] would have said, 'Yo' Momma'" (201), not an ironic "Yeah, you're right"; but the one line is a minimal defining point. The difficulty of transferring ironic attitudes to the screen can be appreciated from two descriptions in the book: the court is like the Roman games with "Christians against lions" (224), but with no one quite sure who the Christians are, and criminal investigators are "like the scientist studying diseases through his microscope" (158). Perhaps if Pakula had chosen a less impressive courtroom and had focused more on humanizing and personalizing the court members, such irony could have been conveyed. As it stands, the film is far too respectful of the court and far too conservative in its rendering of legal niceties. The absence of such a double vision of the court and its representatives is a major fault of the film.

Furthermore, in the novel, very intelligent people are involved in complex actions which must be reduced to simplistic black and white since a trial must provide a simple, credible chain of events that jurors can understand, not the chaos of reality. There is an implicit parallel drawn between the artist and the lawyer, both selecting suitable "facts" to tell a good story. In the courtroom scenes, Turow uses metaphor to spin out the convoluted interpretive possibilities inherent in even the simplest statements of fact. What is normally invisible to the interested observer—sudden shifts of direction and changes in approach—becomes a complex roadmap of alternative routes leading to subpoints of departure for new side-excursions, all of which will take the participants to the final destination, victory for one side or the other. The legal strategies of "proof," in the popular mind a kind of quasi-scientific demonstration of "fact," become evident as a series of persuasive claims on the imagination of judge and jury, claims as much psychological as legal.

Turow's novel demonstrates how the courtroom requires a superimposition of order, a selection of one truth amid a multiplicity of choices, but readers are always kept aware of the real multiplicity that lies behind the coherent courtroom presentation. It is the multiplicity which dominates and intrigues and which is the controlling force of the book; it is the unfortunate selection of one version of truth that drives the film. Here Pakula might have cast doubt in any number of ways enshrined in stagecraft and filmcraft: significant glances, quick cuts to dissonant images, camera angles, musical counterpoint. However, the film's courtroom is almost religious in its reverence, a far cry from the snake pit of the novel.

In "Opening Statement," the initial chapter of the book, Rusty Sabich demonstrates his courtroom style and prepares us for chaos. Speaking as "a functionary of our only universally recognized system of telling wrong from right, a bureaucrat of good and evil," he points out that "people's motives . . . may be forever locked inside them" (2), but that a jury must "at least, try to determine what actually occurred," because, if "we cannot find the truth, what is our hope of justice?" (3). The novel provides some inkling of motives but ultimately proves that these "may be forever locked inside" (2)—unknowable; Rusty Sabich pours out his soul to us as readers, yet at the end we still do not know him fully. The truth remains doubtful and what is just, though seemingly so clear in the courtroom, remains in doubt in the world of Turow's characters. The book's answer to its initial question is, "We cannot find the truth and our hope of justice is slim."

In the film, however, the initial voice-over against a visual backdrop of an empty courtroom is condensed to focus on "justice" to the exclusion of chaos and doubt. Readers are provided with the courtroom's imposition of order, suggestions of a frameup with a focus on political rivals, and a single revelation of truth outside the courtroom. The film too tries to convey that the courtroom activities are merely a surface view of reality and that more complex undercurrents remain hidden, but the plot explains that this is because the evidence has been tampered with and the accused is covering up for someone else. The film loses the novel's sense of peeling layer after layer off the onion only to find no simple kernel of truth at the heart. This loss comes directly from the change in perspective or point of view. In other words, the change in medium from novel to film necessitates a change in perspective that transforms the nature of the two stories. The film depends too heavily on straightforward in-court revelations—a device of plot—when viewers need more short sequences involving schemes, conspiracies, and doubts, the core of Turow's theme rendered through the grammar of film.

Furthermore, in the novel, the reader is inside the head of Rusty Sabich: chief deputy prosecuting attorney, colleague, and once-smitten lover of the dead woman, now her presumed murderer. He narrates his own story. The point of view is blinkered, since readers see only what Sabich chooses to share with them. In contrast, the movie's point of view is the camera's eye. The movie distances the character, showing us his outward action, and we evaluate him in terms of those outward appearances: a manipulated weakling, a victim caught up in events beyond his control, an obsessed lover controlled by others. Perhaps better use could have been made of Lipranzer as friend, supporter, and fellow intriguer, not simply sidekick, to provide a more balanced view of Sabich as a complicated man capable of intrigue himself rather than as simply a dull pawn in the schemes of others.

In the novel, Sabich's style is polished, his voice philosophical. His story builds slowly but inexorably as he reveals characters and relationships, engages in introspective Dostoevsky-like monologues, and reveals unexpected twists and turns of character and event. Our sense of his character grows out of his metaphors, bleak images of shipwrecks, of spiders caught in their own webs, and of life as a constant struggle with darkness. He bares to his readers the depths of his philosophical despair, the roots of his anxieties. Yet his narrative is one of half-truths and deceits that manipulate and at some deep level betray readers, and his sometimes unexpected shifts of voice and tone seem calculated exercises in misdirection.

His musings are the slow ruminations of a troubled man trying to puzzle out the significance of events, to come to terms with his past, to find meaning in act and innuendo. In doing so, he provides capsule biographies of those around him, records the "tough-guy" exchanges of courtroom politicians, recalls the horror of past cases—whether the violation of innocence or the deserved retribution of tough against tough. His flesh-and-blood concerns leave him in an agony of psychic pain, betrayed by his boss and mentor of 12 years, obsessed by a woman who uses, abuses and jilts him, repulsed by and in need of his moody wife, awed by the wonder of his son. He describes himself as "somebody everyone can depend on" (15); his wife calls him a "predictable . . . asshole" (41), a sap.

In the movie, we are shown little of these internal musings. Ford looks shattered, but we have no bleak metaphors to define character, and simply move from discovery to discovery as if sharing in the accused's experiences as they happen. At the end of the film, the cloud of ignorance is dispelled and the truth shines brightly through. In the novel nothing is what it seems and truth is ultimately impossible to know. Layer after layer is peeled away to reveal Byzantine complications, but the human heart remains hidden—sometimes even from itself. Rusty's final lines turn the reader's simple assumptions on end, and his question "What is harder? Knowing the truth or finding it, telling it or being believed?" (418) suggests that ultimately there are no real innocents—only a presumption of innocence. Turow's psychological shrewdness, vivid detail, sense of courtroom finesse, and skill at misdirection capture the imagination, challenge the intellect, and produce unforgettable images of man's hidden darker self and the failure of culture's most vigorous investigative device, the court trial, at plumbing its depths. The film saves its misdirection for a final surprise twist, barely prepared for, a twist that forces viewers to reevaluate what they have seen and heard; but, in effect, the answer is a simple, pat vindication of Sabich's vacillation: he is a loyal spouse after all and bears the brunt of public attack to protect wife and home. This is not Turow's point, and, in fact, undercuts it.

The imagery connected with the two important women in Sabich's life provides a view of relationships and of psychological turmoil that the movie only hints at. In the film the two women are only superficial adjuncts to Sabich's life, with no sense of the complexities involved in their constantly changing love-hate relationships. But the novel's imagery focuses on Sabich's ultimate hatred of or disdain for both the women who have, in their own ways, controlled his life. An examination of these mental pictures shows the distance between prose and film image, and especially the difference in the complexity of Rusty. Despite Rusty's protestations of affection and renewal of conjugal relationships with Barbara at the time of the trial, his images of his wife are all negative. For him "duty and obligation" are hard "like ore deposits," settling in the veins and replacing softer feelings (2). He is irritated by her return to school and describes her dissertation as lingering "like a chronic disease" (37-38). He dislikes her "look of diamond hardness" (121). He complains of "the black forests of her moods" (121), "the rocky currents of her personality" (123). He suggests that she has never understood him and has instead used him for her own purposes, purposes he cannot possibly fulfill: "Barbara hoped I would be like some fairy-tale prince," he says, "a toad she had transformed with her caresses, who could enter the gloomy woods where she was held captive and lead her away from the encircling demons" (123-24). Instead, the couple is caught up in a constant battle: "a tug of war in which we are each maneuvering for position by forever stepping back" (184). Barbara is "volcanic" (44), with continual "momentary eruptions" (185), "in the peak of rage or the dungeons of self-pity" (410), seeking a "monumental act of commitment" or a "miracle cure" (410). Even her courtroom display of loyalty is undercut by images of affectation: "Overall, the effect is a little like the Kennedy widows" (231). Although after the trial Rusty discovers that he needs to travel "a treacherous journey across nearly unspannable chasms to grace and forgiveness" (369), he never really makes this journey.

This is a very different relationship from the film version's. The film begins with an intimate and playful family scene, an exchange over breakfast accompanied by light, upbeat music in a brightly lit suburban setting, and is punctuated by short scenes of family togetherness that belie the few verbal suggestions of tension, pain, and conflict. Barbara is clearly hurt by Rusty's betrayal, but the screen sex scenes suggest a greater warmth and depth of affection than the aggressive gymnastics described in the book. Furthermore, the supportive scenes in court and in the daily activities of ordinary life suggest intimacy, familiarity, and love—a touch of the hand, a sympathetic glance.

In like manner, in the novel, Caroline Polhemus's overpowering physical and emotional effect on Sabich is vital to understanding his character and behavior. Rusty finds her as hard as "flint" (18), with a "hard shell manner" (421) and a "little cat's grin" (34)—"always running one gear too high" (30). Rusty's positive descriptions of the early part of the relationship focus mainly on her sexual effect on him: making him "hum," with a pitch that "rose, vibrated, sang" as she became "a symphonic personality" with a "musical laugh" (33). On her first "date" with Rusty, Carolyn made him feel like "all those gorgeous, poised movietime couples" with "a racing current" between them "that made it difficult to sit in place" (84) and made them "like coquettes with their silk fans [dinner menus]" (84) between them. Soon after his seduction, however, Rusty begins to acknowledge the inherent danger of Carolyn's sexuality: "She seemed like some Hindu goddess, containing all feelings in creation," undamming in Rusty "wild, surging, libidinal rivers" that drew him "over the brink" (60). Through her Rusty struggles "to escape the darkness" (41), but is "lost and high . . . beyond restraint" (106). His sexual conquest of her makes him feel powerful. "Each time I entered her, I felt I divided the world" (106), but he also recognizes a loss of control; like "the mandrake in the old poems," he feels as if he has been "pulled screaming from the earth . . . devastated by . . . passion. . . . shattered. Riven. Decimated. Torn to bits" (105). He adds, "Every moment was turmoil. . . . old and dark and deep. I had no vision of myself. I was like a blind ghost groping about a castle and moaning for love. . . . Now I think of Pandora . . . opening her box and finding that torrent of miseries unloosed" (105). Ultimately, he describes his life as "ransacked" (152) by Carolyn, himself as "lost" (86), and Carolyn as "like a spider caught in her own web" (377), a "demon" to be "exorcised" (43). Her death leaves Rusty a "shipwrecked survivor holding fast to the debris, awaiting the arrival of the scheduled liner" (121). Such images suggest a destructive sexuality that both compels and consumes, that gives Carolyn a much resented power over Rusty, made worse by the ease with which she rejects him.

In the film, Carolyn's obvious superficiality, ambition, and willingness to sleep her way to the top of her profession make viewers ask themselves how Rusty could be so blind, so naive. She is clearly using him; the relationship is purely sexual; the seduction through a condensed series of flashbacks occurs so rapidly and ends so rapidly that Rusty's total infatuation makes little sense. We viewers can see what has happened; why can't he?

In the film we stand outside Rusty, seeing the facade broken only by an anxious glance, a worried look, a frown, a hesitation, a little sweat to betray tensions beneath the surface; Ford mumbles, his body held rigid. In the novel, however, we experience the inner turmoil first-hand through Rusty's images of himself: dark, bleak and full of suppressed rage. Accused of murder, Rusty contemplates "the unsolved maze of my own self, where I am so often lost" (124), feeling rage like "black poison" (141), experiencing "a black vortex of paranoia and rage" (151). While on trial he senses "the wild blackness of some limitless and everlasting panic" that begins "to swallow" (220) him as his spirits descend "in a sickening spiral" toward "bitter lament" (307). Ford's mumbled lines about inner rage set off against a stolid, rarely shifting, facial expression provide no evidence of this inner turmoil.

Ultimately, Turow's spectacular tropes give not a vision of the law, but of humanity. People are complex and impenetrable except by the most directed and disciplined of inquiries, and the law, like the novel itself, provides the structure and means of understanding human motive, however imperfectly. In an American culture given to easy answers and quick and dirty explanations, the novel shows us our own inscrutability, but also leads us to the path to understanding. Metaphor, as is obvious from the passages quoted above, is the only possible way Rusty/Turow can express his feelings, and even the poet's medium is inadequate as image clusters after image in an almost desperate attempt to convey meaning. In the novel, perceptions shift radically from one page to the next, and the final understanding is that there can be no final understanding; in the movie, surprising twists maintain suspense, but the ending provides a simple explanation of the confusions and deceptions. In the novel, the accused narrator is set free but left highly suspect; in the movie, the same character is vindicated, presented as a victim who has maintained silence to protect his guilty wife, whom he has wronged. The novel provides a psychological study of a morose man at home in a world of corruption, betrayal, and psychic pain, something the movie does not even attempt to convey. While the movie version ends with Barbara as the guilty party, and with Sabich's maneuvers ultimately intended to protect both himself and her, Turow's ending is not nearly so definite and clear.

The indeterminacy of the novel's ending depends heavily on the images surrounding the main characters and the legal system. First, defense-lawyer Turow is careful to draw an image of his novel's defense lawyer Sandy Stern as a highly competent master of illusion and deception. This is the high point of the movie as well. Julia captures the sophisticated, skilled, instinctive maneuverings implicit in Stern. With his "brown-eyed spaniel expression" (170), Stern is "caught in a system where the client is inclined to lie" yet where "the lawyer who seeks his client's confidence may not help him do that"; as a consequence, Stern works "in the small open spaces which remain" (157). Turow, through Rusty, argues that watching "Stern work is like tracking smoke, watching a shadow lengthen" (162). His eyes "are penetrating as lasers" (164). The way he puts things makes people take his assertions for granted like "sleight of hand" (169). He "whittles away" (229) at Nico's proof until the "knot between what . . . [Sabich] did not say and what . . . [he] did had been untied; the juncture . . . severed between murder and deceit" (270). In another instance, Sabich notes that "Sandy works like a jeweler, tapping, tapping at his themes of past resentments" (278). Sabich calls Sandy "a magician" (285) with an "odd theatricality . . . pulling rabbits out of hats" (361). His is "not a charted course" but "a matter of intuition and estimation" (381). At the end of the story, even Sabich—canny, experienced prosecutor that he is—is surprised by Stern's strategy and a little disturbed by it. Praise for his lawyerly skill runs over Sandy "with the soothing effect of a bath of warm milk" (371), for he has proven himself the master of indirection, setting up the prosecution and then undercutting them in moves so subtle they don't know what has happened to them. Seeming to focus his attack on one of the prosecuting attorneys, a would-be witness, he lays the groundwork to influence the judge without the court ever realizing he has done so. In Sandy's defense, the unexpected prevails, "facts" require reevaluation and reinterpretation, and new facets of the old "reality" become manifest. Prosecution figures prove base, exploitative, shameless, and even self-deluded.

In the film, Rusty Sabich follows his lawyer's moves and involves himself in his defense, but seems continually astonished by the results; his discovery of the murder weapon and his wife's confession seem to come as surprises, and the missing evidence, the glass with his fingerprints, seems an unsolved mystery to him. But in the novel Sabich has perhaps stacked the whole deck from the very beginning. He has set layers within layers of stratagems to gull even his skilled lawyer, feeding him unexpected material at unexpected times, yielding to his directions, when ultimately it is his secret knowledge that influences the final strategy. At the end, when he toys with his friend Lip, he proves the true master of illusion. Lipranzer, who knows him far better than anyone else and who has been loyal to him throughout his trial, believes he is guilty. For this reason he has kept from the prosecution the glass with Sabich's fingerprints on it. Sabich, understanding Lip's doubts, provides a scenario to fill in puzzling gaps, the scenario the film takes as its ending: Sabich's wife Barbara committed murder as a jealous act of premeditated revenge; she planted the glass with his fingerprints on it (Carolyn and Barbara had a matching set of glasses); she used sperm from her diaphragm to give the murder the appearance of rape; she made the disputed phone call from the Sabich home to Carolyn; and unbeknownst to herself, she left carpet fibers from the Sabich home as evidence. The hammer she finds him cleaning in the laundry tub is the murder weapon, with Carolyn's blood and hair still on it.

Furthermore, Sabich suggests that if he had told the "truth," he would not have been believed. When Sabich claims that Barbara did not intend him malice and only wanted him to understand what she had done, Lip provides a second explanation to make the scenario credible to him: "I figure she wanted Carolyn dead and you in the slammer for doing it. I'd say the only thing that happened that she never counted on was that you beat it" (416).

But Turow toys with readers just as Sabich does with Lipranzer: "Fifteen minutes ago you thought I was the one who killed her" (417). Sabich presents another scenario, the case that prosecutor Nico would have argued against Sabich if Barbara had been involved: Nico, says Sabich, would argue that Carolyn's murder was instead the perfect crime. Nico's reasoning, argues Sabich, would be that, as "a prosecutor who knows the system inside out" (4118), Sabich has gotten rid of a lover who has discarded him and a wife who despises him, has laid the ground work for eventual custody of his son and for political vindication and success, has used his wife as a "fail-safe," the person he'd like to see nabbed "in case the whole house of cards fell in" on him, and has in effect made it impossible to know the truth (418). Thus, just when they have smugly settled on a comfortable explanation that seems to explain Sabich's peculiar behavior, Lip and readers are left to puzzle over the possibility that this toss-away scenario might be the truth, that Carolyn Polhemus and her whole corrupt way of life was indeed a "progressive disease" (375), caught by Sabich and manifested by tampering with evidence, setting up an intricate frame, and getting away with murder. Sabich's narration of these scenarios relies on the passive voice, the standard verbal ploy of criminals to evade responsibility. But there is no way of knowing for sure.

Ultimately, then, Scott Turow proves an even greater magician than Sandy Stern because he gives readers the chance to accept the magic and believe in Sabich's innocence, or to be cynics and suspect the worst. Stern's unwillingness to see Sabich again socially, Barbara's decision to take her son and leave, Lip's initial belief in Sabich's guilt and his final doubts about his vindication leave the reader with no clear final explanation. In fact, what Turow has really proven is the inability of man to ever know the heart of another. He has told story after story, provided scenario after scenario, only to reveal that the truth remains elusive, with a single emphasized detail transforming the kaleidoscope into a new pattern. Knowing the truth or finding it, telling it or being believed are only layers in a complicated organic whole.

Throughout the novel, Sabich has bared his soul to his readers, shown them the depths of his philosophical despair, and explored with them the roots of his anxieties. Consequently, the discovery of his having held back information disturbs most readers' secret sense of right. Though inured to the lies, half-truths, and deceits of the other characters, most readers come to know Sabich so intimately that it is painful to concede—as does his faithful friend and associate Lip—a doubt, a fear that we have been manipulated and at some deep level betrayed.[1] We are willing to accept a *Hamlet*-like world of seems, but in a mystery we expect the cloud of ignorance to be dispelled and the truth to shine brightly through. Instead, Rusty's "struggle to escape the darkness" (421) leaves readers with "an idle doubt" and the question, "What is harder? Knowing the truth or finding it, telling it or being believed?" (418). Again, Turow suggests there are no real innocents—only a presumption of innocence.

The film presents a far more black-and-white interpretation of events: justice prevails, albeit a rough street justice. The final talk with Lipranzer is limited: a friend confessing his fears and explaining how the glass went missing; Sabich belying his suspicions and asserting innocence. Sabich is not guilty and, therefore, is rightly freed by the court, which fulfills its social obligation correctly. The scenario Sabich proposes to Lip as one of several possible interpretations becomes Barbara's direct confession and the final interpretation of the film. Barbara is guilty, but she is a woman wronged, revenging herself on rival and husband. Sending her to jail will right no wrongs. The film's closing scene explains the main character's peculiar behavior and brings a surprising close to a case that has left puzzling questions. The confusions and the unexpected twists that maintained suspense are provided a simple explanation. Corruption in high places has been exposed, but the deeper corruption of the main character's soul is never mentioned. Instead, Sabich is totally vindicated: an innocent victim who has been betrayed by colleagues and who has maintained silence to protect his guilty wife, whom he has wronged. His return to political life seems only right, rather than a deeply cynical, manipulative action fueled by a sly, or perhaps even self-deceptive, ambition.

Both novel and movie capture the sights and smells, the intimacy and the clinical distance of the investigation scene, the drama, the suspense and some of the internal maneuverings of a headline trial; but the novel much more vividly captures the moral ambiguity of those who participate in and are touched by such a case. Turow's psychological shrewdness, vivid detail, sense of courtroom subtleties, and skill at multiple levels of interpretation capture the imagination, challenge the intellect, and produce unforgettable images of man's hidden darker self. His narrative voice provides a meticulous gloss on speech, testimony, and human behavior, with the analysis moving skillfully from lawyerly explication of legal points to precise and careful observation of the interpretive possibilities of everyday communication. This prose is admirably precise, metaphorical, and elegantly classic in quality and structure, sometimes achieving the intensity of poetry; his characterizations are fully rounded and fully believable. In short, Turow combines mystery and suspense with style and vision to produce a spellbinding plot and furnish penetrating analyses of the justice system and of family life. The film, in contrast, has impressive vignettes, sharp characterizations, and captivating suspense but fails to make use of cinematic strategies for suggesting psychological complications and for calling into doubt motive and act. As a result, it falls short of the double vision and the intellectually challenging analysis that make the book a special experience for readers.

NOTES

[1]A number of critics are profoundly disturbed by Turow's ending. For example, Jane Stewart Spitzer complains about the "troubling moral ambiguity" of the novel's resolution and is clearly disturbed that there are no simple final answers.

WORKS CITED

Denby, David. Rev. of *Presumed Innocent. New York* 6 Aug. 1990: 45.

Donahugh, Robert H. *"Presumed Innocent." Library Journal* 1 June 1987: 130.

Presumed Innocent. Dir Alan Pakula. Warner Brothers. 1990.

Pym, John. Rev. of *Presumed Innocent. Sight & Sound.* Autumn 1990: 279.

Rice, Anne. "She Knew Too Many, Too Well." *New York Times Book Review* 28 June 1987: 1.

Schickel, Richard. Rev. of *Presumed Innocent. Time* 30 Aug. 1990: 57.

Spitzer, Jane Stewart. "Scott Turow." *Christian Science Monitor* 13 Aug. 1987: 18.

Turow, Scott. *Presumed Innocent.* 1987. New York: Warner, 1988.

"Twenty Questions: Scott Turow." *Playboy* Aug. 1993: 113-14, 132.

It's Scarier at the Movies: Jonathan Demme's Adaptation of *The Silence of the Lambs*

Joan G. Kotker

Both Thomas Harris's novel The Silence of the Lambs *and Director Jonathan Demme's film adaptation exemplify the excellence possible in works intended for mass audiences. While Harris posits a world where evil can be contained and at least to some degree defeated by those determined and self-disciplined enough to acquire the skills that will allow them to do so, in Demme's world it seems that the vulnerable can rely on little more than luck.*

With reference to film adaptations screenwriter-novelist William Goldman says, "When people say, 'Is it like the book?' the answer is, 'There has never in the history of the world been a movie that's really been like the book.' Everybody says how faithful *Gone with the Wind* was. Well, *Gone with the Wind* was a three-and-a-half hour movie, which means you are talking about maybe a two-hundred-page screenplay of a nine-hundred-page novel in which the novel has, say, five hundred words per page; and the screenplay has maybe forty, maybe sixty, depending on what's on the screen, maybe one hundred and fifty words per page. But you're taking a little, teeny slice; you're just extracting little, teeny *essences* of scenes. All you can ever be in an adaptation is faithful in spirit" (326).

In the case of Thomas Harris's *Silence of the Lambs*, a 367-page novel is reduced by Ted Tally's screenplay to 120 pages. Obviously, much has been left out. However, critics have given high marks to Tally: Dan Persons says, "In light of the scripts that go through an infinity of rewrites and an army of authors (in the process keeping mediators at the Writer's Guild very, very, busy), Tally's singular effort stands as one of the most faithful, and successful, screen translations in recent years" (31).[1] One would, therefore, assume that what Goldman calls "the spirit" of the novel has been accurately rendered, but this is only partly true. Harris's

Silence of the Lambs has two texts, the surface text of chronology, character, and events, and a well-articulated subtext reflecting a particular world-view. Director Jonathan Demme has transferred Harris's surface text from the page to the screen, but Harris's subtext is missing, replaced in the film by a more pessimistic vision that ultimately adds to its horror.

The plot of *Silence of the Lambs* is one that crosses genres: the story is both a chilling horror tale and a well-researched police procedural. The hero, Clarice Starling, is an FBI agent-in-training who has been sent to interview an imprisoned serial killer, the notorious (and thanks to Anthony Hopkins's superb portrayal of him, beloved) Hannibal Lecter. Lecter is a mad psychiatrist who killed his victims out of boredom and then used various parts of their internal organs for his gourmet dishes, a practice that has earned him his nickname, "Hannibal the Cannibal." Starling's superior, Jack Crawford, has assigned her the interview because he believes that Lecter may know the identity of another serial killer, Buffalo Bill, who abducts women, keeps them in a well in his basement for three days, then kills them, skins them, and dumps their bodies in rivers.

To no viewer's or reader's surprise, Lecter does indeed have information on Bill (the world of serial killers seems to be a small one, where everybody knows everybody else), and he trades bits of this information to Starling in return for her telling Lecter about herself. Meanwhile, Bill has kidnapped his sixth victim, and the story becomes a classic race against the clock: the FBI has only 72 hours to discover the identity of Bill, and both reader and viewer are kept on the edge of their seats through the device of the countdown. Starling persuades Crawford to assign her to the case, and the audience then follows her through forensic work on the body of one of Bill's victims, further interviews with Lecter, and fieldwork on the previous killings.

At this point Lecter escapes from prison in one of the most imaginatively gory scenes in recent fiction, a scene that is handled faithfully in the film and at the same time is presented without unnecessary violence—not an easy feat, as any reader of the book can verify. Lecter's escape ratchets up the tension: there are now not one but two serial killers on the loose, Bill's latest victim is still in the well, and time is running ever shorter. As in all good procedurals, the careful, workmanlike investigating of the FBI agents slowly uncovers the identity of the killer but it is a laborious process. While the agents are on a cold trail, surrounding a house

Bill once lived in, Starling finds Bill in another city through her background check on his first victim. This part of both film and novel is brilliantly done: the real agents with their weapons, their armor, and expertise go room by room through an empty house at the same time that trainee Starling stands talking with the killer in a house that is anything but empty. Starling ultimately disposes of Bill and rescues his captive, but Lecter remains free, planning God knows what for his next meal.

Both the novel and the film are utterly terrifying, and in some ways the film is the more so. Demme's cinematographer Tak Fujimoto has done a superb job of photographing the film, particularly Lecter's prison cell and Buffalo Bill's basement.[2] In the novel, Lecter's cell is in a prison for the criminally insane, and the reader might well imagine it as being an antiseptic, shiny, hospital-like place flooded with bright fluorescent light. In the film, the cell is dark, wet-looking, and underground, lit with low-watt bulbs that cast a dim, yellowish glow. The walls look as though one's hands would slither off them. Overall, it reminds one of an abandoned sewer. This visual tone is repeated in the well in Bill's basement, and people's hands have indeed slithered off the walls of this pit—we see the bloody trails left by his previous victims in their attempts to claw their way out. These wet, underground images bring to mind creepy, slimy creatures who live in dark places and cannot bear the light of day: not a bad analogy for serial killers.

Howard Shore's music also adds to the terror of the film. In an interview on *Sixty Minutes* with FBI agent John Douglas, the real-life counterpart of Jack Crawford, Douglas is asked if he thinks the movie is good. He says, "I thought it was a tremendous movie. It was scary as heck." The interviewer says, "*You* were scared? Oh, that's great. That's great." "Oh sure," Douglas says, "'cause . . . in real cases we don't have the music in the background." Other sounds contribute to the fear: we hear the hum of Bill's sewing machine as he works away making himself a girl suit out of the skin of his victims, and we hear the newest victim's screams from the well (the actress who plays her, Brooke Smith, does a fine job of re-creating both her terror and her bravery[3]), noises we can only imagine—or choose not to imagine—when reading the novel.

The first scenes of both film and book prefigure their differences. The film opens to a stark, blue-black winter's day in the woods. It is cold, the leaves have fallen off the trees, and there is dirge-like music. As the music builds in intensity, we see a young girl who appears to be pulling herself up out of somewhere, and then we see her running faster and faster. Viewers know full well how to respond to young women running as fast as they can through bleak woods, and the opening image thus emphasizes danger, particularly danger for young women, and the need to escape. Only at the end of this sequence do we learn that instead of running from something, the girl, who turns out to be Clarice Starling, is just working out on an obstacle course. This is in sharp contrast to the novel's opening scene in which Starling is walking into Jack Crawford's office in response to his summons, with no preliminary running through the woods. And whereas Crawford's film office shocks us with its wall of pictures and clippings about Buffalo Bill, the novel's office has no such items; it is just a dull, bureaucratic room.

In both film and novel Crawford has called Starling to his office to give her the interviewing assignment, but first there is background chat establishing how she came to be in the FBI Academy and detailing her relationship to Crawford. The way Demme handles this meeting sets the pattern for the creation of a more vulnerable Starling than Harris's. In each version, Crawford asks Starling about her grades at the Academy and refers to her background at the University of Virginia, and in each we learn that she met Crawford when he was a guest lecturer there. But in the film Crawford goes on to say, "I gave you an A," to which Starling responds, "No sir, an A minus." This sets up Starling's subordinate role vis-à-vis Crawford and also her spirit: the truth is important to her and she's not afraid to correct a superior on a matter of fact. However, the scene lacks credibility to the extent that it uses language most instructors are careful not use—we like to think of our students as earning grades rather than having grades given to them. And it undermines Starling even before she became a trainee: with her A minus she was almost at the top, almost as good as you can get, but not quite.

This subtle undermining of Starling's abilities and skills is continued throughout the film. Visually, her smallness is emphasized, making her seem waiflike and fragile. Certainly Jodie Foster, the actress who plays Starling, is a small woman, but the film makes her seem even more so, surrounding her in an opening scene with men who tower over her and crowd around her in an elevator. They are all dressed in red FBI shirts so that they give the impression of a single large mass in which she is nearly lost. There is no conversation; Starling gets on the elevator and then off at its next stop, and the men continue on to wherever they were going.

This scene is not in the novel, plays no part in the plot of the film, and has no function other than to locate Starling among her bigger male colleagues. A scene that is in the novel—Starling's visit to a funeral home to study the body of a victim of Buffalo Bill—again is photographed to emphasize Starling's size. Here she is seen dwarfed by big, bulky, black-leather-clad West Virginia State Troopers. Like the men in the elevator, the troopers are so similar as to be a single massive entity, a second image that makes Starling seem petite, frail and vulnerable.[4]

In contrast, the Starling of the novel is never referred to as small, and from the evidence at hand is probably taller than average. At one point she and Jack Crawford, who is wearing moccasins, are standing speaking and Harris writes, "their eyes were almost on level" (253), and when Buffalo Bill is examining her, he decides "she was too slender to be of great utility to him" (346), suggesting that her height is such that 6'1" Bill, who seeks big women, would consider her. When Hannibal Lecter is impressing Starling with what he knows about her from having observed her just once, he says, "Good nutrition has given you some length of bone, but you're not more than one generation out of the mines, Officer Starling" (22). This line has been retained in the film, and the viewer watches bemused, wondering what on earth Lecter is talking about. Length of bone? In this waif? The camera can make people look virtually any way it wants, as witness the film portrayals of Alan Ladd, Dustin Hoffman, Robert Redford, et al., and here the film has chosen to emphasize smallness and frailty even though these are not characteristics of the hero in the novel.

The film then goes on to raise doubts about Starling's skills as a trainee in the academy. We see her during an arrest exercise and are jolted by a loud voice shouting, "You're dead, Starling!" The members of her class are next given a short lecture on how to cover oneself when entering a room, with Starling as the object lesson in how not to do it. This scene does not appear in the book, but the novel has a similar scene in which Starling is being tested on hand strength in front of her class by seeing how many times in 60 seconds she can pull the trigger on a Model 19 Smith & Wesson. She manages 74 with her left hand and 90 with her right, after which her instructor says to the class, "All right, you people . . . I want you to take note of that. Hand strength's a major factor in steady combat shooting. Some of you gentlemen are worried I'll call on you next. Your worries would be justified—Starling is well above average with both hands. That's because she works at it" (34). Later, this instructor loans Starling his own gun so that she will be armed when she is out in the field working on the case, and when he does this he says to her, "Listen, what I teach is something you probably won't ever have to do. I hope you won't. But you've got some aptitude, Starling. If you have to shoot, you can shoot" (69). This is backed up by Starling's being chosen for the FBI team that will shoot against the DEA and Customs in the interservice match, and the team she's to be on is "Not the Women's [team]. The Open [team]" (277). Thus, while the film has Starling held up to her classmates as the bad example, the failure, the novel presents her as outstanding, the model of what a trainee should be.

Another way the film undermines Starling's competence is by giving to a different character skills that in the novel are not only Starling's but that provide the rationale for Jack Crawford's continued use of her, a trainee, on a major investigation. Demme does this by creating a character not in the novel, an FBI technician who performs much of what are Starling's tasks in the novel. Harris has her included on the trip to West Virginia because she was a "lab grunt" before she was in the Academy and has the technical skills Crawford needs: she can print a floater; she knows how to photograph a corpse, including taking dental photographs; and she is the only person with such knowledge who is immediately available. However, in the film, the technician performs all these tasks. Starling inks a roller but is never seen using it; she records her observations of the body into a microphone in a hesitant, questioning tone that suggests Crawford has brought her along to train her in how to do this; and she examines the photographs the technician has taken. Starling does make an important discovery in looking at these pictures, but she does so in a context that suggests that anyone examining them would have made the same discovery. The horror of the partially flayed body on the slab rivets our attention so that we don't think about why Starling has been brought here, but the overall effect of the transference of tasks from Starling to the technician is again to make Demme's Starling less competent than the character Harris created.

Also in this vein, much has been said about Jodie Foster's convincing use of a West Virginia accent in the film, an accent so well done that the *National Review*'s John Simon says, "let me hope she isn't a native West Virginian, which would minimize the achievement" (57). Demme uses the accent as a marker for her rural background and, by implication, her lack of sophistication, her inexperience, and her naivete. In the novel Harris uses the accent differently, as yet another example of Starling's skill: she can turn it on and off at will, as circumstances dictate, making her a person very much in control of herself at all times, a person who can do what she needs to do in order to get results. Here Harris's version is the more plausible: an adult who moved far away from home at the age of ten—as Starling did—is not likely to retain the regional accent of her first few years, although she may indeed be able to mimic it.

While the changes in the film make Demme's Starling a weaker, smaller, less-skilled, and less-controlled character than the novel's, the most significant difference between the two versions is their use of the title. Both works explain that ten-year-old Starling (orphaned in the film but not in the book) lived in Montana with relatives who fattened horses and sheep for slaughter, and in both versions she is wakened very early one morning by the screaming of the spring lambs, which are being killed. Demme has the young Starling attempting to save one of the lambs; she takes it and runs away from the ranch, but the lamb is heavy and she is only a little girl who cannot carry it very far. She is caught, the relatives put her in an orphanage, and the lamb is returned to the ranch, where it is killed. This is a radical departure from the novel, where Starling makes no attempt to save the lambs but, instead, runs away with an old horse named Hannah, who like the lambs is headed for slaughter. She takes the horse to a livery stable and asks to board the horse in return for working there. The upshot is that, as in the film, Starling is sent to an orphanage in Bozeman, but as orphanages go, this has to be one of the best: it allows Starling to bring Hannah the horse along too. Starling explains to Lecter, "They already had a barn at the orphanage. We plowed the garden with [Hannah]. . . . And we led her around pulling kids in a cart." Hannah lived to be 22, "pulled a cart full of kids the last day she lived, and died in her sleep" (229).[5] Thus, while Demme's Starling was a failure at saving an animal threatened with death, Harris's Starling not only saved such an animal but in doing so improved her own life too. In both cases Starling is troubled by the creatures she did not save, symbolized by the crying of the lambs. However, in the film, Starling has achieved nothing, while in the novel, she has achieved much. And there is an element of foreshadowing here. In the novel Starling has demonstrated that she is capable of rescuing large creatures sought for their hides, an underlying reassurance that Harris gives his reader but Demme denies his viewer.

The differences in Starling's skills and experience make for significant differences in the credibility of the respective endings of the two versions of *Silence*. In both, Buffalo Bill is killed by Starling in a tense, terrifying scene in which he stalks her through his dark basement wearing eerie, infrared goggles that stand out from his eyes like those of a mutated being, emphasizing the fact that he is indeed a monster, something that is profoundly other. The light that Demme uses here is a cold green, and it suffuses the screen with a marine glow so that we feel that we are looking underwater, into the depths. This effect subliminally increases the scariness of the film because of the association of water with wells and rivers, the sites Bill chooses for his victims. The fear in the scene is further heightened by the fact that only we know that Bill can see Starling. She thinks that he too cannot see, so we watch him stalking someone who doesn't know she's being stalked.

At this point in the novel, Starling uses all her training, going over and over it in her head, to stay in control of herself and of the situation. She enters a room in this maze of a basement and the lights go out. Harris describes her response this way: "Her heart knocked hard enough to shake her chest and arms. Dizzy dark, need to touch something, the edge of the tub. The bathroom. Get out of the bathroom. If he can find the door he can hose this room, nothing to get behind. Oh dear Jesus go out. Go out down low and out in the hall. Every light out? Every light. He must have done it at the fuse box, pulled the lever, where would it be? Where would the fuse box be? Near the stairs. Lots of times near the stairs" (346). In this same scene in the film, Starling also enters the bathroom, the lights go out, and she "cries out, turns blindly, reaching for the door, can't find it, free hand clawing desperately . . . [She] stumbles, goes to her knees, rights herself, finally clutches the door frame . . . " (114).

Once out of the bathroom, Harris's Starling continues talking herself through the situation. "She moved, quietly, her shoulder barely brushing the wall, brushing it too lightly for sound, one hand extended ahead, the gun at waist level, close to her in the confined hallway. Out into the workroom now. Feel the space opening up. Open room. In the crouch in the open room, arms out, both hands on the gun. You know exactly where the gun is, it's just below eye level. Stop, listen. Head and body and arms turning together like a turret. Stop, listen. In absolute black the hiss of pipes, trickle of water" (347). Demme does the scene this way: Starling "emerges from the bathroom in a half-crouch, arms out, both hands on the gun, extended just below the level of her unseeing eyes. She stops, listens. In her raw-nerved darkness, every SOUND is unnaturally magnified—the HUM of the refridgerator [sic] . . . the TRICKLE of water . . . her own terrified BREATHING . . . Moths smack against her face and arms" (114).

Because Harris's Starling has moved with such care, because she has stopped and listened as she has been trained to, she hears the "snick-snick" of Buffalo Bill's Colt Python when he cocks it to shoot her, and instantly she turns and shoots in the direction of the noise. Harris writes, "**The sound** of a revolver **being cocked** is like no other. She'd fired at the sound" (347); and although Starling does not yet know it, she has killed Buffalo Bill. Certainly there's an element of luck in Starling's hitting Bill with a fatal shot under these circumstances, but we accept it because we have been so well prepared by Harris to view her as exceptionally skilled with guns and very much in control of what she does.

In the film Bill is also killed by Starling, but the structure makes the ending less credible than in the novel. Demme has prepared us to be very frightened here by the earlier scene at the academy in which Starling has failed in the arrest exercise, and he repeats a key image from that scene when he has Bill holding a gun behind her head in exactly the same way as did the instructor who shouted, "You're dead, Starling." Now, instead of Harris's careful, controlled Starling talking herself through her training routines, we are given Demme's Starling flailing around the basement, bumping into things, being smacked by moths, her breath coming out in such loud, ragged gasps that it is difficult to believe she could hear the sound of Bill cocking his gun. When this Starling turns and shoots at Bill, she seems completely out of control. The fact that she hits him is far more credible as chance than skill, creating a resolution that Stanley Kauffmann sees as one of "the weakest elements of the film." He says, "The way the danger is resolved, in the dark, is past belief" (48). At this point in the film the tension is so high that the viewer craves a release, and is satisfied when it is dramatically provided by the death of Bill. However, a careful examination of the scene substantiates Kauffmann's charge, suggesting that we accept Demme's climax not because it is inherently believable but because it puts an end to our terror.

On the surface level, then, the film is faithful to the spirit of the novel. Both forms of the story create a text in which the world is a place where, for their own perverse pleasures, creatures of evil destroy the innocent. We cannot predict who will be victim; we can never know if or when we ourselves will be next, but we can surely predict that in the world of Thomas Harris and Jonathan Demme, it is young women who are likely to be objectified and sought out and who are, therefore, the most vulnerable of us all. However, despite the agreement in surface text, Harris's and Demme's subtexts have little in common. Harris is specific that one can choose not to be a victim, a point that he emphasizes by having his hero be a young woman who is overtly aware of herself as one of those preyed upon. He has Starling say of Bill, "All of [his] victims were women, his obsession was women, he lived to hunt women" (292), a litany that she uses to drive herself on in the ultimately successful search in which she, a woman, removes by the use of her skills and training someone who is a source of evil to all women.

Like Harris's Starling, Demme's performs this same act, and according to critic Chris Lehmann (who questions the feminist message of the film), Demme is well aware of the feminist implications of the young woman as hero here. Lehmann says, "Demme's film clearly is struggling to make a feminist statement; Demme has said as much himself, calling it a challenge to what he calls 'the patriarchy.' Demme proudly points out that he has . . . reversed the 'genre base' of the slasher film by portraying a woman's successful pursuit of a man—in the daring, heroic effort, moreover, to prevent yet another woman's violent death at the hands of a sexually deranged man" (78). However, the feminist qualities Demme rightly sees in Starling's character are ironically undermined by his darker interpretation of her, one in which Starling is shown to lack skills, where we know nothing of her self-discipline, and where she has only her courage to sustain her. Ultimately this leaves her in the traditional female role of victim, since she must depend on fate rather than shape it.[6]

Overall, both Thomas Harris and Jonathan Demme have succeeded in creating outstanding works, with both novel and film serving as examples of the excellence that can be achieved in popular media intended for mass audiences. However, in terms of their respective visions, Harris posits a world where evil can be contained and at least to some degree defeated by those determined and self-disciplined enough to acquire the skills that will allow them to do so. In contrast, it is tempting to say that in Demme's world the vulnerable can only be saved by, literally, blind luck, and while this would be an overstatement, it is not far off the mark from his actual subtext as it is played out in the defeat of Buffalo Bill. Thomas Harris is credited with being a careful researcher, a writer who can be counted on to be accurate in his technical details. It would be well if he is equally accurate in his description of the effectiveness of procedures and training: a world in which victims can by their own actions defend themselves against victimizers, where we can all, by extension, defend ourselves against Buffalo Bill, is far preferable to one in which our best hope is that we will be lucky.

NOTES

[1]Tally's peers agree with the critical assessments of his screenplay: he won the Writer's Guild award for Best 1991 Screenplay Written Directly for the Screen, the Mystery Writers of America award for Best Mystery Movie, and the Oscar for Best Adapted Screenplay.

[2]Fujimoto's work on *Silence* earned him an Oscar nomination for Best Cinematography.

[3]The film is beautifully acted, with Anthony Hopkins and Jodie Foster winning Oscars for Best Actor and Best Actress. In an otherwise mixed review—one of the few negative responses to the film—critic John Simon comments on Jonathan Demme's "exact casting," his skill at "fitting the right actors into even the smallest parts, down to Bill's toy poodle, perkily enacted by Starla" (56).

[4]But note that while I see an emphasis on weakness and frailty in these scenes, Chris Lehmann believes that Demme's intent was "to frame Clarice in scenes where she is surrounded by men in uniform, thereby suggesting that she is an ambitious pioneer in the authoritarian male hierarchy of the law-enforcement bureaucracy" (78).

[5]Harris does not explain why Starling, who has been sent to live with the relatives by her widowed mother, goes into an orphanage. He leaves us to assume that the adult Starling is an orphan, but exactly when she became one is not established.

[6]Jodie Foster also sees the film as one that makes a feminist statement: in her acceptance speech at the Oscars, she thanked the Academy "for embracing such a strong feminist hero that I'm proud to have portrayed" ("And the Winner"). And in an interview with Lawrence Grobel, she says, "A movie like *Silence of the Lambs* will do more for the inequities of women on the marquee than federally funded campaigns. *Silence of the Lambs* in a weird way is a more important film than anything that has happened in a long time—for a film to make $125 million and the hero to be a woman. This movie will change the next 20 copycat films that are made after that" (32). Surely Foster is correct that the film would open up more strong leading roles for women. However, it seems to me that what

both Demme and Foster are doing here is equating action films in which women are the central, heroic figures with feminist films, and while the two can be the same, they are not necessarily so.

WORKS CITED

"And the Winner Is . . . 'Silence of Lambs' Sweeps 5 Top Oscars." *Journal American* [Bellevue, WA] 31 Mar. 1991, B1.

Boggs, Joseph M. *The Art of Watching Films*. Mountain View, CA: Mayfield, 1991.

Douglas, John. Interview. "The Psycho Squad." *Sixty Minutes*. CBS. KIRO, Seattle. 17 Nov. 1991.

Grobel, Lawrence. "Anything is Possible." *Movieline* Oct. 1991: 28-33, 75-76.

Harris, Thomas. *The Silence of the Lambs*. 1988. New York: St. Martin's, 1989.

Kauffmann, Stanley. "Gluttons for Punishment." *The New Republic* 18 Feb. 1991: 48-49.

Lehmann, Chris. "Jonathan Demme and the Aesthetics of Contempt." *Tikkun* July-Aug. 1991: 74-79.

Persons, Dan. "Scripting the Bestseller." *Cinefantastique* Feb. 1992: 31.

The Silence of the Lambs. Dir. Jonathan Demme. Jodie Foster, Anthony Hopkins, and Scott Glenn. Orion, 1991.

Simon, John. "Horror, Domestic and Imported." *National Review* 29 Apr. 1991: 55-58.

Tally, Ted. *The Silence of the Lambs*. North Hollywood, CA: Hollywood Scripts, 1989.

Reflections on Film Adaptation of Fiction

Michael Cox

British filmmaker Michael Cox discusses the various formats available to film producers, explains why so many films are adaptations of fiction, and describes in depth the difficult process of successfully adapting fiction to film. Cox stresses his view that film adaptations should maintain fidelity not simply to the letter of the original text but to the author's style and tone.

Fiction is not only the most prominent source material for film screenplays; it has, in fact, provided the principles which govern the films I make. J.D. Salinger's "Seymour: An Introduction" provided a signpost which guides me in my work. In this story, Seymour tells his brother, Buddy, that the only way to do the work that you most want to do as a writer is to write what you want to read.[1] I recognize that as the best advice that anybody who makes films could receive, and I always try to follow it: make the films that you want to see. That has been, as far as possible, my watchword. My whole list of credits is characterized by one particular enthusiasm of mine: exploring different ways to tell a story. That's what provides a unifying thread. I don't really think there is any other, no matter what genre of film I make.

Adaptation of fiction is only one of several genres of television film which studios might produce. All of us in television would, I guess, like to tell original stories if we can, but the hardest work to get into production is primary television, material which exists only in terms of the medium and was specifically written for it—in the way that *Citizen Kane* can only be a movie. One would like to work on pieces that can only be television. They exist, but they are not the most bankable projects in the world because the overseas market for them is often a small one.

One of the most exciting things I have ever worked on was a piece of original television called *After the War*, by Frederic Raphael. He's an interesting example of a novelist and film writer whose novels are published, but whose screen plays don't always see the light of day—he has probably been paid to write three times as many movies as have ever been produced from his work. He came to Granada Television to sell us an adaptation of one of his novels, but because of his most famous television work, an original series for the BBC called *The Glittering Prizes*, we found it much more exciting to go for another original piece. He wanted to cover the immediate post-World War II years and try to show how what happened in the 1950s and 1960s made us what we are today. A hugely ambitious project—originally conceived as thirteen hours, it eventually boiled down to ten. It was a wonderful adventure because from day to day Freddy's ideas of what he was going to write would change. He always said, "I will give you an outline of what is to come"; but of course he never did. What he wrote today decided what he was going to write tomorrow, so he couldn't tell you what he was going to be writing in six weeks. That's the kind of thing one would love to be doing frequently, and only once in a while gets the chance to do.

Another type of television which balances between original screenplays and adaptation is drama-documentary or "faction." There is a valid reason for this as a film or television mode, because it often opens the door to material which is otherwise unavailable. It's hugely limiting, of course, because of the imperative to use only documented ingredients and to try to weave those into a coherent pattern. What one longs to do is to try to imagine explanations, motives—using the documented evidence as responsibly as possible, but filling the inevitable gaps in it. Drama-documentaries set a hundred years ago allow one a little more latitude in imagining explanations for people's conduct, something you can't actually have when you are talking about recent figures such as Britain's last Prime Minister or the Watergate tapes. There you have to be absolutely letter-perfect, true to the material. However, because living people like Margaret Thatcher and Richard Nixon are not going to be particularly forthcoming or honest on the record about their motives in doing certain things, one longs to speculate about what went on between those people and their closest associates. But unless you have a way into that, unless there is someone who is prepared to describe the process—and that has to be someone you can trust—then you can't simply plunge in and dream it up, because that will devalue the rest of your fabric. But perhaps the excitement in doing these things is to stir up the public conscience and bring into the light of day things that might otherwise be conveniently brushed under the carpet. I guess a film like Oliver Stone's *J.F.K.*, which is highly speculative, I imagine—I haven't seen it—does that kind of service, reopening the case without necessarily providing absolutely, finally the answer to the question. So whether you're adapting fact or indeed fiction for television, I think what you long to do is expand.

When one does turn to adapting fiction to film, the first thing one needs guiding the expansion is a devotion to good writing. Although television executives don't read books very often, at least they know they are there and they can look at the best-seller lists. If something has worked well in one medium, there is a sporting chance it will work well in another. That's why I think so much adaptation has been on the screen—both in the movies and in television since both those media began: adaptation is much safer than original work from the corporate point of view, and thus is accepted much more frequently, especially once someone vouches for the literature in question.

I developed my devotion to literature as a voracious reader from an early age. A British university education cannot give one the very best way of approaching literature; I think you have to learn it for yourself. I devoured the kind of adventure stories and thrillers which kids of my age read in the 1940s. They would include the work of John Buchan, Leslie Charteris, the Bulldog Drummond books, and Doyle's Holmes tales and the other adventure stories and historical novels he wrote. My own leap from that kind of reading into adult fiction was via American writers, oddly enough. John Steinbeck, John O'Hara, Ernest Hemingway, and Scott Fitzgerald were authors who showed me what books could do. From Britain, Graham Greene, Evelyn Waugh, George Orwell, Robert Louis Stevenson, and H.G. Wells. Then there are surprise books which you come across and have a huge influence on you, like the novels of J.D. Salinger or Heller's *Catch-22*—one of the great novels of the century.

But what is the creative work to transfer a story from one medium to another? If you are confronted with a piece of literature which you admire, then you admire it because it succeeds on its own terms. Why monkey around with it? The answer, I think, is something I've hinted at before. Whether you're dealing with fact or with fiction, I think what you long to do is to flesh it out. I believe that is why we do it. For instance, the writer and director of *The Devil's Foot* episode of the Holmes series added the sequence which embodies the ordeal that Holmes went through on a frightening hallucinatory drug. That rhapsody, that extension of what Doyle had proposed, but didn't actually expand on, was perhaps the most interesting part of the film. If you've got nothing to add, nothing to say about the original, then it's better simply to direct people to it. And you hope to direct them towards it anyway. But if you don't have some kind of gloss, even a minor one, to put on the work, then leave it alone.

Of course, simply the desire to expand on a work through adaptation is not enough to bring the project into production. The executive process involved in choosing which fiction to adapt to film is complicated and curious. There are certain novelists whose work seems to defy adaptation. In general, the best fiction of the second rank is probably the most adaptable, by which I mean, the Forsyte novels of John Galsworthy, for instance. There is a huge difference between the way Galsworthy wrote and the way Proust wrote. I don't think Proust's *Remembrance of Things Past* would make a particularly successful television series, though there is a fascinating film script by Harold Pinter which distills some of the essence of Proust, but it's never been made. I mentioned that *Catch-22* is a favorite novel of mine. I don't think the film of *Catch-22* is particularly successful, and as far as I know, Joseph Heller has not had any other successes in the camera medium. J.D. Salinger, of course, has resisted it apart from one short story he sold to Hollywood, probably when he needed the money. I don't think *Catcher in the Rye* would make a very good movie; I am sure it would be screwed up by whoever did it, whereas the *Forsyte Saga* was a huge success both in this country and in the States. That's the sort of thing that one immediately thinks is going to be the most successful kind of adaptation, because it has a very strong and rich story line, well-explored relationships between characters, and of course a theme which is perennially fascinating: the whole Edwardian obsession with property, money, position in society, and respectability at war with the more passionate sides of human nature. And Galsworthy dealt with it at great length which is wonderful for television, because people are always saying don't just give me 6 of those, I'd like to have 13 or 52 or 104. His works made 26 hours of television for the BBC, which is quite a good rate of striking.

Curiously, however, some novelists who have a very personal, often convoluted technique adapt rather well. I'm thinking, for instance, of Ford Madox Ford's *The Good Soldier*, which became a successful television film, although the original is a most unusual piece of storytelling—a gradual removal of layers of truth to reveal what has actually happened in a relationship, not told in a normal or particularly accessible linear order. You have to concentrate. You have to work when he takes you backwards and forwards. Paul Scott's huge novel sequence, *The Raj Quartet*, works in the same way. This is again not a linear narrative. It goes backwards and forwards in time and it changes its viewpoints, and again you have to concentrate very much on the work. But it adapted amazingly well to television, under the title *The Jewel in the Crown*, despite the fact that, on the face of it, it had many disadvantages. For instance, after the first couple of hours you have to abandon a couple of characters, for one of them is dead. You have adopted them as your viewpoint for the story; then you have to get to know a whole new cast of characters. Things like that are a great deterrent, because whether we underestimate the audience or not, there is always the danger that viewers will come in late and not find the story easy to pick up. Of course in film or television there's no chance to turn back to the beginning and have a look at the pages you missed. Nevertheless, Paul Scott's piece worked astonishingly well; it was probably one of the most admired adaptations that British television has produced.

I have to emphasize that the choice of such a complex piece is an unusual one. A piece of fiction usually appeals to executives for adaptation if it can be distilled into one or, at the most, two sentences. There is a firmly held belief amongst the people who control the purse strings that if you can describe a story in about twenty-five words, then it must be a story that is going to work on television. I don't quite know why that is. I suppose it's because time is short. You could tell the idea of Tarzan or Batman or Superman in that kind of form, so people believe only stories which can be distilled in that way are going to work. This method does put something of a limit on one's imagination, but it is often used.

After deciding if the story is a coherent one which audiences can easily accept, producers have to concentrate on what a film version of the fiction will cost. For instance, period pieces are not being produced as often as they used to be. The one that really drove a nail into their coffin was the Granada version of *A Tale of Two Cities*, I think. Because of the economic climate in which it was made, this had to be a co-production with a French partner. Besides, if ever Dickens wrote a novel for co-production, that had to be it, didn't it? So the piece was made by a multi-national team, as it were, a French director, British writer, some French casting, some British casting; and that relationship enabled the team to go to France and shoot the French bits there, and build sets in this country for the eighteenth-century London. It was sensibly set up in that way. But because it didn't have one overriding vision, and the success of any piece mostly depends on a single overriding vision, it failed. It had a good cast and a good director, but in the end it was a patchwork quilt which didn't really please anybody.

The next important consideration in choosing a piece of fiction for adaptation is successful precedent, especially in terms of length and shape. The enormous success of the Inspector Morse series has affected the format of other productions, because it has worked rather well in the two-hour feature-length segments. Now, two-hour segments are the only things that people want. You will notice that the Sherlock Holmes stories that are in production now, for instance, are no longer 60-minute films, which happened to suit the short stories very well—and that is chiefly what Conan Doyle wrote. What Granada is making now are two-hour films, and stories long enough to support that length are difficult to find. So the producers are having to expand and blow up stories to satisfy a scheduling need which derives from the success of another product. At the same time, *Morse* has made John Thaw an enormously important actor. And there aren't too many internationally bankable actors like Thaw or Jeremy Brett around, which means that anything in which you could credibly cast either will probably get made in this country.

Both powerful actors and format influence the possibility of a pre-sale overseas which can greatly enhance the production budget. The economics of the business are such that if you can sell your work ahead of production, you always get a better price for it than if you sell it after the event. For some reason, once you are out there in the market place with a finished piece, however successful it's been, its value is diminished. I suppose that's understandable—it's been done, so you don't actually need the money to do it. But someone who comes in on the ground floor and agrees to buy the piece in advance of production knows that they are an essential ingredient of the budget, and, therefore, they are prepared to pay a little more. So sales to America are a vital part of the game. When I set up the Sherlock Holmes series, I knew that an American sale would bring in a sum of money which would enhance the budget by say 20 percent. Now that 20 percent would be the part of the budget that actually paid for the quality. The rest of the budget paid for the necessities—the film stock, the cost of the crew, the transportation, the meals, and accommodations. The American 20 percent paid for the better costumes, the farther-flung locations, the higher quality casting—the elements, I think, that made it solid and more highly polished.

Of course, British producers have to pay a price for that extra 20 percent from America, but we have been exceedingly lucky in our relationship with the Public Broadcasting Service in the States over the last 10 to 15 years. We have dealt with sympathetic people who have allowed us to make television drama according to our own standards and not forced us to conform to someone else's. That doesn't mean that you ignore the taste of the American audience. Far from it. For instance, I thought that the Sherlock Holmes stories formed a viable proposition because I knew of their terrific popularity in the States, perhaps even greater than in this country. I built in a little insurance when I started the series by asking John Hawkesworth to be senior script consultant on the piece. John had had several successes in the States: a slightly surprising one called *Danger UXB*, which was about unexploded bombs in World War II, but, more understandably, *Upstairs Downstairs*, which was brilliant. I know it was a great success for PBS as it was for London Weekend Television here. So I asked John if he would help, and happily he turned out to be a Sherlock Holmes fan too and was very happy to come in on the production. That gave me insurance, as I say, an "in" with our American partners so that they were convinced that we would be doing something of the kind of taste and quality that they were looking for. Their enthusiasm brought us the extra money which guaranteed that the source material could be properly served.

Once a story is chosen for production, much work must be done to it before filming actually begins. I believe that the principle which should govern adaptation is fidelity to the original spirit of the piece if not always to the letter, because the letter does not always necessarily work on film. The target must be to do what the novelist might have done if he had been writing a film script. I try to remember the oldest movie adage: don't tell me, show me. Words matter, heaven knows, but in a film words are juxtaposed with images. "Watch my lips" is not actually drama. Drama is "watch my eyes" or "watch my hands" while words are said. So the guiding principle is to make into the stuff of camera-drama what the author intended.

Perhaps the most important element in making a film which will carry the author's narrative intent and still be cinematically successful is structure; a story must be told at the right pace and in the right order, and transferring actions from descriptions to dramatizations can change the timing of a narrative completely. For this, one needs a built-in clock to produce something that plays not only at the right length but has got the right proportions. All of the Holmes episodes began with a kind of teaser sequence at the beginning so that we had a flavor of the crime, our own mystery to puzzle over before Holmes was given it. This splendid idea came from John Hawkesworth. It pulls an audience in by tantalizing them. But then I worried about the inevitable second scene, the second paragraph, which is generally Doyle's first paragraph, which is the client arriving at the door and Holmes, having perhaps briefed Watson with a sentence or two, saying, "Ah, here comes our man now. I think that's his knock." And up the 17 stairs to 221B comes the client, who sits down and tells a story. Now that is a rather repetitive structure. But Hawkesworth said, "No, don't throw that away. That is what the audience expects. That's what they have learned to enjoy in the story. When they get that, they will feel at home and secure and know that they are in the right place." And of course he's absolutely right. You can't monkey with that element of Doyle, but you can add a little flourish at the beginning without altering the spirit.

Other elements of the story must be altered because of budgetary limitations, and one of the first changes which may occur in adaptation is the consolidation of minor incidents, settings, and characters. The original writer, Conan Doyle in our case, can propose anything. The most exotic location, the biggest crowd scene, adds not a penny to the cost of ink and paper, but in a film it's a major consideration. Take, for instance, the story of Silver Blaze, the missing racehorse. In fact, the horse-race at the end is not a necessary part of the story, but try to stop a director from showing it. He will say, "That is a natural climax, when the horse has been returned, when the mystery's been solved. You expect to see the horse win the race." And, of course, he's right. There is an audience expectation there. In theory the mystery would be just as compelling a mystery without the race and it would be much more economical to make. But we didn't remove the horse race, as I'm sure you noticed.

Also, if you can get away from the "Charing Cross Hotel" or a "Scene at the Opera," then you are going to save an enormous amount of money on crowd artists. And they cost twice as much in a period piece as they do in a contemporary piece. If you're paying them 50 pounds a day to be there, you're probably paying 50 pounds a day to costume them, as well, aside from feeding them and paying their national insurance money and all of the things that go with it. It's tedious to have to keep saying so much about money, but I suppose it is the producer's job to a very large extent. So shaping a story to be told with the minimum necessary number of scenes and characters and the most contained list of locations is a necessary part of the game. There is considerable economy in the Sherlock Holmes stories in spending a considerable amount of time in front of the fire at Baker Street. It does tend to produce howls of agony both from the actors and the directors, because they say it's all talk—there are these two chaps or two chaps and a client in front of the fireplace simply making conversation. It's not the stuff of which exciting movies are made. They are right, of course, but a few minutes of that can pay for quite a lot of stunts and railway trains elsewhere.

In addition to money, time also strictly controls the possibilities within an adaptation. The director, the producer, and the writer often will sit down and discuss ways in which things might be changed, shortened, or lengthened in order to respect the tyranny of the 51-minute film. The most latitude you have either way is, perhaps, 30 seconds. That can present serious problems if, during filming, you realize your work will run over. I've been watching recently one of the Holmes films called *Wisteria Lodge*. One of the sad things about the final version of *Wisteria Lodge* is that the whole explanation of what John Scott Eccles is doing at Wisteria Lodge and why Garcia invited him there has been omitted from the edited version. Obviously that was not a decision that was lightly taken. In the editorial process something had to go. There were probably 53, 54, or 55 minutes, and what went, of course, was one of those scenes which a director friend of mine calls the "There's one thing I don't understand, Inspector" scenes. By the time you need the explanation, Eccles has disappeared from the story. Other concerns have taken over, so it must have seemed to others legitimate to omit the explanation. It seems to me to be a flaw, and I blame myself for not having noticed it and corrected it.

During the actual filming even more changes might be made to the scripted adaptation, changes which may remove it further from or bring it closer to the original story. One would like to think that all directors worked as I'm told Alfred Hitchcock worked, in that every shot, every angle, every pause and movement was planned down to the last detail before he ever went on location or into a studio. That's asking an awful lot, because very few people are as meticulously aware of exactly what they want as Hitchcock was. I think you also need someone who can respond to the input of other people. It would be sad if a director was not able to respond to what an actor suggests. And it would also be sad if he was unable to respond to what a location offers. You might go to a particular place one day when the sun is shining and decide that you will shoot a scene in the sunshine. But because of the wonderfully entertaining English climate, by the time you come to do it, it may be black skies and pouring with rain. The guy who can respond to that change in the climate and make use of it and integrate it into the scene he is doing is obviously someone to treasure.

One of the least tangible concerns in translating a piece of fiction from the page to the screen is a concern to satisfy the audience, including those who have never read the original and, perhaps more importantly, those who have. This is perhaps where fidelity to the spirit of the original text is most important. Persuading people who have not read the original to pick it up is one of the great satisfactions that can come from adaptation. It seems to happen frequently, because if any kind of classic is adapted for the big screen or the small, sales of that book tend to rise dramatically, which suggests we're doing a useful job. But readers can be more difficult to please. I think we all know that we've read a book ourselves and had in our minds the kind of person, the kind of setting, that story brings to mind. It's not always possible to match that. I suppose the best example in the world is *Gone With the Wind*. I think everybody who read *Gone With the Wind*, as far as I can judge, thought that Rhett Butler had to be played by Clark Gable. And fortunately he *was* played by Clark Gable. One can't always satisfy the original reader as neatly as that. What is most liable to disappear from an adaptation is the writer's style, and if it does, you're in desperate trouble.

For example, Evelyn Waugh's *Brideshead Revisited* inspired a remarkably successful adaptation of fiction to film; however, the success lay not simply in the translation of setting and character and plot. I think if you have sufficient money you can create Oxford (or Paris or Venice or London) in the 1920s. If you get the casting right—and I think that the casting of Jeremy Irons and Anthony Andrews was magically right—then Evelyn Waugh is not so hard to do. But to put it all together, you need to trust Waugh's tone of voice. In *Brideshead Revisited* the adapter, John Mortimer, and the producer and director wisely decided to use a great deal of voice-over in the narrative so that Charles Ryder, who really embodies the Evelyn Waugh voice as the narrator, articulated that style, and there was no danger that Waugh's particular tone—whether ironic or romantic or whatever—would be lost.

Our success with fans of Doyle's work comes from the fact that in most of the scripts that we have done for the series, we have been more faithful to Doyle's unique tone than any other filmmakers. When there was either a compelling need or the possibility of adding to the stories that Doyle had written, we could be as agile as anybody else, but we always attempted to build on what Conan Doyle provided without betraying him. For instance, I suggested that we put *The Red-Headed League* in the twelfth slot in *The Adventures* and that we credit the infamous Moriarty with that wonderful device for distracting a man from his work. This would then lead up to *The Final Problem*, which was our number 13, the grandstand finale. The writer, John Hawkesworth, built Moriarty into *The Red-Headed League*, which Doyle had not done, and then tackled the problem of adapting "The Final Problem," which is not a very good Sherlock Holmes story, alas, as any student of the canon knows. It doesn't have very much for Holmes to do except take Watson on a continental holiday and apparently try to avoid Moriarty. Remember, Doyle was tired of his hero at this point, and while he was writing the story, he's supposed to have written a letter to his mother, saying something to the effect that "I'm in the middle of the last Sherlock Holmes story now. After this, the man disappears forever. I'm weary of his name." So he wrote a story which disposes of Sherlock Holmes, and John and I were confronted with the problem of how to make that into a coherent and attractive film script. John came up with the notion of Moriarty trying to steal the *Mona Lisa*. He built all that into the beginning and made what, in detection terms, is one of Doyle's less satisfactory pieces into a film script which I think combines the best of Hawkesworth and the best of Doyle, because you get the detective story to begin with, and you get this extraordinary elegy for the end of a friendship, which is what Watson feels about the death of Holmes at the end of the piece.

One adaptive change which I got criticized for involved the end of *The Greek Interpreter*. I think Conan Doyle loved the idea of one man who, because he speaks the same language as another, can communicate with him in a room full of enemies who have no idea what they're saying—and Doyle used it brilliantly and imaginatively. But when he used it, he allowed the rest of the story—the whole structure of character and incident—to fall apart. He says at the end of the story, and I'm quoting, "Months afterwards a curious newspaper cutting reached us. . . . It told how two Englishmen who had been travelling with a woman had met with a tragic end. . . . [Holmes] holds to this day that, if one could find the Grecian girl, one might learn how the wrongs of herself and her brother came to be avenged" (I, 446). Well, it's a puzzling situation, isn't it, that the girl, who was the sister of a man who had been appallingly treated by the villains, had fled with them. First of all, I think, one has to decide whether the girl was guilty or innocent. Then, perhaps, one has to tackle the need to give the story a satisfying ending by showing what happened to those three people. That's what we chose to do. We pursued them onto a railway train. We even took Mycroft Holmes with us, Mycroft, who is alleged never to move further than a few hundred yards either from his apartment or his club, and we showed what happened on a very exciting train journey. It's not in the story. It involves an extension or an imaginative leap, which I think is justified.

In *The Norwood Builder* we were even more justified in doing what we did. That episode depends upon a man disappearing by faking his own death in a fire where some charred bones are discovered. When Holmes discovers the man still alive at the very end of the story, he says to him, "By the way, what was it you put into the wood-pile besides your old trousers? A dead dog, or rabbits, or what? You won't tell? Dear me, how very unkind of you! Well, well, I daresay that a couple of rabbits would account both for the blood and for the charred ashes. If ever you write an account, Watson, you can make rabbits serve your turn" (II, 510). Well, with all respect to Conan Doyle, I think that's nonsense; and, as a medical man, he should have known it was nonsense. Forensic science had been a serious study for most of the nineteenth century. I don't think any police doctor would have been taken in by animals' bones serving as human remains. So we changed the story, using a clue that Doyle provided about the disappearance of an old tramp. We made it, I suppose, a more serious crime, but a more believable one in that the Norwood builder had killed a tramp and used the tramp's body to fake his own death rather than using a dog or rabbits. So where changes like that have been made, they've been made in order to support the stories.

The story that we changed most of all is "The Disappearance of Lady Frances Carfax," which, like "The Greek Interpreter," has a very good central device: two bodies in one coffin as a way of disposing of somebody. This is a very tricky device to stage because you do need an unusually deep coffin, and presumably it would be more obvious than Doyle allows it to be in the story. That's a good mystery to introduce, but the mechanics by which we reach it are not quite so satisfactory. We never meet Lady Frances Carfax before she's discovered in the coffin. She never appears in the story as Watson pursues her from city to city across Europe, eventually being saved from a blunder by Holmes, who has been pursuing her also, while disguised as a French artisan. So having decided to do it and to stick somewhere near the original, we found a location for one of the places where Watson goes, which is a Swiss spa. Then we thought, well, if we're going to go to the English Lake District and pretend it's a Swiss spa, why bother? Why not use what's a beautiful stretch of country anyway and say that it is exactly what it is and construct a story in which Watson is there for a good reason. That way we can meet Lady Frances, build up a couple suspects, and simply reorder and relocate the piece in a different setting so that one preserves the mystery. I hope we actually enhanced the mystery and made an exciting investigation out of a story that is just a little lame in its original form.

I must admit that in the Holmes films I never consulted a professional in textual analysis for guidance on the adaptation. It's not because of a prejudice against experts in that field, but I've never actually felt the need of it. That may show enormous conceit on my part, but I'm not sure that someone whose main concern is the analysis of a text in literary terms—and goodness knows those are now pretty abstruse—is going to be a great help to people who want to translate that onto the screen. A professional in the field of history, however, yes. I think one always needs to go to such a source for exact reference on costume, behavior, appearance—all of those things—and we do. I was interested that John Hawkesworth has a technique with writers which is a useful one, I think. As soon as they are commissioned, he gives them a precise date for the story they are writing and asks them to go off and read the newspapers for the week or month around that date. Nothing they read may emerge in the script, but I think that process of absorbing what was happening in a particular month of 1891, or whatever it may be, is going to pay off in some way or other.

So, finally, I suppose it is worth saying why one does it. If it doesn't sound too pretentious, I can only say that I wanted to put these stories onto film and to dramatize them simply to add to the sum of human happiness. I'm able to enjoy them in more than one form. I enjoy the story on the printed page. I enjoy a film version of it, which may be a little different or substantially different. I would also enjoy a musical about Sherlock Holmes, although I've not yet seen a good one. I enjoyed cartoon strips based on Sherlock Holmes. I think that all these activities are defensible if they are done with some kind of loyalty and if they entertain. I must say that when I was producing *The Adventures of Sherlock Holmes*, and when I returned to the front line to produce *The Casebook* a year or so ago, I thought myself exceedingly lucky. I think that while I was doing it I probably had the best job in television.

NOTES

¹The passage from "Seymour" reads as follows: "If only you'd remember before ever you sit down to write that you've been a *reader* long before you were ever a writer. You simply fix that fact in your mind, then sit very still and ask yourself, as a reader, what piece of writing in all the world Buddy Glass would most want to read if he had his heart's choice. The next step is terrible, but so simple I can hardly believe it as I write it. You just sit down shamelessly and write the thing yourself. . . . Trust your heart. You're a deserving craftsman" (187).

WORKS CITED

Doyle, Arthur Conan. "The Adventure of the Norwood Builder." *The Complete Sherlock Holmes* II, 496-510.

____. *The Complete Sherlock Holmes.* 2 vols. Garden City, New York: Doubleday, 1927.

____. "The Greek Interpreter." *The Complete Sherlock Holmes* I, 435-46.

Salinger, J.D. *"Raise High the Roof Beam, Carpenters"* and *"Seymour: An Introduction."* Boston: Little, Brown, [1959].

Works Cited

The Abbey Grange. Exec. Prod. Michael Cox. Dir. Peter Hammond. Dram. Trevor Bowen. Granada Television. 1986. *MYSTERY!* PBS. WGBH, Boston. 12 Feb. 1987.

After The Thin Man. Dir. W.S. Van Dyke. Prod. Hunt Stromberg. Writ. Albert Hackett and Frances Goodrich. With William Powell, Myrna Loy, James Stewart, Jessie Ralph, and Sam Levene. Metro-Goldwyn-Mayer, 1936.

"And the Winner Is . . . 'Silence of Lambs' Sweeps 5 Top Oscars." *Journal American* [Bellevue, WA] 31 Mar. 1991, B1.

Another Thin Man. Dir. W.S. Van Dyke. Prod. Hunt Stromberg. Writ. Albert Hackett and Frances Goodrich. With William Powell, Myrna Loy, C. Aubrey Smith, Otto Kruger, and Nat Pendleton. Metro-Goldwyn-Mayer, 1939.

Anthony, Carolyn. "Crime Marches On." *Publishers Weekly* 13 Apr. 1990: 24-25.

Archer, Eugene. "Laura." *Movie* Sept. 1962: 12-13.

Auerbach, Nina. *Communities of Women.* Cambridge: Harvard UP, 1978.

August, Lissa. "Picks & Pans." *People Weekly* 23 May 1983: 9-23.

Bakerman, Jane. "Vera Caspary's Chicago, Symbol and Setting." *Midamerica* 11 (1984): 81-89.

____. "Vera Caspary's Fascinating Females: Laura, Evvie, and Bedelia." *Clues* 1.1 (1980): 46-52.

Barton, Sabrina. "'Crisscross': Paranoia and Projection in *Strangers on a Train.*" *camera obscura* Jan.-May 1991: 75-100.

Behlmer, Rudy. *America's Favorite Movies: Behind the Scenes.* New York: Ungar, 1982.

Beja, Morris. *Film and Literature: An Introduction.* New York: Longman, 1979.

Benenson, Laurie Halpern. "Kathleen Turner: Going Public as a Private Eye." *New York Times* 14 Apr. 1991: 20.

Berger, John. *Ways of Seeing.* London: British Broadcasting Corporation; Harmondsworth: Penguin, 1972.

Bergstrom, Janet. "Alternation, Segmentation, Hypnosis: Interview with Raymond Bellour—An Excerpt." Penley 186-95.

Bluestone, George. *Novels into Film.* Baltimore: Johns Hopkins UP, 1957.

The Body in the Library. Dram. T.R. Bowen. Dir. Silvio Narizzano. MYSTERY! PBS. WGBH, Boston. 2, 9, 16 Jan. 1986.

Boggs, Joseph M. *The Art of Watching Films.* Mountain View, CA: Mayfield, 1991.

Bok. "Travis McGee." *Variety Television Reviews.* Ed. Howard H. Prouty. 15 vols. to date. New York: Garland, 1989- . 13: n.p.

Borzello, Frances, Annette Kuhn, Jill Pack, and Cassandra Wedd. "Living Dolls and 'Real Women.'" *The Power of the Image: Essays on Representation and Sexuality.* Ed. Annette Kuhn. London: Routledge, 1985. 9-18.

Boyum, Joy Gould. *Double Exposure: Fiction into Film.* New York: Universe Books, 1985.

Brill, Lesley. *The Hitchcock Romance: Love and Irony in Hitchcock's Films.* Princeton: Princeton UP, 1988.

A Caribbean Mystery. Dir. Robert Michael Lewis. With Helen Hayes, Maurice Evans, Bernard Hughes. CBS. WCBS, New York. 22 Oct. 1983.

Caspary, Vera. *Laura.* 1943. New York: Avon Books, 1970.

____. "Mark McPherson." *The Great Detectives.* Ed. Otto Penzler. Boston: Little, Brown, 1978. 143-46.

____. "My Laura and Otto's." *Saturday Review* 26 June 1971: 36-37.

Cawelti, John G. *Adventure, Mystery, and Romance: Formula Stories as Art and Popular Culture.* Chicago: U of Chicago P, 1976.

Chodorow, Nancy. *The Reproduction of Mothering: Psychoanalysis and the Sociology of Gender.* Berkeley: U of California P, 1978.

Christie, Agatha. *An Autobiography.* 1977. New York: Berkley, 1991.

____. *At Bertram's Hotel.* 1965. New York: Harper, 1992.

____. *The Body in the Library.* 1942. New York: Harper, 1992.

____. *4:50 from Paddington.* 1957. New York: Pocket Books, 1958.

____. *Funerals Are Fatal.* 1953. New York: Harper, 1992.

____. *The Mirror Crack'd from Side to Side.* 1962. New York: Harper, 1992.

____. *Mrs. McGinty's Dead.* New York: Dodd, 1952.

____. *The Murder at the Vicarage.* 1930. New York: Dodd, 1977.

____. *Nemesis.* 1971. New York: Harper, 1992.

____. *A Pocket Full of Rye.* 1953. New York: Pocket Books, 1955.

____. *Sleeping Murder.* New York: Dodd, 1976.

____. *They Do It with Mirrors.* New York: Dodd, 1952.

Clark, Randall. "Stirling Silliphant." *American Screenwriters.* Ed. Robert E. Morseberger, Stephen O. Lesser, and Randall Clark. Detroit: Bruccoli Clark-Gale, 1984. 294-99.

Cleveland, Carol. "Travis McGee: The Feminists' Friend." *The Armchair Detective* 16 (1983): 407-13.

Clouse, Robert, dir. *Darker than Amber*. Writ. Ed Waters. Rod Taylor, Suzy Kendall, and Theodore Bikel. National General, 1970.

Cox, Michael. Personal Interviews. 28 Nov. 1990 and 12 Feb. 1991.

Craig, Patricia, and Mary Cadogan. *The Lady Investigates: Women Detectives and Spies in Fiction*. 1981. New York: Oxford UP, 1986.

Crist, Judith. "This Week's Movies." *TV Guide* 14 May 1983: A5, A56.

Crowther, Bosley. "*Laura*." *New York Times* 12 Oct. 1944: 24.

The Dead of Jericho. Adapt. Anthony Minghella. Dir. Alastair Reid. Prod. Kenny McBain. *MYSTERY!* PBS. WGBH, Boston. 4, 11 Feb. 1988.

Death on the Nile. Dir. John Guillin. With Peter Ustinov, Mia Farrow, Bette Davis, Maggie Smith, David Niven, and Angela Lansbury. EMI. 1978.

Deceived by Flight. Writ. Anthony Minghella. Dir. Anthony Simmons. Prod. Chris Burt. *MYSTERY!* PBS. WGBH, Boston. 30 May and 6 June 1991.

De Lauretis, Teresa. *Alice Doesn't*. Bloomington: Indiana UP, 1984.

Denby, David. Rev. of *Presumed Innocent*. *New York* 6 Aug. 1990: 45.

Desowitz, Bill. "Life With Video: Strangers on Which Train?" *Film Comment* May-June 1992: 4-5.

The Devil's Foot. Exec. Prod. Michael Cox. Dir. Ken Hannam. Dram. Gary Hopkins. Granada Television. 1985. *MYSTERY!* PBS. WGBH, Boston. 3 Nov. 1988.

Dexter, Colin. "Criminal Dexterity: An Interview with Colin Dexter." With Markman Ellis. *Waterstone's New Books*. London: Blackmore, 1991.

———. *The Dead of Jericho*. 1981. London: Pan, 1983.

———. *The Jewel that was Ours*. London: Macmillan, 1991.

———. *Last Bus to Woodstock*. 1975. New York: Bantam, 1989.

———. *The Riddle of the Third Mile*. 1983. New York: Bantam, 1988.

———. *Service of All the Dead*. 1979. London: Pan, 1980.

———. *The Silent World of Nicholas Quinn*. 1977. New York: Bantam, 1988.

Dick, Bernard F. *Anatomy of Film*. 2nd ed. New York: St. Martin's, 1990.

Dmytryk, Edward. *On Screen Writing*. Boston: Focal-Butterworth, 1985.

Doane, Mary Ann. "*Caught* and *Rebecca*: The Inscription of Femininity as Absence." Penley 196-215.

———. *Femmes Fatales: Feminism, Film Theory, Psychoanalysis*. New York: Routledge, 1991.

Donahugh, Robert H. "*Presumed Innocent*." *Library Journal* 1 June 1987: 130.

Douglas, John. Interview. "The Psycho Squad." *Sixty Minutes*. CBS. KIRO, Seattle. 17 Nov. 1991.

Doyle, Arthur Conan. "The Adventure of the Devil's Foot." *The Complete Sherlock Holmes* II, 954-70.

____. "The Adventure of the Illustrious Client." *The Complete Sherlock Holmes* II, 984-99.

____. "The Adventure of the Norwood Builder." *The Complete Sherlock Holmes* II, 496-510.

____. *The Complete Sherlock Holmes*. 2 vols. Garden City, New York: Doubleday, 1927.

____. "The Greek Interpreter." *The Complete Sherlock Holmes* I, 435-46.

____. "A Scandal in Bohemia." *The Complete Sherlock Holmes* I, 161-75.

Driven to Distraction. Writ. Anthony Minghella. Dir. Sandy Johnson. Prod. David Lascelles. MYSTERY! PBS. WGBH, Boston. 23, 30 Apr. 1992.

Durgnat, Raymond. *The Strange Case of Alfred Hitchcock, Or The Plain Man's Hitchcock.* Cambridge, MA: MIT, 1974.

Dyer, Richard. "Resistance through Charisma: Rita Hayworth and *Gilda.*" Kaplan, *Women* 91-99.

Farrel, Manny. "Murdered Movie." *The New Republic* 30 Oct. 1944: 568.

Fat Chance. Writ. Alma Cullen. Dir. Roy Battersby. Prod. David Lascelles. MYSTERY! PBS. WGBH, Boston. 8, 15 Apr. 1993.

Foote, Harold. "Writing for Film." *Films and Literature: A Comparative Approach to Adaptation.* Eds. Wendell Aycock and Michael Shoenecke. Lubbock, TX: Texas Tech UP, 1988. 5-20.

4:50 from Paddington. Dram. T.R. Bowen. Dir. Martyn Friend. MYSTERY! PBS. WGBH, Boston. 9, 16 Mar. 1989.

Fraser, C. Gerald. "Television Week." *New York Times* 16 Oct. 1982: 84.

Garber, Marjorie. *Vested Interests: Cross Dressing and Cultural Anxiety.* New York: Routledge, 1992.

Gaudy Night. Dir. Michael Simpson. Prod. Michael Chapman. Writ. Philip Broadley. BBC2. 13, 20, 27 May 1987. *MYSTERY!* PBS. WGBH, Boston. 19, 26 Nov. and 3 Dec. 1987.

Geherin, David. *John D. MacDonald.* New York: Ungar, 1982.

The Ghost in the Machine. Writ. Julian Mitchell. Dir. Herbert Wise. Prod. Chris Burt. MYSTERY! PBS. WGBH, Boston. 17, 24 May 1990.

Gilbert, Sandra M., and Susan Gubar. *The Madwoman in the Attic: The Woman Writer and the Nineteenth-Century Literary Imagination.* New Haven: Yale UP, 1979.

Gill, Gillian. *Agatha Christie: The Woman and Her Mysteries.* New York: Free, 1990.

Goodman, Walter. "A Sterling Gallery of Sleuths." *New York Times.* 13 Mar. 1988: Section 2, 31+.

Gorbman, Claudia. *Unheard Melodies: Narrative Film Music.* Bloomington: Indiana UP, 1987.

Grimes, Larry E. "The Reluctant Hero: Reflections on Vocation and Heroism in the Travis McGee Novels of John D. MacDonald." *Clues: A Journal of Detection* 1.1 (1980): 103-08.

Grobel, Lawrence. "Anything is Possible." *Movieline* Oct. 1991: 28-33, 75-76.

Hammett, Dashiell. *The Thin Man*. 1934. New York: Alfred A. Knopf, 1962.

____. *The Thin Man*. 1934. New York: Random House, 1972.

Hardwicke, Edward. "Edward Hardwicke on Conan Doyle's Popularity." Interview. PBS. WGBH, Boston. Attached to *The Problem of Thor Bridge*.

Harris, Thomas. *The Silence of the Lambs*. 1988. New York: St. Martin's, 1989.

Haskell, Molly. *From Reverence to Rape: The Treatment of Women in the Movies*. New York: Penguin, 1973.

Have His Carcase. Dir. Christopher Hodson. Prod. Michael Chapman. Writ. Rosemary Anne Sisson. BBC2. 15, 22, 29 Apr. and 6 May 1987. *MYSTERY!* PBS. WGBH, Boston. 22, 29 Oct. and 5, 12 Nov. 1987.

Herbert, Rosemary. "Aiming Higher." *Publishers Weekly* 13 Apr. 1990: 30-32.

Highsmith, Patricia. *Plotting and Writing Suspense Fiction*. New York: St. Martin's, 1983.

____. *Strangers on a Train*. Baltimore: Penguin, 1950.

Himmelstein, Hal. *On the Small Screen: New Approaches in Television and Video Criticism*. New York: Praeger, 1981.

Hitchcock, Alfred, dir. *Strangers on a Train*. Warner Brothers, 1951.

Hjortsberg, William. *Falling Angel*. New York: Harcourt Brace Jovanovich, 1978.

The Illustrious Client. Prod. Michael Cox. Dir. Tim Sullivan. Dram. Robin Chapman. Granada Television. 1991. *MYSTERY!* PBS. WGBH, Boston. 14 Nov. 1992.

The Infernal Serpent. Writ. Alma Cullen. Dir. John Madden. Prod. David Lascelles. *MYSTERY!* PBS. WGBH, Boston. 16, 23 May 1991.

Jackson, Rosemary. *Fantasy: The Literature of Subversion*. London: Methuen, 1981.

James, P.D. *A Taste for Death*. London: Faber, 1986.

Johnson, Diane. *Dashiell Hammett: A Life*. New York: Random House, 1983.

Kaminsky, Stuart. *American Film Genres*. 2nd ed. Chicago: Nelson-Hall, 1985.

Kaplan, E. Ann. *Women and Film: Both Sides of the Camera*. London: Methuen, 1983.

____, ed. *Women in Film Noir*. London: British Film Institute, 1980.

Kauffmann, Stanley. "Gluttons for Punishment." *The New Republic* 18 Feb. 1991: 48-49.

Kenney, Catherine. *The Remarkable Case of Dorothy L. Sayers.* Kent, Ohio: Kent State UP, 1990.

Klein, Kathleen Gregory. "Patricia Highsmith." *And Then There Were Nine . . . More Women of Mystery.* Ed. Jane S. Bakerman. Bowling Green, OH: Bowling Green State University Popular Press, 1985: 170-97.

Krupp, Charla. "Word On . . . " *Glamour* Dec. 1991: 131.

Krutnik, Frank. *In a Lonely Street: Film Noir, Genre, Masculinity.* New York: Routledge, 1991.

Kuhn, Annette. *Women's Pictures: Feminism and Cinema.* London: Routledge & Kegan Paul, 1982.

The Last Enemy. Adapt. Peter Buckman. Dir. James Scott. Prod. Chris Burt. *MYSTERY!* PBS. WGBH, Boston. 31 May and 7 June 1990.

"Laura." *Daily Variety* 11 Oct. 1944: 3.

Laura. Prod. and dir. Otto Preminger. With Gene Tierney, Dana Andrews, Clifton Webb, Vincent Price, and Judith Anderson. Twentieth Century-Fox, 1944.

Leese, Elizabeth. "Laura." *Magill's Survey of Cinema: English Language Films, First Series.* Ed. Frank N. Magill. 4 vols. Englewood Cliffs, NJ: Salem P, 1980. 2: 948-51.

Lehmann, Chris. "Jonathan Demme and the Aesthetics of Contempt." *Tikkun* July-Aug. 1991: 74-79.

Leonardi, Susan J. *Dangerous by Degrees.* New Brunswick: Rutgers UP, 1989.

Luhr, William, and Peter Lehman. *Authorship and Narrative in the Cinema: Issues in Contemporary Aesthetics and Criticism.* New York: Putnam, 1977.

MacDonald, John D. *Cinnamon Skin: The Twentieth Adventure of Travis McGee.* 1982. New York: Fawcett, 1983.

____. *Darker than Amber.* 1966. New York: Fawcett, 1982.

____. *The Deep Blue Good-by.* 1964. New York: Fawcett, 1982.

____. *The Empty Copper Sea.* New York: Fawcett, 1978.

____. "Introduction and Comment." *Clues: A Journal of Detection* 1.1 (1980): 63-74.

____. *A Tan and Sandy Silence.* New York: Fawcett, 1971.

Marrill, Alvin H. *Movies Made for Television: The Telefeature and the Mini-Series: 1984-1986.* New York: Zoetrope-Baseline, 1987.

Masonic Mysteries. Writ. Julian Mitchell. Dir. Danny Boyle. Prod. David Lascelles. *MYSTERY!* PBS. WGBH, Boston. 9, 16 Apr. 1992.

McDougal, Stuart Y. *Made Into Movies: From Literature to Film*. New York: Holt, Rinehart and Winston, 1985.

McFadyean, Melanie. "The Man for the Job." *The Guardian* 19 Sept. 1991: 24.

McLaglen, Andrew V., dir. *Travis McGee: The Empty Copper Sea*. Writ. Stirling Silliphant. Sam Elliott, Gene Evans, and Katharine Ross. Warner Bros., 1983.

McNamara, Eugene. *Laura as Novel, Film, and Myth*. Lewiston, NY: Edwin Mellen, 1992.

____. "Preminger's *Laura* and the Fatal Woman Tradition." *Clues* 3.2 (1982): 24-29.

Mellen, Joan. *Women and their Sexuality in the New Film*. New York: Dell, 1973.

Meyers, Richard. "*TAD* on TV." *The Armchair Detective* 16 (1983): 428-30.

Miller, William. *Screenwriting for Narrative Film and Television*. New York: Communication Arts-Hastings House, 1980.

The Mirror Cracked. Dir. Guy Hamilton. With Angela Lansbury, Geraldine Chaplin, Tony Curtis, Rock Hudson, Kim Novak, and Elizabeth Taylor. EMI. 1980.

Monaco, James. *How to Read a Film: The Art, Technology, Language, History and Theory of Film and Media*. New York: Oxford UP, 1977.

Moran, Peggy. "McGee's Girls." *Clues: A Journal of Detection* 1.1 (1980): 82-88.

Morgan, Janet. *Agatha Christie: A Biography*. New York: Knopf, 1984.

Mulvey, Laura. "Visual Pleasure and Narrative Cinema." Penley 57-68.

Murder Ahoy! Dir. George Pollock. With Margaret Rutherford and Stringer Davis. MGM. 1964.

Murder at the Gallop. Dir. George Pollock. With Margaret Rutherford and Stringer Davis. MGM. 1963.

Murder Most Foul. Dir. George Pollock. With Margaret Rutherford and Stringer Davis. MGM. 1964.

Murder on the Orient Express. Dir. Sidney Lumet. With Albert Finney, Lauren Bacall, Ingrid Bergman. EMI. 1974.

Murder She Said. Dir. George Pollock. With Margaret Rutherford and Stringer Davis. MGM. 1962.

Murder with Mirrors. Dir. Dick Lowry. With Helen Hayes, Bette Davis, John Mills, and Leo McKern. CBS. WCBS, New York. 20 Feb. 1985.

The Naval Treaty. Prod. Michael Cox. Dir. Alan Grint. Dram. Jeremy Paul. Granada Television. 1984. *MYSTERY!* PBS. WGBH, Boston. 28 Mar. 1985.

Nemesis. Dram. T.R. Bowen. Dir. David Tucker. MYSTERY! PBS. WGBH, Boston. 10, 17 Dec. 1987.

O'Connor, John J. "TV: Three-Part Series on Blacks in the Military." *New York Times* 18 May 1983: C27.

Osborne, Charles. *The Life and Crimes of Agatha Christie*. New York: Holt, 1982.

Paretsky, Sarah. *Deadlock*. New York: Dial, 1984.

____. *Guardian Angel*. New York: Delacorte, 1992.

____. *Indemnity Only*. New York: Dial, 1982.

Parish, James Robert, and Michael R. Pitts. *The Great Detective Pictures*. Metuchen, NJ: Scarecrow, 1990.

Parker, Alan, dir. *Angel Heart*. Prod. Alan Marshall and Elliot Kasner. CAROLCO. 1987.

Peary, Danny. *Cult Movies 2*. New York: Dell, 1985.

Penley, Constance, ed. *Feminism and Film Theory*. New York: Routledge, 1988.

____. "Introduction." Penley 1-24.

Persons, Dan. "Scripting the Bestseller." *Cinefantastique* Feb. 1992: 31.

Pitts, Michael R. *Famous Movie Detectives*. Metuchen, NJ: Scarecrow, 1979.

Place, Janey. "Women in Film Noir." Kaplan, *Women* 35-67.

Pratley, Gerald. *The Cinema of Otto Preminger*. New York: Castle Books, 1971.

Prendergast, Roy M. *A Neglected Art: A Critical Study of Music in Films*. New York: New York UP, 1977.

Presumed Innocent. Dir. Alan Pakula. Warner Brothers, 1990.

The Problem of Thor Bridge. Prod. Michael Cox. Dir. Michael Simpson. Dram. Jeremy Paul. Granada Television. 1991. *MYSTERY!* PBS. WGBH, Boston. 28 Nov. 1992.

Promised Land. Writ. Julian Mitchell. Dir. John Madden. Prod. David Lascelles. *MYSTERY!* PBS. WGBH, Boston. 22, 29 Apr. 1993.

Pym, John. Rev. of *Presumed Innocent*. *Sight & Sound* Autumn 1990: 279.

The Resident Patient. Prod. Michael Cox. Dir. David Carson. Dram. Derek Marlowe. Granada Television. 1985. *MYSTERY!* PBS. WGBH, Boston. 13 Feb. 1986.

Rice, Anne. "She Knew Too Many, Too Well." *New York Times Book Review* 28 June 1987: 1.

Rich, Adrienne. *Of Woman Born: Motherhood as Experience and Institution*. New York: Bantam, 1977.

Richardson, Robert. *Literature and Film*. Bloomington: Indiana UP, 1969.

Riley, Dick, and Pam McAllister, eds. *The Bedside, Bathtub, & Armchair Companion to Agatha Christie*. New York: Ungar, 1979.

Rosen, Marjorie. *Popcorn Venus: Women, Movies and the American Dream*. New York: McCann & Geoghegan, 1973.

Rowan, Dan, and John D. MacDonald. *A Friendship: The Letters of Dan Rowan and John D. MacDonald: 1967-1974*. New York: Knopf, 1986.

Salinger, J.D. *"Raise High the Roof Beam, Carpenters" and "Seymour: An Introduction."* Boston: Little, Brown, [1959].

Sanders, Dennis, and Len Lovallo. *The Agatha Christie Companion*. New York: Avenel, 1984.

Sanderson, Mark. *The Making of Inspector Morse*. London: Macmillan, 1991.

Sayers, Dorothy L. *Gaudy Night*. London: Gollancz, 1935.

____. "Gaudy Night." *Titles to Fame*. Ed. Denys K. Roberts. London: Nelson, 1937. 75-95.

____. *Have His Carcase*. London: Gollancz, 1932.

____. Introduction. *Great Short Stories of Detection, Mystery, and Horror*. Ed. Dorothy L. Sayers. London: Gollancz, 1928. 9-47.

____. Introduction. *Tales of Detection*. Ed. Dorothy L. Sayers. London: Dent, 1936. vii-xiv.

____. "The Present Status of the Mystery Story." *The London Mercury* Nov. 1930: 47-52.

____. *Strong Poison*. London: Gollancz, 1930.

A Scandal in Bohemia. Prod. Michael Cox. Dir. Paul Annett. Dram. Alexander Baron. Granada Television. 1984. *MYSTERY!* PBS. WGBH, Boston. 14 Mar. 1985.

Schickel, Richard. Rev. of *Presumed Innocent*. *Time* 30 Aug. 1990: 57.

Schine, Cathleen. "Inspector Morse." *Vogue* May 1990: 174.

The Second Stain. Exec. Prod. Michael Cox. Dir. John Bruce. Dram. John Hawkesworth. Granada Television. 1986. *MYSTERY!* PBS. WGBH, Boston. 26 Feb. 1987.

Second Time Around. Writ. Daniel Boyle. Dir. Adrian Shergold. Prod. David Lascelles. *MYSTERY!* PBS. WGBH, Boston. 25 Mar. and 1 Apr. 1993.

The Secret of Bay 5B. Writ. Alma Cullen. Dir. Jim Goddard. Prod. Chris Burt. *MYSTERY!* PBS. WGBH, Boston. 13, 20 June 1991.

The Settling of the Sun. Writ. Charles Wood. Dir. Peter Hammond. Prod. Kenny McBain. *MYSTERY!* PBS. WGBH, Boston. 3, 10 May 1990.

Shadow of the Thin Man. Dir. W.S. Van Dyke. Prod. Hunt Stromberg. Writ. Irving Brecher and Harry Kurnitz. With William Powell, Myrna Loy, Barry Nelson, Donna Reed, Dicky Hall, and Sam Levene. Metro-Goldwyn-Mayer. 1941.

Shales, Tom. "ABC's Tired 'Travis McGee.'" *Washington Post* 18 May 1983: B13.

Shaw, Marion, and Sabine Vanacker. *Reflecting on Miss Marple*. London: Routledge, 1991.

Shine, Walter, and Jean Shine, comps. and eds. *A Bibliography of the Published Works of John D. MacDonald with Selected Biographical Materials and Critical Essays*. Gainesville: Patrons of the Libraries, U of Florida, 1980.

The Silence of the Lambs. Dir. Jonathan Demme. Jodie Foster, Anthony Hopkins, and Scott Glenn. Orion, 1991.

The Silent World of Nicholas Quinn. Adapt. Julian Mitchell. Dir. Brian Parker. Prod. Kenny McBain. *MYSTERY!* PBS. WGBH, Boston. 18, 25 Feb. 1988.

Silverman, Kaja. *The Acoustic Mirror: The Female Voice in Psychoanalysis and Cinema*. Bloomington: Indiana UP, 1988.

____. "Dis-Embodying the Female Voice." *Re-Vision: Essays in Feminist Film Criticism*. Eds. Mary Ann Doane, et al. Los Angeles: American Film Institute, 1984. 131-49.

Simon, John. "Horror, Domestic and Imported." *National Review* 29 Apr. 1991: 55-58.

Sins of the Fathers. Writ. Jeremy Burnham. Dir. Peter Hammond. Prod. David Lascelles. *MYSTERY!* PBS. WGBH, Boston. 7, 14 May 1992.

Sinyard, Neil. *Filming Literature: The Art of Screen Adaptation*. New York: St. Martin's, 1986.

Song of the Thin Man. Dir. Edward Buzzell. Prod. Nat Perrin. Writ. Steven Fisher, Nat Perrin, James O'Hanlon, and Harry Crane. With William Powell, Myrna Loy, Keenan Wynn, Gloria Grahame, and Jayne Meadows. Metro-Goldwyn-Mayer, 1947.

Spitzer, Jane Stewart. "Scott Turow." *Christian Science Monitor* 13 Aug. 1987: 18.

Spoto, Donald. *The Art of Alfred Hitchcock*. New York: Hopkinson & Blake, 1976.

Stasio, Marilyn. "Crime." *New York Times Book Review* 19 Apr. 1992: 17.

Strong Poison. Dir. Christopher Hodson. Prod. Michael Chapman. Writ. Philip Broadley. BBC2. 25 Mar. and 1, 8 Apr. 1987. *MYSTERY!* PBS. WGBH, Boston. 1, 8, 15 Oct. 1987.

Symons, Julian. "The Mistress of Complication." *Agatha Christie: First Lady of Crime*. Ed. H.R.F. Keating. New York: Holt, 1977. 25-38.

Tally, Ted. *The Silence of the Lambs*. North Hollywood, CA: Hollywood Scripts, 1989.

Taylor, John Russell. *Hitch: The Life and Work of Alfred Hitchcock*. London: Faber & Faber, 1978.

Tennenbaum, Michael. "Margaret Rutherford: The Universal Aunt." Riley and McAllister 249-51.

The Thin Man. Dir. W.S. Van Dyke. Prod. Hunt Stromberg. Writ. Albert Hackett and Frances Goodrich. With William Powell, Myrna Loy, Maureen O'Sullivan, Nat Pendleton, and Cesar Romero. Metro-Goldwyn-Mayer, 1934.

The Thin Man Goes Home. Dir. Richard Thorpe. Prod. Everett Riskin. Writ. Robert Riskin, Dwight Taylor, and Harry Kurnitz. With William Powell, Myrna Loy, Harry Davenport, Gloria DeHaven, and Donald Meek. Metro-Goldwyn-Mayer, 1944.

Thompson, Howard. "Screen: 'Darker than Amber' Opens." *New York Times* 15 Aug. 1970: 16.

Thompson, Kristin. "Closure within a Dream: Point-of-View in *Laura*." *Film Reader* 3 (1978): 90-105.

Truffaut, Francois. *Hitchcock*. Rev. ed. New York: Simon & Schuster, 1983.

Turow, Scott. *Presumed Innocent*. 1987. New York: Warner, 1988.

"Twenty Questions: Scott Turow." *Playboy* Aug. 1993: 113-14, 132.

V.I. Warshawski. Dir. Jeff Kanew. Prod. Jeffrey Lurie. Hollywood Pictures, 1991.

Van Dine, S.S. "Twenty Rules for Writing Detective Stories." *The Art of the Mystery Story*. Ed. Howard Haycraft. New York: Grosset and Dunlap, 1946. 189-93.

Weiler, A.H. Rev. of *Murder Ahoy!*. *New York Times* 23 Sept. 1964: 55.

Williams, Linda. "Feminist Film Theory: *Mildred Pierce* and the Second World War." *Female Spectators: Looking at Film and Television*. Ed. E. Deidre Pribram. London: Verso, 1988. 12-30.

Wolfe, Peter. "The Critics Did It: An Essay Review." *Modern Fiction Studies* 29 (1983): 389-433.

The Wolvercote Tongue. Adapt. Julian Mitchell. Dir. Alastair Reid. Prod. Kenny McBain. *MYSTERY!* PBS. WGBH, Boston. 15, 22 Dec. 1988.

Wood, Robin. "*Strangers on a Train*." *A Hitchcock Reader*. Ed. Marshall Deutelbaum and Leland Poague. Ames, IA: Iowa State UP, 1986: 170-81.

Contributors

A graduate of The City College of New York, the University of Wisconsin, and New York University, **Iska Alter** is Associate Professor of English at Hofstra University. She has written on such authors as William Shakespeare, Bernard Malamud, John Updike, and Arthur Miller, and on such subjects as ethnicity, feminism, and cultural history. A long-time mystery fan, she is now working with the fiction of Anne Perry, P.D. James, and Agatha Christie.

Liahna Babener is Head of the English Department at Montana State University. She has published articles on a variety of topics in popular culture, particularly *film noir*, detective fiction, and women writers. She has edited an anthology, "*Fatal Attraction*: Feminist Readings," published as a special number of *The Journal of Popular Culture* (Winter 1992), to which she contributed an essay. Her current work on the subject focuses on feminist critical approaches to the literature of detection.

Before becoming involved in television, British producer **Michael Cox** worked as actor, stage manager, member of an advertising company, and served on the staff of a theatrical agent. In the 1960s he joined Granada Television as a director's assistant, eventually earning the opportunity to train as a director himself. He worked on news programs and local documentaries, ultimately graduating to production of drama and comedy series. He is perhaps best known for his work as producer and executive producer of the Sherlock Holmes films featuring Jeremy Brett, which originally aired in the United States on PBS's *Mystery!*

A member of the Department of English at Ball State University, in Muncie, Indiana, **Joanne Edmonds** has a special interest in the twentieth-century British novel. She has delivered papers on Dorothy L. Sayers and on Colin Dexter at meetings of the Popular Culture Association and is at work on a study of sense of place in contemporary British crime novels.

Frederick Isaac is Head Librarian at the Jewish Community Library of San Francisco. A long-time member of the Popular Culture Association and its Detective and Mystery area, he has written papers on many aspects of detective fiction, covering such topics as moral issues in the hard-boiled novel, Great Detectives in World War II mysteries, and such authors as Nicolas Freeling and Richard Lockridge. He has also published articles on several San Francisco Bay Area writers, including Bill Pronzini and Julie Smith.

Kathleen Gregory Klein is the author of *The Woman Detective: Gender and Genre* (Urbana: University of Illinois Press, 1988; Tokyo: Shobun Sha, forthcoming). She is the editor of *Great Women Mystery Writers: A Bio-critical Dictionary* (Greenwood, forthcoming) and *Women Times Three: Writers, Detectives, and Readers* (Popular Press, forthcoming). She is also a member of the Advisory Boards of *Clues, The Oxford Companion to Crime and Mystery Writing*, and *Twentieth Century Crime and Mystery Writers*, for which she wrote the Preface to the third edition.

Joan G. Kotker is an Instructor and Director of the Writing Lab at Bellevue Community College, Bellevue, Washington, where she has developed and taught a course on mystery and detective fiction. She has contributed reviews and articles to such publications as *The Armchair Detective* and has regularly presented papers on mystery and detective fiction at national Popular Culture Association conferences.

Andrew Macdonald's interest in literature about the underworld began with his University of Texas doctoral dissertation on Ben Jonson. Since then he also has written about modern crime and mystery writers, including Patricia Highsmith, Frederick Forsyth, Ken Follett, Graham Greene, James Hall Roberts/Robert Duncan, Ralph McInerny, Kenneth Benton, and Frederick Forsyth. He is an Associate Professor at Loyola University, New Orleans.

Gina Macdonald's interest in mystery, detection and underworld literature began with her University of Texas doctoral dissertation on Robert Greene's Coney-catching Pamphlets. She has contributed articles on detective fiction to *Twentieth Century Crime and Mystery Writers*; the *Dictionary of Literary Biography*; the *Concise Dictionary of Literary Biography*; and *Magill's Critical Survey of Mystery and Detective Fiction*. She teaches at Loyola University, New Orleans.

MaryKay Mahoney is an Associate Professor at Merrimack College in North Andover, Massachusetts. She has presented papers on detective fiction at national Popular Culture Association conferences, and participated in a panel on detective fiction at the annual New England Association of Teachers of English conference. She has contributed articles on detective fiction to *The Baker Street Journal* and *Kansas English*.

Lewis D. Moore is a Professor in the Department of English Studies at the University of the District of Columbia. He has published articles on John D. MacDonald's Travis McGee series and since 1984 has given talks on MacDonald at many conferences, including the Popular Culture Association National Meeting and the John D. MacDonald Conference on Mystery and Detective Fiction. He is working on a book on MacDonald's Travis McGee series.

William Reynolds is a Professor of English at Hope College in Holland, Michigan. In addition to articles on Old English and Middle English literature, he has published several essays on detective fiction. While he has written on such recent and contemporary figures as Anthony Price, Marian Mainwaring, and C.H.B. Kitchin, his principal interest is in Golden Age British Detective Fiction, in particular Dorothy L. Sayers.

Sharon A. Russell is a Professor of Communication at Indiana State University in Terre Haute, Indiana. She has contributed an essay to *Mysteries of Africa* (1991) and has published other articles on horror literature and film. Former chair of the mystery and detection fiction interest area of the Popular Culture Association, she is editor of *Animals in Mysteries* (Popular Press, forthcoming).

Elizabeth A. Trembley specializes in psychological approaches to gothic and detective fiction and modern literature. Since receiving her Ph.D. from the University of Chicago, she has published and presented papers on Conan Doyle, Dorothy L. Sayers, James Joyce, D.H. Lawrence, Virginia Woolf, and Frank Miller's *Batman*. She currently serves as Head of General Education at Davenport College in Holland, Michigan.